MONEY AND POLITICS

DR JOO-CHEONG THAM is a senior lecturer at the Melbourne Law School and a leading expert on Australian political finance. He has written extensively on this topic in academic publications and newspapers. Joo-Cheong regularly gives expert evidence to parliamentary inquiries into political funding. Political parties across the political spectrum have also relied upon his research.

MONEY AND POLITICS

THE DEMOCRACY WE CAN'T AFFORD

Joo-Cheong Tham

UNSW
PRESS

A UNSW Press book

Published by
University of New South Wales Press Ltd
University of New South Wales
Sydney NSW 2052
AUSTRALIA
www.unswpress.com.au

© Joo-Cheong Tham 2010
First published 2010

10 9 8 7 6 5 4 3 2 1

National Library of Australia
Cataloguing-in-Publication entry
    Author: Tham, Joo-Cheong.
    Title: Money and politics: the democracy we can't afford/
    by Joo-Cheong Tham.
    ISBN: 978 192141 009 3 (pbk.)
    Notes: Includes index.
    Subjects: Campaign funds – Australia.
        Financial disclosure – Australia.
        Australia – politics and government.
    Dewey Number: 324.780994

Design Avril Makula
Cover Di Quick
Printer Ligare

This book is printed on paper using fibre supplied from plantation or sustainably managed forests.

CONTENTS

To my parents, from whom
I learnt the value of integrity

ACKNOWLEDGMENTS

More than three years have passed from the time of the book's conception to its publication. During this time, I have incurred many debts. I am grateful to the Melbourne Law School for providing me with a congenial environment to undertake research in, and to my law school colleagues, who make this place a vibrant and stimulating place for scholarship. The publication of the book was facilitated by financial assistance from the Law School's Research Support Fund and a Melbourne University publication grant.

My work on political finance has been greatly enriched by the discussions and interactions I have had with scholars working in this field. Special mention should be made of Brian Costar, Keith Ewing, Graeme Orr, Jacob Rowbottom and Sally Young. Keith, Graeme, Jacob and Sally were generous enough to review draft chapters of the book, and so was my law school colleague, Anna Chapman. Catherine Dow, Emily Long, Stephen Sempill and Jesse Winton provided indispensable research assistance – it was a distinct privilege to be able to work with such talented individuals. Particular thanks to Julian Sempill for our enduring friendship and also the days he spent reviewing a draft of the book. Former Democrats Senator Andrew Murray also kindly reviewed a draft of the book and provided insightful comments (and criticisms). Many thanks too to Andrew and to Dr Carmen Lawrence, former WA Premier, Federal Health Minister and ALP President, for endorsing the book. Their courageous, passionate and intelligent efforts over many years in working for a more democratic Australia are a source of inspiration.

I would like to thank the team at UNSW Press, in particular Chantal Gibbs and Heather Cam; I am particularly grateful to Phillipa McGuinness for her unstinting support for the book. Thanks too to David Hudson for his proofreading.

I would like to express my deep gratitude to my family, who have always provided support to me – especially my parents, who made many sacrifices, emotional and financial, so that I could reach my potential through a proper education. Finally, and most importantly, my gorgeous partner and best friend, Paula O'Brien, with whom I have many discussions – and arguments – over the question of money in politics, has been a tremendous source of support and encouragement (even to the extent of undertaking the laborious task of reviewing a draft manuscript).

PREFACE

Australia's democracy is in the grip of a financial crisis, but the crisis is not about lack of money. Far from it. The major parties are flush with funds from businesses and trade unions. They are also subsidised by the public purse, to the tune of millions of dollars. The crisis is about how such money is raised and spent. First, money flows into the political system under the cover of secrecy. Second, the selling of access and influence is entrenched in the major parties. Third, there is shameless use of public money for partisan gain, with parliamentary entitlements and government advertising costing millions of dollars being used to enhance the electoral prospects of incumbents.

This crisis is not one of dramatic revelations or front-page headlines or money changing hands. It is a scandal of inequitable rules and insidious practices. Most of all, it reflects a debased political culture in which the key players are complicit in creating and maintaining a system geared to their mutual benefit. This has spawned a sanguine acceptance of corrupt and unethical practices that undermine the public interest. As the major parties grow rich on private money and public funds, Australia's democracy is impoverished. In the emphatic words of Eric Roozendaal, former general secretary of the NSW Australian Labor Party (ALP) and current Treasurer of the NSW government, the status quo is 'dangerously unsustainable'.[1]

The key aims of this book are to understand and challenge this state of affairs. Its subject matter is the role of money in Australian politics. Its principal focus is on those who run for elected office (the political parties and candidates), those who succeed in winning such office (the parliamentarians and the parties in government), and other organisations and individuals that seek to influence the political process through the spending of money (in electoral law, third parties).

Chapter 1 sets the scene by proposing four primary purposes for a political finance regime in a democracy: protecting the integrity of representative government, promoting fairness in politics, supporting parties in performing their functions, and respecting political freedoms. These goals provide the benchmark for evaluating the role of money in Australian politics. Chapter 1 also identifies the key ways of regulating political finance.

Later chapters provide fuller analysis of these regulatory means. Chapters 2 to 4 deal with the topic of private political money. Chapter 2 examines the extent to which such money is adequately disclosed. The way in which such money flows into Australian politics, its regulation and the challenges it poses are taken up by Chapter 3 and Chapter 4. Public funding of politics is the focus of Chapters 5 and 6. Chapter 5 analyses election funding, tax subsidies and parliamentary entitlements, and Chapter 6 examines government advertising.

The book considers election spending in Chapter 7. Chapters 8 and 9 study a key way in which money can influence the political process: lobbying. The book concludes with Chapter 10, which issues a blueprint for reform.

By the time this book is published, nine years will have passed since I began researching and writing about Australian political finance. Initially, my study was prompted by a vague sense of its importance ... and its neglect. This sense has only sharpened and deepened over time: there is little doubt that the funding of politics goes to the heart of democracy, yet one can (still) count on one hand the number of academics who have expertise in Australian political finance. The imperative to write and speak out in this area also became pressing as I kept coming across the smug view that Australia is a 'clean' democracy and things are fine as they are. Convincing politicians, particularly, that there are serious problems to be addressed posed a challenge in itself, and it remains a challenge. The influence of such views is, however, lessening somewhat. At the time of writing, there is a push at the federal level and in two states, New South Wales and Queensland, to radically reconfigure their political funding regimes. These developments present both opportunities and dangers. While generally welcome, there is also the risk that the major parties will set up a system that further entrenches their position − this danger is one of the principal targets of the book. I hope that this book charts a course between complacency and self-interest masquerading as reform, and so contributes to a more democratic funding of Australian politics.

Note: The law as stated is, to the best of my knowledge, accurate as at 1 February 2010.

1

THE ENDS AND MEANS OF DEMOCRATIC POLITICAL FINANCE REGIMES

When money makes its way into politics, suspicions are aroused and red lights start flashing; accusations, or at least suspicion, of corruption rarely seem far from consciousness. Why? Clearly, the running of Australia's democracy requires money. Without adequate funding, parties and candidates would not be able to campaign. And elected representatives should be properly resourced to perform their duties: developing law and policy, being responsive to the citizenry. Put simply, money plays a necessary role in Australian politics.

And in Australia, money plays a limited role in politics. We are not a country where people are blatantly offered cash to vote in particular ways, for instance. Moreover, money is only one of the many factors that determine political outcomes. Election results, for instance, are shaped by a range of things – ideas, campaign strategies, organisational unity and efficiency, candidate charisma and appeal, strength of the support base, media coverage, the design of the electoral system, historical circumstances and demographic factors. So the question must be asked again: why single out money as a source of evil in politics?

The answer lies first in the special characteristics of money. Unlike other campaign resources (such as the appeal of leaders and ideas), it is by its very nature convertible into other goods. It is also highly mobile. Unlike candidates and party workers, money can be moved with a few clicks of a mouse. Compared with other campaign resources, money is also easy to move anonymously. In the absence of mandatory disclosure, a financial contribution from a company to a party can remain completely private. Other campaign resources tend to have a public element. Indeed, for some, their efficacy depends on their having a public face: policies and candidates can hardly be assets if they are wrapped in layers of secrecy.[1]

Second, the advantages of money are never equally shared. Economic inequalities are a defining feature of a capitalist economy like Australia's,[2] and this gives rise to the possibility of wealthy individuals, groups and businesses translating their economic power into political power. As former Democrats Senator Andrew Murray has observed, 'Some moneyed people will always attempt to speak louder and will often succeed as a result.'[3] Further, access to public money largely resides with those in political office. The risk is that those in power will use these resources for partisan ends. It is these two general characteristics of money — its *mobility* and its *unequal distribution* — that together result in its posing particular threats to the health of Australia's democracy.

But what definition of democracy are we using here? As a mantra, 'democracy' attracts broad support, but the word alone offers little guidance in relation to the funding of politics. And once we delve into specific meanings and theories, it becomes clear that 'democracy' is a complex and contested political ideal.[4] However, if there is to be meaningful discussion of the funding of politics in Australia, we must first flesh out our meaning of democracy. The next section will do just this in order to develop a set of principles – the ends of democratic political finance regimes.[5] The discussion that follows will set out the various methods of regulating political money – the means of democratic political finance regimes.

The ends

Protecting the integrity of representative government

As the Royal Commission on WA Inc. rightly observed, the 'architectural principle' of the Australian governmental system is that elected officials are accountable to Australian citizens and expected to act in the public interest.[6] The first element of this principle, accountability, requires that elected officials be in 'a constant condition of responsiveness' to the citizens.[7] There is no such responsiveness without regular elections.[8] However, there should be responsiveness both *during* elections and *between* elections, as was recognised by High Court Chief Justice Mason in *Australian Capital Television Pty Ltd v Commonwealth (Cth)*:

> the representatives who are members of Parliament and Ministers
> of State are not only chosen by the people but exercise their
> legislative and executive powers as representatives of the people.
> And in the exercise of these powers the representatives of
> necessity are accountable to the people for what they do and have
> a responsibility to take account of the views of the people on
> whose behalf they act.[9]

Public accountability is also fundamentally concerned with public confidence – accountability to the public implies their trust or confidence. Hence elected officials 'should act so as to create and maintain public confidence in their actions and in the legislative process'.[10]

The second element of this principle, acting in the public interest, can have various meanings and is (and should be) hotly contested in the political arena.[11] The part that is perhaps central and uncontroversial is the merit principle: elected officials 'should act on reasons relevant to the merits of public policies or reasons relevant to advancing a process that encourages acting on such reasons'.[12]

Political funding, specifically funding of political parties and candidates, can undermine these two principles by leaving in its wake particular kinds of corruption.[13] Keeping such funding secret, in terms of who is contributing and how much they are contributing, can lead to corruption of electoral processes. Effective accountability through elections requires informed voting – citizens who are in the dark as to the finances of parties and candidates are missing information that could be crucial to their decision. A democratic political finance regime should remove the possibility of this type of corruption 'by providing details of the funding sources of political parties'.[14] As Kim Beazley emphasised when proposing, as Special Minister for State, the federal funding and disclosure regime:

> The whole process of political funding needs to be out in the open … Australians deserve to know who is giving money to political parties and how much.[15]

The other way political funding threatens the integrity of representative government is through corruption of public office: the 'improper use of public office for private purposes'.[16] There are three main forms of such corruption. First, there is corruption through graft, when the receipt of private funds leads directly to political power being improperly exercised in favour of contributors. Bribery of public officials, for instance. Such corruption was at issue in WA Inc. and in the Fitzgerald Inquiry into the Joh Bjelke-Petersen Queensland government. Former Queensland Minister Gordon Nuttall was also found guilty of this kind of corruption.[17]

Second, there is corruption through undue influence. There is a risk of such corruption with most, if not all, large political contributions. The danger is that a donor secures influence simply by virtue of paying money to an elected official (or, more often, the party to which the elected official belongs). Such influence is undue because of its source – the payment of money – does not bear upon the merits of public decision-making. Because the making of political contributions is irrelevant to acting in the public interest, public officials who exercise their powers or make decisions by reference to such contributions are engaging in a form of corruption. They are improperly using their public office for private purposes.[18]

Corruption through undue influence is one species of conflict of interest. Substantial political contributions[19] create the risk that holders of public office will give extra weight to the interests of their financiers rather than deciding matters on their merits and in the public interest;[20] when this risk eventuates, there is corruption through undue influence. In contrast with corruption through graft, corruption through undue influence does not require explicit bargains or that a specific act result from the receipt of funds. Rather, it arises when the structure of incentives facing public officials results in implicit bargains of favourable treatment, or a culture of delivering preferential treatment to moneyed interests. As the Bowen Committee on Public Duty and Private Interest explained:

> Conflict of interest generally differs from bribery because it
> does not require a transaction between two parties. It needs only
> one person, the officeholder possessing the interest in point.
> The distinction between bribery and this category … is that,
> whilst a benefit conferred as a bribe is directed to a particular
> transaction or series of transactions, gifts, hospitality or travel may
> be provided to create *a general climate of goodwill* on the part of the
> beneficiary. The 'debt' might not be called in for years or ever
> (emphasis added).[21]

Corruption through undue influence manifests itself in various ways. More blatant forms involve the sale of political access and influence (see Chapter 3). Here, formal and informal ways for money to influence politics come together in an unsavoury mix: some businesses secure favourable hearings by buying access and influence and also through the lingering effect of their contributions (a phone call from a big donor, for example, being more likely to be returned than one from a constituent). With perceptions of the merits of any issue invariably coloured by the arguments at hand, preferential hearings mean that when judging what is in the 'public interest', the minds of politicians will be skewed towards the interests of their financiers.[22] Notice here that undue influence can be present even when the influence is not decisive (that is, even if the donor does not succeed in securing its desired result). This does not, however, mean that such influence is worthless – there is tremendous value in being able to receive a favourable hearing from politicians – or that such influence does not corrupt public decision-making. The payment of money to elected officials remains an illegitimate source of influence, regardless of the final result.

The third form of corruption of public office is through the misuse of public resources. This occurs when public resources are used for illegitimate purposes. Such purposes could be grounded in personal or party interests. For instance, the party in government might use public monies to pay for advertising that is principally aimed at boosting its electoral fortunes (see Chapter 6). More subtly, a governing party might use information secured through public office in its efforts to fundraise through, for instance, 'off the record' briefings given by Ministers to fee-paying businesses, rather than for public purposes.

Clearly, these forms of corruption of public office are not mutually exclusive. They may overlap – briefings by Ministers to their business patrons involve not only corruption through the misuse of public resources but also corruption through undue influence. Similarly, this example highlights how corruption stemming from private funding can intertwine with corruption related to public resources; this is not surprising, because motivation for corruption related to private funding is most likely to arise when the party or politician enjoys some public power (and therefore, access to public resources).

A political finance regime should aim to prevent all of these forms of corruption of public office. This was a point well recognised by Kim Beazley. In his Second Reading Speech for the Commonwealth's Political Broadcasts and Political Disclosures Bill 1991 – the Bill that introduced a ban on political advertising and annual disclosure returns – Beazley noted that:

> There is no greater duty upon the representatives of the people in a democratic society than the duty to ensure that they serve all members of that society equally. This duty requires government which is *free of corruption and undue influence* (emphasis added).[23]

Not only should governments be free of graft and undue influence; also:

> The public is entitled to be assured that *parties and candidates* which make up the government or *opposition of the day* are free of undue influence or improper outside influence (emphasis added).[24]

These various forms of corruption of public office can be more fully understood through the distinction between individual corruption and institutional corruption. Individual corruption is when public officials render undeserved services in exchange for personal gain.[25] In these cases, the necessary link between the services and the gain is provided by corrupt motives, that is, an intention to improperly gain from public office.[26] Graft (for example, bribery of public officials) typically involves cases of individual corruption. With institutional corruption, on the other hand, 'the gain a [public official] receives is political rather than personal, the service the member provides is procedurally improper, and the connection between the gain and the service has a tendency to damage the legislature or the democratic process'.[27]

While graft tends to be a form of individual corruption, the other forms of corruption – of electoral processes, through undue influence or through the misuse of public resources – can take either individual or institutional form. For example, the misuse of public resources such as parliamentary entitlements and government advertising often involves institutional corruption (see Chapters 5 and 6).

A democratic political finance regime should aim to tackle both individual and institutional corruption. A focus or preoccupation with individual corruption (like corruption through graft) can lead to the dangerous neglect of institutional corruption through undue influence and misuse of public resources. While institutional corruption is 'more ambiguous', it is 'often [a] more corrosive kind of corruption that takes place within the heart of the institution'[28] because it can be 'so closely related to conduct that is a perfectly acceptable part of political life'[29] or 'the way things are done'.

In terms of institutional corruption, a political finance regime should be based on the 'appearance' standard. As the Bowen Committee stated:

> there is a test ... in judging what is proper in particular
> circumstances: the test of appearance. Does that interest look to
> the reasonable person the sort of interest that may influence?[30]

The appearance standard rests on two grounds. First, it protects an essential element of accountability: public confidence in governmental processes. Its premises are that 'under certain institutional conditions the connection between contributions and services *tends to be improper*' (emphasis in original),[31] and that this tendency erodes public confidence in representative institutions. In this context, as the then Queensland Integrity Commissioner Gary Crooke put it, 'Perception is reality.'[32] The second ground is that 'when confronted with a connection that exhibits these tendencies, citizens cannot be reasonably expected to obtain the evidence they need to judge whether the connection is actually corrupt'.[33] This explains why a breach of the appearance standard is seen by some as 'a distinct wrong, independent of and no less serious than the wrong of which it is an appearance'.[34] The secrecy of political funding leads to automatic breaches of the appearance standard: political contributions given in secret defeat reasonable attempts by citizens to properly assess whether or not there was corrupt conduct.

Promoting fairness in politics

The principle of political equality lies at the heart of democracy. By insisting that each citizen has equal political status, this principle implies that political freedoms be formally available to all citizens and, as political philosopher John Rawls has argued, that such freedoms have 'fair value'.[35] As Rawls writes, 'fair value of ... political liberties [means] that citizens similarly gifted and motivated have roughly an equal chance of influencing the government's policy and of attaining positions of authority *irrespective of their economic and social class*' (emphasis added).[36] The aim here is to ensure that all citizens have 'a genuine chance to make a difference'[37] in the political process.

This aim is perhaps the most difficult challenge for political finance regimes in capitalist countries such as Australia. Social and economic inequalities undermine the value of these freedoms for those who are marginalised – the poor, the disadvantaged, the powerless – so that though the rights are formally available, they cannot be meaningfully exercised.[38] Indeed, Rawls is of the view that laissez-faire capitalism 'rejects ... the fair value of equal political liberties'.[39]

Ensuring the fair value of political freedoms will involve a radical redesign of Australia's social, economic and political institutions, a task that clearly cannot be borne by our political finance regime alone. At the same time, proper design of a political finance regime is crucial to ensuring fair value of political liberties.[40]

This aim has several key elements. First, a political finance regime should facilitate fair access to the public arena: that is, to the forums in which public opinion and policy are articulated, influenced and shaped. Citizens and their organisations will only have leverage when they have that access. Such access also provides the principal guarantee that the public agenda is responsive to the opinions of the citizenry.[41] In other words, fair access to the public arena secures public accountability.

The 'public arena' is, of course, a complex notion, because public opinion and policy are expressed and shaped in numerous ways – by door-to-door campaigning, party newsletters, lobbying and, increasingly, advertisements through the mass media and the internet. It is also a 'limited space',[42] where the loudness of one voice can drown out others. In particular, those with superior means of communication can exclude less resourced citizens or groups. In elections, for example, parties with enough money to pay for advertising that reaches mass audiences will tend to receive a better hearing among the public than less well-off competitors who rely on letter-boxing and door-knocking. Preventing such unfairness is one of the central aims of a democratic political finance regime.

The importance of access to the public arena stems from the deliberative nature of democracy. Democracy is not simply a matter of the majority getting what it wants. Political competition involves, at its core, a battle of rival ideas, policies and ideologies: politics is conducted through debate and discussion. That deliberation is how citizens engage in the making of laws. Deliberation also plays another role. Citizens will be bound by laws they disagree with, as well as by those they agree with, and public deliberation plays a role in justifying laws and policies to the public. It is through such justification that respect is accorded to citizens as subjects of laws who may or may not agree with those laws.[43] In this sense, citizens are 'the "makers" and the "matter" of politics'.[44]

So political equality (each citizen having equal political status) does not imply equal political power for each citizen. In rare situations, equal political power is mandated. Voting rights are a relatively uncontroversial example. With these rights, political equality finds expression (at least in relation to the House of Representatives), thus fulfilling a key objective advanced by the original *Commonwealth*

Electoral Act 1918: that of 'equality of representation throughout the Commonwealth'.[45]

In the realm of franchise, we can see the force of Harrison Moore's observation that the 'great underlying principle' of the Constitution is that citizens have 'each a share, and an equal share, in political power'.[46]

In other realms of political activity (including political funding), equal political power, however, is generally not a requirement of political equality. Democratic deliberation means that not all ideas or voices are given equal weight. Ideally, superior ideas gain greater support while their lesser competitors fall by the wayside. In the context of political deliberation, what political equality generally requires is conditions of fair deliberation,[47] conditions that only exist with fair access to the public arena (discussed above).

Most importantly perhaps, a political finance regime should promote fairness in electoral contests. As the Royal Commission on WA Inc. emphasised:

> The first institution of representative government, the
> Parliament, must be constituted in a way which fairly represents
> the interests and aspirations of the community itself. *The electoral
> processes must be fair* (emphasis added).[48]

Fairness in this context relates to the competition among candidates and parties.[49] First, it means that a political finance regime should ensure open access to electoral contests. It should prevent the costs of this access escalating to prohibitive levels, and be alert to the danger that access will be placed beyond the reach of most citizens through the 'competitive extravagance'[50] of parties that seek to outbid each other in their campaign spending. This may warrant election spending limits (see Chapter 7). More than a century ago, Senator O'Connor, when introducing the original *Commonwealth Electoral Act*, justified the candidate expenditure limits set by the Act in this way:

> If we wish to secure a true reflex of the opinions of the electors,
> we must have ... a system which will not allow the choice of the
> electors to be handicapped for no other reason than the inability
> of a candidate to find the enormous amount of money required to
> enable him [sic] to compete with other candidates.[51]

Ensuring meaningful access to the public arena may require 'compensating steps',[52] such as public funding so that the electoral contest is open to 'worthy parties and candidates [that] might not [otherwise] be able to afford the considerable sums necessary to make their policies known'.[53] New candidates and parties may need to be financially assisted (see Chapter 5).

A political finance regime should also promote fair electoral competition by advancing 'fair rivalry'[54] among the main parties. First, fair rivalry implies an absence of '[a] serious imbalance in campaign funding'[55] between the major and minor political parties. As political funding expert Keith Ewing has argued, 'no candidate or party should be permitted to spend more than its rivals by a disproportionate amount'.[56] Second, fair rivalry between the major parties – that is, the parties contending for government – may demand more than the absence of a gross disparity in resources. The most important choice citizens make in an election is of the party or parties that will form government. For this choice to be meaningful in Australia's predominantly two-party system, the two alternatives may need to be equally represented in electoral contests. If so, then fair rivalry among the major parties would imply something approximating 'equality of arms'.

Also, there should be fairness among all the electoral contestants and players: political parties and candidates, and other political participants, such as lobby groups, trade unions, businesses and other non-government organisations. The latter, often referred to as third parties in electoral law, should have adequate access to the public arena, as they play an essential role in elections. Their role should, however, be understood within the context of the central function of elections, which is to determine who is to govern and who is to represent the electors. The electoral contestants – the parties and candidates – have a privileged (but not dominant) position during election time. At the very least, third parties should not be able to outspend political parties and candidates. Neither should political parties and candidates be subject to unfair speech by third parties: for example, political attacks made by groups whose identities are not publicly known.

The principle of fairness extends beyond electoral contests to governmental processes between elections. Elections are usually contested on broad issues, and the policies of parties espoused during elections are sometimes vague, allowing them significant room to manoeuvre once in office. This means that electoral politics does not always govern what parties do in parliament (parliamentary politics), or what a party in office does in relation to executive action (policy politics).[57] All these types of politics should be subject to the principle of fairness. This underscores the importance of fair access to the public arena, including to avenues of influence such as lobbying (see Chapters 8 and 9).

In this context, we can see a close connection between unfairness in politics and the various forms of corruption. Remember, individual corruption occurs when public officials provide undeserved services in exchange for personal gain, and institutional corruption occurs when a public official receives a political gain as a result of providing some procedurally improper service. In the case of individual corruption, the service will be undeserved if it involves a departure from the merit principle. Proper adherence to this principle requires observance of fair processes; it is only fair processes that can ensure that a robust notion of merit is articulated and applied. Similarly, in the case of institutional corruption, fair processes are an imperative of procedural propriety.

Supporting parties in performing their functions

In his major study of Australian political parties, political scientist Dean Jaensch observed:

> There can be no argument about the ubiquity, pervasiveness and centrality of party in Australia. The forms, processes and content of politics – executive, parliament, pressure groups, bureaucracy, issues and policy making – are imbued with the influence of party, party rhetoric, party policy and party doctrine. Government is party government. Elections are essentially party contests, and the mechanics of electoral systems are determined by party policies and party advantages. Legislatures are party chambers. Legislators are overwhelmingly party members. The majority of electors follow party identification. Politics in Australia, almost entirely, is party politics.[58]

Parties are central to Australia's democracy and, indeed, 'modern democracy is unthinkable save in terms of parties'.[59] So Australia's political finance regime must reflect this. It should ensure that parties are adequately funded. Adequacy, though, does not mean what the parties want (or think they need for campaigning purposes); it must be strictly judged against the functions that parties ought to perform.

It may be said, however, that the only functions parties perform are as vehicles to gain political power. This is true, but only in part. What it obscures are the various democratic functions that parties perform. Foremost, political parties have representative functions: that is, functions aimed at reflecting public opinion. They perform an electoral function when, in their efforts to secure voter support, they respond to the wishes of the citizenry. They also have a participatory function, as they offer a vehicle for political participation through membership, meetings and engagement in the development of party policy. The relationship between political parties and the citizenry is not, however, one way. As political scientist Giovanni Sartori has noted, '[p]arties do not only *express;* they also *channel*' (emphasis in original).[60] Political parties also perform an agenda-setting function, as they shape the terms and content of political debates: the platform of a major party both influences and is influenced by public opinion. Political parties also perform a governance function. This function largely relates to parties that succeed in having elected representatives. These parties determine the pool of people who govern through their recruitment and preselection processes. They also participate in the act of governing. This is clearly the case with the party elected to government but is equally true of other parliamentary parties, as they are involved in the lawmaking process and scrutinise the actions of the executive government.

There are, of course, many other organisations which perform one or more of these functions. The media, for example, clearly has an agenda-setting role and, to a lesser (and contested) extent, a responsive function. Non-government organisations, such as interest groups, also have responsive and agenda-setting functions, and the public service obviously has a governing function. But no other institution or group combines these various functions. That is why Sartori is correct to argue that 'Parties are *the* central intermediate and intermediary structure between society and government' (emphasis in original).[61]

Respecting political freedoms

The aim of promoting fairness in politics implies respect for political freedoms. This deserves standing as a distinct end of a political finance regime, and it has several aspects.

Respecting freedom of political expression

Freedom of political expression is essential if citizens are to be able to participate in democratic decision-making.[62] Such decision-making depends upon citizens being able to argue their own views, listen to the opinions of others, debate and dissent. At a most fundamental level, democratic deliberation depends on freedom of political expression.

Political funding can connect to political expression in two ways. The giving of money by donors itself tends to be an act of political expression, with the political contribution signalling support for a party or candidate (although not necessarily in a public manner). Moreover, money is an enabling resource for political expression: most of the essential tools of campaign communications (pamphlets, posters and advertisements) have to be paid for. It follows that regulation of political funding throws up challenges for freedom of political expression. In Australia, these challenges also have constitutional significance, as the High Court has implied a freedom of political communication into the Commonwealth Constitution (see Chapters 4 and 7).

In understanding these challenges, it is useful to distinguish two aspects of freedom of political expression. There is, first, 'freedom from', which emphasises the absence of state regulation of political expression or, put differently, freedom from state interference in political discussion (this is the aspect the constitutional freedom is centrally concerned with). The other aspect, 'freedom to', is about the ability of citizens to actually engage in political expression. While 'freedom to' of course depends on 'freedom from', it requires more than just the absence of state regulation. It requires, notably, adequate resources to engage in political expression. Both aspects of freedom of political expression need to be taken into account – citizens should be significantly free from legal constraints on political activity and should have a meaningful capacity to engage in such activity. In Rawls' phraseology, freedom of political expression should not only be formally available to all citizens but should also have a fair value.

Respect for freedom of political expression does not dictate any particular formula or combination of 'freedom from' and 'freedom to'. The desirable balance often depends not only on normative principles, but also on the specific factual context. Because proper respect for freedom of political expression is contingent on such specifics, such freedom does not create an in-principle bar against state regulation of political expression.[63]

This point is sometimes obscured by excessive emphasis on the metaphor of the 'marketplace of ideas'. This metaphor likens the political forum to a market for goods and services and suggests that a 'free' market of political debate, based on the absence of state regulation, will result in a rich diversity of ideas. In this picture, freedom of political expression is typically equated to 'freedom from'. The essential flaw here is that while the picture correctly takes into account state regulation, it ignores the structures of private power. It neglects the way financial inequalities between citizens (in the context of expensive means of communications such as radio and television) can block access to the public realm. These blockages mean that 'freedom from' (the absence of state regulation of political expression) in fact produces a political agenda biased in favour of powerful interests.[64] The result, for most citizens, is that whilst freedom of political expression is formally available, it has little or negligible value.

More useful metaphors for the public realm are those of a 'town hall' meeting[65] or 'public square' meeting. These metaphors suggest that the public realm is a limited space (only a limited number of persons can speak at a public meeting) that is governed by state regulation *and* structures of private power. Further, it implies that state regulation has a role in setting the rules and procedures for fair deliberation (like the rules of a public meeting).[66] Importantly, such regulation might be required to counteract the silencing effects of 'private aggregations of power'.[67] As law professor Owen Fiss eloquently put it:

> It [the state] may have to allocate public resources – hand out megaphones – to those whose voices would not otherwise be heard in the public square. It may even have to silence the voices of some in order to hear the voices of the others.[68]

In terms of specific measures, protecting freedom of political expression may very well require state funding of parties and candidates and limits on political spending.

Clearly, then, the characterisation of the debate between those who favour state regulation of political expression and those who oppose it as a conflict between political equality and liberty is misleading. This characterisation is based on an unduly narrow conception of liberty, one that reduces freedom of political expression to 'freedom from'. A more expansive and plausible understanding of freedom of political expression that combines 'freedom from' with 'freedom to' reveals that 'what at first seemed to be a conflict between liberty and equality [is] a conflict between liberty and liberty'.[69]

Even when there is a genuine conflict between freedom of political expression and equality (or, more accurately, political fairness), its resolution does not imply the absence of state regulation. Like all political freedoms, freedom of political expression is not absolute; it can be legitimately limited on the grounds of competing public interests, whether they be political fairness or protecting the integrity of government. Whether such limitation is justifiable will depend on a complex set of factors, including the weight of the countervailing public interest, the extent to which the limitation is properly tailored to advancing this interest and the severity of the limitation (including the risk that the limitation will lead to an abuse of state power).

Respecting freedom of political association

Various types of political associations are active in Australian politics. As well as the political parties, there are also groups which do not seek public office but do aim to influence the outcomes of elections or public debate more generally. These political associations are fundamental to the proper workings of Australian democracy. In a mass democracy, leverage is usually secured through acting collectively. It is very rare for a citizen of ordinary means to have political leverage

on her or his own accord. It is only through mobilising in groups –
parties, interest groups, community groups – that a citizen is capable
of securing meaningful political power. In particular, associations are
necessary in order to engage in meaningful political expression. As
political philosopher Amy Gutmann put it:

> organized association is increasingly essential for the effective use
> of free speech ... Without access to an association that is willing
> and able to speak up for our views and values, we have a very
> limited ability to be heard by many other people or to influence
> the political process, unless we happen to be rich or famous.[70]

Such associations, and the freedom to form and act through them, are
therefore crucial to fairness in politics and to protecting the integrity of representative government, in particular by ensuring accountability in the exercise of public power.[71]

Underlying the importance of freedom of political association is
the principle of pluralist politics: citizens should have diverse avenues
through which to combine to influence the political process and
to express their views. This principle is also implicit in the functions to be performed by political parties: party politics should provide citizens with different ways to engage in political activity and
be represented; parties' policies and programs should offer clear and
meaningful choices.

The principle of pluralist politics provides further justification
for freedom of political association.[72] Political associations require
a meaningful degree of freedom from state regulation in order to
develop their identities, messages and activities. This applies in particular to political parties: pluralism in party politics cannot be sustained without parties having genuine autonomy in organising their
affairs.[73]

As with freedom of political expression, freedom of political
association does not imply an absence of state regulation. State regulation might be necessary in order to promote 'freedom to' associate,

for instance, through state funding to help disadvantaged sectors of society form organisations. Freedom of political association is also not absolute, and can be properly limited in certain circumstances. The functions of the parties themselves may, for example, furnish reasons for limiting such freedom. For instance, parties cannot properly discharge their participatory functions if their membership rolls have been corrupted, a problem that may require state intervention. State regulation might be necessary in order to secure pluralism and fairness in politics. It might also be needed as an antidote to the '[t]he monopolistic position of parties'[74] or the 'oligopoly' status of major parties.[75] Whether these rationales justify limitation of freedom of political association will depend (as with freedom of political expression) on the weight of such rationales, the extent to which the limitation is adapted to advancing this rationale and the severity of the limitation (including the risk that the limitation will lead to an abuse of state power).[76]

The means

There are four major objectives of a political finance regime:
1   protecting the integrity of representative government;
2   promoting fairness in politics;
3   supporting parties in performing their functions; and
4   respecting political freedoms.

These ends can be pursued in various ways with regulatory choices, choices that involve a complex interplay between the principles of the regime and the means it relies upon.

One choice is to adopt a laissez-faire policy. Under such a policy, there is no direct state regulation of the funding of politics. Rather, the influence of money on politics will be determined by the self-regulation of candidates, parties and other political actors, such as the media and third parties, in the context of electoral contests. Often this position reflects the view that electoral accountability is sufficient discipline. This assumption, however, is deeply flawed. For electoral accountability to police the funding of politics in even a minimal sense, there needs to be transparency of political funding so that voters can be fully informed. This transparency is not likely to be forthcoming through self-regulation.

Moreover, electoral accountability can only be effective if there is fairness in elections. It is improbable that such fairness will spontaneously emerge – rules and regulations, including those relating to political finance, will be necessary to provide a level playing field. Also, elections are too blunt a tool to ensure integrity of government in the area of political funding. They are usually fought over broad policies and platforms. A single incident of graft, for instance, may not irretrievably damage the prospects of the governing party and yet the integrity of government insists that such conduct be prevented.

Importantly, the view that electoral accountability is sufficient discipline fails to properly acknowledge the strict limits on such accountability in a system of representative government. It is these understandings that provide 'a form of popular rule that keeps the people at a considerable distance from the actual work of government'.[77] As Senator John Faulkner has noted:

> one of the internal strains and contradictions in democratic
> government [is that] power may belong to the people but it is
> exercised on their behalf – by both public servants charged with
> administration, and by politicians authorised by electoral success
> to implement their policies and programs.[78]

Aiming to prevent corruption and promote fairness in politics, most countries have adopted some form of state regulation. Transparency measures are usually at the top of the regulatory menu and are the most uncontroversial: many countries, including Australia, require that parties, candidates and other political actors disclose their funding details (see Chapter 2).

Then there are supply-side measures that directly regulate the flow of money into politics. These measures generally take two forms: source restrictions which regulate who (or what entities) can make financial contributions; and amount restrictions that limit the sums that can be given. Source restrictions are typically directed at preventing corruption (for example, by banning contributions from government contractors to parties). Amount restrictions share this aim but also seek to promote political fairness (see Chapter 4).

Demand-side measures, on the other hand, seek to deal directly with the demand for campaign funds that is driving the constant efforts of parties and candidates to raise money. The objectives here are to prevent corruption by staunching the appetite for funds and to promote fairness by levelling the playing field. To this end, some countries have established campaign expenditure limits. Others have gone further, banning the most expensive item of campaign expenditure: political advertising (see Chapter 7).

Another regulatory option is state support. Public funding of this kind is animated by various aims. It can be a demand-side measure that seeks to meet the demand for campaign funds by providing cash subsidies to parties or in-kind support such as the provision of 'free' broadcast time. An often-cited aim of public funding is also to provide fairer contests than would occur if private sources alone funded parties and candidates. Other forms of state support are aimed explicitly at supporting parties in performing their functions. Parliamentary entitlements, for instance, support the main parties in their governing function, and tax subsidies have sometimes been used to stimulate smaller contributions from citizens and, therefore, greater public participation in the parties (see Chapters 5 and 6).

While adopting any of these measures means that a country has gone beyond laissez-faire or complete reliance on self-regulation (in the context of electoral contests), no political finance regime can entirely dispense with self-regulation. State regulation has a vital but limited role to play, and needs to be complemented by self-regulation, because its effectiveness depends on the conduct of parties and other political actors. Its effectiveness will be shaped by their attitudes towards compliance: will they see the law as providing minimum standards of behaviour to be conscientiously complied with or as cumbersome constraints on behaviour with loopholes to be exploited? The 'bite' of regulation also relies on parties policing each other. Also, some ends of a political finance regime cannot be fully achieved by state regulation (for instance, the prevention of corruption through undue influence). In these situations, the conduct of parties and other political actors will be decisive. And finally, respect for political freedoms implies meaningful freedom from state regulation and ample room for political actors to develop their own characteristic practices and policies. While all this points to a continuing role for self-regulation, it is a long way from granting carte blanche to political actors. On the contrary, freedom from state regulation implies placing the burden of responsibility squarely upon these actors.

An Antipodean anomaly?

Among English-speaking liberal democracies, Australia stands out. Unlike Canada, New Zealand and the United Kingdom, it has no real demand-side measures; in particular, there are no limits on election spending except in Tasmania. Moreover, the High Court in the early 1990s foiled an attempt to institute a ban on federal political advertising[79] like the one in New Zealand and the United Kingdom. Supply-side measures are also largely absent. Canada and the United States have extensive limits on the amounts that can be contributed by individuals and organisations, but in Australia, unfettered freedom to contribute largely prevails. Even Australia's disclosure regime compares unfavourably. For instance, the schemes in Canada, the United Kingdom and the United States mandate far more frequent disclosure than the annual disclosure required in Australia and New

Zealand. Not surprisingly, Australia has been described as being 'by international standards ... decidedly laissez faire'.[80]

To identify Australia as an outlier amongst the countries we are usually compared with is not, however, to make an argument, let alone a persuasive one, that Australia should follow the lead of these countries. Keith Ewing and Samuel Issacharoff have identified a (non-exhaustive) list of factors that determine the choice of regulatory method in the area of political finance. These factors relate to history, geography, class structures, constitutional systems, party systems, electoral systems and ideological traditions.[81] If we take such complexity seriously – and we should – it is obvious that questions about whether Australia should adopt particular regulatory measures are only properly answered by an in-depth inquiry into Australia's specific circumstances; they cannot (and should not) be read off simplistic comparisons. We should abandon the notion that there is an international 'best practice' system or that there is a continuum along which we can locate regulatory models as 'strong' or 'weak'. Such understandings not only decontextualise and flatten the complexity involved in devising the best system for Australia but also, at times, seem to speak of a cultural cringe.

To make these points is not, however, to advocate a parochial stance closed off to overseas influence – indeed, this book regularly makes reference to regulation in other countries. The aim is not to deprecate the importance of comparative analysis but rather to point to its limits: it broadens our horizons by gesturing to what is possible, but often says very little as to what is desirable.

Nor is the characterisation of Australia's political finance system as laissez-faire (or relatively so) a compelling case for increased regulation. As suggested above, the absence of regulation is in itself not sufficient cause for concern. We should resist what legal expert Graeme Orr has perceptively described as the 'regulatory instinct'[82] that automatically deems such absence a lack that needs to be remedied by more legislation – not least because more regulation does not necessarily produce better outcomes. Indeed, if the parties and candidates were able to self-regulate to ensure fairness and integrity, this would be cause for celebration and testimony to a deep and robust democratic culture. The facts, however, speak to the failure of self-regulation in the area of political finance. As the chapters of this book will document, this failure traverses the whole spectrum of political funding: private funding and public funding, political contributions and political spending. It is this gross failure in the context of a laissez-faire system that makes the case for reform.

2
DISCLOSURE SCHEMES

The laissez-faire character of Australia's political finance regime is vividly illustrated by its lack of regulation of political funding from private sources. At the moment, there are no restrictions on the *source* of such funding, except for a Queensland ban on receiving gifts of foreign property[1] and a NSW ban on receiving money from property developers.[2] The only restriction on the *amount* of political funding appears in the *Electoral Act 2002* (Vic): holders of casino and gambling licences and their related companies are prohibited from making political donations exceeding $50,000 in a financial year to each registered political party.[3]

The main way in which private political funding is regulated in Australia is through disclosure schemes. They are the focus of this chapter. The key principle underlying these schemes is transparency, which aims to protect the integrity of representative government in three ways. First, it aids informed voting, thereby buttressing the integrity of electoral processes. Second, it is a crucial tool for preventing corruption. Third, such transparency in itself protects public confidence in representative government (see Chapter 1). Besides these broader rationales, transparency of political funding is also necessary to ensure the effectiveness of specific regulatory measures. Contribution and election spending limits, for instance, can only work effectively if there is adequate disclosure of political contributions and spending.

The chapter begins with a definition of the key terms used in disclosure schemes, then analyses the federal, state and territory disclosure schemes. All these schemes seriously fail to provide proper transparency of private funding: they offer partial coverage, half measures and lax compliance, and their disclosure obligations sit alongside avenues for concealment and evasion. Local government disclosure schemes are not any better: there is only ramshackle regulation in most jurisdictions. The result is that the flow of private money into Australian politics remains murky and opaque.

The chapter then turns to the question of solutions. It critically evaluates the Commonwealth Electoral Amendment (Political Donations and Other Measures) Bill 2009 (Cth), a Bill that will significantly improve the disclosure of political funding in Australia (if it is passed), and then proposes further improvements to the disclosure of such funding. The chapter concludes by emphasising that robust disclosure schemes, though vital, are not sufficient. In particular, it sounds a cautionary note on two inherent limitations of disclosure schemes.

Federal, state and territory disclosure schemes

The federal scheme is found in the *Commonwealth Electoral Act 1918*. Under this Act, registered political parties[9] and their associated entities[10] have to submit annual disclosure returns, regardless of their obligations under their own state or territory laws. The registered political parties and associated entities have virtually identical disclosure requirements. The returns have to be in a form approved by the Australian Electoral Commission (AEC) and must disclose

Definition of key terms

ASSOCIATED ENTITIES

Disclosure schemes generally define an 'associated entity' as an entity that is either controlled by one or more registered political parties or that operates wholly or to a significant extent for the benefit of one or more registered political parties.[4] With the enactment of the *Electoral and Referendum Amendment (Electoral Integrity and Other Measures) Act 2006* (Cth), the definition of 'associated entity' under the federal scheme has been extended to include organisations that are financial members of or have voting rights in a political party.[5]

ELECTORAL EXPENDITURE

Under disclosure schemes, this term is generally defined to mean expenditure, during election periods (which typically begin on the days the election is called and end at the close of the ballot), on: publishing, broadcasting, displaying or producing electoral advertisements; producing and publishing electoral matter; carrying out opinion polls relating to the election; and payments made to consultancies for services relating to the election.[6]

GIFTS (POLITICAL DONATIONS)

Under disclosure schemes, a 'gift' is defined as any disposition of property made with inadequate or no consideration.[7] When public commentary refers to 'political donations', it is typically referring to that definition of 'gifts'. This book will use these terms as synonyms.

RECEIPTS (INCOME/CONTRIBUTIONS)

Under disclosure schemes, 'receipts' refers to all payments received. These include gifts, membership subscriptions, payments received as a result of commercial transactions (such as investments) and, under the federal scheme, payments made at fundraisers.[8] This book will use 'income' and 'contributions' as synonyms for 'receipts'.

THIRD PARTIES

'Third parties' is a non-legal term that refers to entities other than registered parties, their associated entities, candidates (and groups of candidates) and donors with disclosure obligations. Examples include non-government organisations (NGOs) that engage in political campaigns during election time, such as the Australian Council of Trade Unions, the Business Council of Australia and GetUp!

---

the total amount received, paid or owed by, or on behalf of, the registered political party or associated entity for the financial year. In addition, registered political parties and associated entities are required to make further disclosure if they have received from, or owe, a particular person or organisation a sum exceeding an indexed threshold.[11] In 2009–10, the indexed threshold stood at $11,200. In calculating whether this sum has been reached amounts below the indexed threshold can be disregarded – this means that a group of donations that exceed the threshold when added together can be disregarded unless one or more of these donations is over the threshold. So I could give a political party $1500 per month for one financial year, a total of $18,000, and the party would not have to disclose that because none of the individual payments was over $11,200 and therefore they can all be disregarded. However, if I gave $600 for 11 months and $11,201 in the last month, a total for the year of $17,801, the party would have to disclose all those payments. Once the indexed threshold has been reached, registered political parties and associated entitles must disclose certain particulars: the amount of the sum (that is, all payments) or debt and the name and address of the person (or organisation) who paid or is owed the sum.

Persons who give a registered political party an amount exceeding the indexed threshold in any particular year are subject to annual disclosure obligations themselves. They have to lodge a statement with the AEC disclosing all such gifts, and they have to itemise those exceeding the indexed threshold; they also have to itemise gifts exceeding the indexed threshold that were used to make the gifts to the political party.[12] Third parties that have spent more than the indexed threshold in a financial year on political expenditure must disclose to the AEC details of such expenditure,[13] as well as the gifts received exceeding the indexed threshold that were used for such spending.[14]

Candidates and groups of candidates, after every election, have to give the AEC a statement detailing the amount of gifts received during the period between elections if the gifts exceeded the indexed threshold, together with the names and addresses of the donors,[15] as well as details of their electoral expenditure.[16] Persons who have donated amounts exceeding the indexed threshold to candidates (and groups of candidates) must disclose similar details of such gifts to the AEC after the relevant election.[17]

Table 2.1 summarises the funding disclosure obligations under the *Commonwealth Electoral Act*. Table 2.2 does the same in relation to expenditure disclosure obligations.

Five of the eight states and territories have their own funding disclosure schemes. Two states, South Australia and Tasmania, do not have such schemes, which makes the federal scheme the only source of funding disclosure obligations in these states. Victorian electoral law does not include a funding disclosure scheme but does require registered Victorian political parties to comply with federal disclosure obligations.[18] The federal disclosure scheme is also of crucial significance in the Northern Territory[19] and in Western Australia:[20] they both allow registered parties and associated entities to lodge returns under the federal scheme instead of under their own schemes, which have more onerous obligations.

Table 2.3, on pages 34–39, sets out the key features of state and territory funding disclosure schemes. As a result of amendments made in 2008, the Queensland[21] and NSW[22] schemes provide the most

TABLE 2.1: FUNDING DISCLOSURE OBLIGATIONS UNDER THE *COMMONWEALTH ELECTORAL ACT*

Entity	Details to be disclosed	Frequency	Reporting deadline
Registered political parties	Total amount received Itemise receipts exceeding $11,200 (indexed)	Annual	16 weeks after end of financial year
Associated entities	Total amount received Itemise receipts exceeding $11,200 (indexed) Itemise contributions made to capital used to generate income paid to registered political party	Annual	16 weeks after end of financial year
Candidates, and groups of candidates not endorsed by a registered political party	Total amount of gifts received Itemise gifts exceeding $11,200 (indexed)	Post-election	15 weeks after polling day
Donors	Total amount of gifts given to candidates if total exceeds $11,200 (indexed) Itemise gifts exceeding $11,200 (indexed) received by donor used for making above gifts	Post-election	15 weeks after polling day
	Total amount of gifts given to registered political party/ies if total exceeds $11,200 (indexed) Itemise gifts exceeding $11,200 (indexed) received by donor used for making above gifts	Annual	20 weeks after end of financial year
Third parties	Itemisation of any gifts given that exceed $11,200 (indexed) if the third party made political expenditure exceeding $11,200 (indexed) and at least one of the gifts used for such expenditure exceeded $11,200 (indexed).	Annual	20 weeks after end of financial year

Source: *Commonwealth Electoral Act 1918* (Cth), Part XX – Election Funding and Financial Disclosure, ss 304, 305A, 305B, 314AB, 314AC, 314AEA, 314AEC.

TABLE 2.2: EXPENDITURE DISCLOSURE OBLIGATIONS UNDER THE *COMMONWEALTH ELECTORAL ACT*

Entity	Details to be disclosed	Frequency	Reporting deadline
Registered political parties	Total amount paid	Annual	16 weeks after end of financial year
Associated entities	Total amount paid	Annual	16 weeks after end of financial year
Candidates, and groups of candidates not endorsed by a registered political party	Details of electoral expenditure	Post-election	15 weeks after polling day
Third parties	Details of political expenditure if such expenditure exceeds $11,200 (indexed)	Annual	20 weeks after end of financial year

Source: *Commonwealth Electoral Act 1918* (Cth) ss 309, 314AB, 314AEA, 314AEB.

robust disclosure obligations. Key features of the Queensland scheme include biannual returns by registered political parties and associated entities and 14-day disclosure by donors, registered political parties and associated entities when a donor makes a gift (or gifts) totalling $100,000 within a 6-month reporting period. The NSW scheme, on the other hand, requires all key political participants, except for associated entities, to submit biannual returns.

In terms of expenditure disclosure schemes, South Australia is the outlier, in that it does not impose any obligation to disclose details of political expenditure. The effect again is that only the federal scheme provides information on the political expenditure of SA political parties and other participants. Table 2.4, on pages 38–41, which identifies the key features of the schemes in other states and territories indicates that, as with funding disclosure schemes, there is considerable variation. Again, as a result of amendments made in 2008, Queensland[23] and New South Wales[24] are most demanding.

Transparent failures[25]

The disclosure of private political funding in Australia falls seriously short of transparency. Both South Australia and Tasmania do not have funding disclosure schemes; South Australia is clearly at the bottom of the league, because it does not have its own expenditure disclosure scheme either. Even in jurisdictions that have disclosure schemes, some give only partial coverage of the key political actors. The NSW disclosure scheme, while exemplary in many respects, fails to cover associated entities. The effect is that NSW political parties have a readily available way to avoid disclosure – front organisations. The Tasmanian and Victorian expenditure disclosure schemes do not extend to third parties such as lobby groups, trade unions and businesses; the Tasmanian, Victorian and WA funding disclosure schemes leave out registered parties, candidates and donors respectively.

Timeliness of disclosure is also necessary if these schemes are to prevent graft and undue influence, and ensure that citizens have the information they need before they cast their votes. There is, however, a lack of timeliness in most of the disclosure schemes. While post-election disclosure obligations might help provide information that will prevent graft and undue influence, they clearly cannot aid voters, as information is only provided after the election.

Even annual disclosure obligations do not provide timely information. The AEC has observed in relation to federal annual returns that '[t]his form of … reporting and release can result in delays that can discount the relevance of making the information public'.[26] For example, in late September 2004, barely a fortnight before the October 2004 federal election, British Lord Michael Ashcroft donated $1 million to the federal Liberal Party.[27] Citizens casting their votes in that election were completely unaware of this contribution and only found out more than 15 months later, on 1 February 2005, when the AEC released the disclosure returns.

Biannual returns, which are currently required under the NSW

TABLE 2.3: STATE AND TERRITORY FUNDING DISCLOSURE SCHEMES

Jurisdiction	ACT	NT
Registered parties	Annual returns disclosing total amounts received Defined 'particulars' for amounts received from a person or organisation equal to or greater than $1000 in a financial year (e.g. name and address of the organisation that paid the amount)	Annual returns disclosing total amounts received Defined particulars for amounts received from a person or organisation equal to or greater than $1500 in a financial year
Associated entities	Annual returns disclosing total amounts received from a particular person or organisation, including defined 'particulars' for the amount, where the sum of all amounts received from that person or organisation is equal to or greater than $50 in a financial year	Annual returns disclosing total amounts received Defined particulars of amounts received where amount received from an entity is equal to or greater than $1500 in a financial year
Elected candidates	Annual returns disclosing total amounts received Defined particulars for amounts received from a person or organisation equal to or greater than $1000 or more in a financial year	None

NSW	QLD	WA
Biannual returns disclosing details of gifts received totalling $1000 or more and details of non-reportable donations, subscriptions and fundraising functions. Returns to be accompanied by auditor's certificate These obligations apply to political parties whether or not registered under the Act	Biannual returns disclosing total amounts received Details for amounts received from, and owed to, a person or organisation where amounts to/from that organisation are equal to or greater than $1000 in the six-month reporting period Where a political party, related political parties and associated entities together receive $100,000 or more from a single donor in a 6-month reporting period, receipt of gifts must be disclosed within 14 days of receipt	Annual return disclosing details of gifts received totalling $2100 (indexed) or more in the financial year
None		Annual return disclosing details of gifts received totalling $2100 (indexed) or more in the financial year
Biannual returns disclosing details of gifts received totalling $1000 or more and details of non-reportable donations, subscriptions and fundraising functions Returns to be accompanied by auditor's certificate	None	None

Jurisdiction	ACT	NT
Candidates	Post-election disclosure of the total amount of all gifts received and the total number of persons who made gifts Defined particulars required where the sum of gifts received from one person during the period between elections is equal to or greater than $1000	Post-election disclosure of the total amount of all gifts received and the total number of persons who made gifts Defined particulars required where the sum of gifts received from one person during the period between elections is equal to or greater than $200
Groups of candidates	None	None
Donors	Post-election return disclosing details of gifts if gifts made to a candidate, non-party group, political party, associated entity or parliamentarian total $1000 or more in the period between elections Specifically included in disclosure obligation: if donor received a gift/s totalling $1000 or more and then used all or part of that gift/s to make their own gift/s of $1000 or more to a political party, associated entity or parliamentarian, donor must disclose	Post-election return disclosing details of gifts if gifts to a candidate total $200 or more, or gifts to a party total $1500 or more, in the period between elections Specifically included in disclosure obligation: if donor received a gift/s of $1000 or more and then used all or part of that gift/s to make their own gift/s of $1500 or more to a registered party, donor must disclose

NSW	QLD	WA
Biannual returns in the case of reportable political donations totalling $1000 or more Must disclose details of gifts received totalling $1000 or more and details of non-reportable donations, subscriptions and fundraising functions Returns to be accompanied by auditor's certificate	Post-election disclosure of the total amount of all gifts received and the total number of persons who made gifts Defined particulars required where the sum of gifts received from one person is equal to or greater than $1000 Particulars not required if the gift was made in a private capacity for personal use and was not/will not be used solely or substantially for a purpose related to an election or by-election	Post-election disclosure of the total amount of gifts received and the total number of persons who made gifts Defined particulars required where the sum of gifts received from one person in the period between elections is equal to or greater than $2100 (indexed)
As above	None	Post-election disclosure of the total amount of gifts received and the total number of persons who made gifts Defined particulars required where the sum of gifts received from one person in the period between elections is equal to or greater than $2100 (indexed)
As above	Post-election return disclosing details of gifts if gifts to a candidate total $1000 or more in the period between elections If gifts to a party totalling $1000 or more in 6-month reporting periods, then biannual returns detailing such gifts If made gift of $100,000 or more to political party, related political parties and associated entities as a whole in 6-month reporting period, obligation to disclose gifts within 14 days	None

Jurisdiction	ACT	NT
Third parties	Post-election return disclosing details of gifts if incurred $1000 or more in electoral expenditure and received gift/s valuing $1000 or more, all or part of which was used to enable the electoral expenditure	Post-election return if incurred $1000 or more in electoral expenditure and received gift/s valuing $1000 or more, all or part of which was used to enable the electoral expenditure

Source: *Electoral Act 1992* (ACT) ss 217, 220–221A, 230, 231B, 232(3)–(4); Electoral Regulation 1993 (ACT), r 6; *Electoral Funding and Disclosure Act 1981* (NSW) ss 88(1)–(2), 89–92, 96K; *Electoral Act 2004* (NT) ss 191–194, 205, 208, 210; *Electoral Act 1992* (Qld) Schedule – 'Election Funding and Financial Disclosure Based on Part XX of the Commonwealth Electoral Act' – ss 304, 305–305C, 314AB–AEA, Act'; Electoral Act 1907 (WA) ss 175, 175N–175Q.

TABLE 2.4: STATE AND TERRITORY EXPENDITURE DISCLOSURE SCHEMES

Jurisdiction	ACT	NT	NSW
Registered parties	Annual return stating total amount paid Post-election return detailing electoral expenditure if expenditure more than $1000	Annual return stating total amount spent	Biannual returns detailing electoral expenditure Returns to be accompanied by auditor's certificate These obligations apply to political parties whether or not registered under the Act
Associated entities	Annual return stating total amount paid Post-election return detailing electoral expenditure if expenditure more than $1000	Annual return stating total amount spent	None
Elected candidates	Annual return stating total amount paid	None	Biannual returns detailing electoral expenditure Returns to be accompanied by auditor's certificate

	NSW	QLD	WA
	Biannual returns if incurred electoral expenditure of $1000 or more; must disclose details of gifts received totalling $1000 or more and details of non-reportable donations, subscriptions and fundraising functions Returns to be accompanied by auditor's certificate	Post-election return disclosing details of gifts if incurred $1000 or more in electoral expenditure and received gift/s valued at $1000 or more, all or part of which were used to enable the electoral expenditure	Post-election return disclosing details of gifts if incurred $2100 (indexed) or more in electoral expenditure and received gift/s valued at $1000 or more, all or part of which were used to enable the electoral expenditure

	QLD	TAS	VIC	WA
	Biannual returns detailing amounts paid of $1000 or more Claims for election funding must detail electoral expenditure	None	Claims for election funding must provide statement of electoral expenditure with auditor's certificate	Post-election return detailing electoral expenditure Claims for election funding must detail electoral expenditure
	Biannual returns detailing amounts paid of $1000 or more	None	None	None
	None	None	None	None

Jurisdiction	ACT	NT	NSW
Candidates	Post-election return detailing electoral expenditure if expenditure is $1000 or more	Post-election return detailing electoral expenditure if expenditure is $200 or more	Biannual returns disclosing details of electoral expenditure if reportable political donations totalled $1000 or more Returns to be accompanied by auditor's certificate
Groups of candidates not endorsed by a registered political party	None	None	As above
Donors	None	None	As above
Third parties	Post-election return detailing electoral expenditure if expenditure more than $1000	Post-election return detailing electoral expenditure if expenditure is $200 or more	Biannual returns disclosing details of electoral expenditure if incurred electoral expenditure totals $1000 or more Returns to be accompanied by auditor's certificate

Source: *Electoral Act 1992* (ACT) ss 161, 224, 230(4)(b), 231B(2)(b); *Electoral Act 2004* (NT) ss 200(1)–(2), 205, 208; *Election Funding and Disclosure Act 1981* (NSW) ss88(1)–(2), 89–91, 93, 96K; *Electoral Act 1992* (Qld) Sch – 'Election funding and financial disclosure based on part XX of the Commonwealth Electoral Act'– ss 297–298, 309(4), 314AD; *Electoral Act 2002* (Vic) ss 208–209; *Electoral Act 1907* (WA) s175LD(5), 175SA–175SD.

	QLD	TAS	VIC	WA
	Post-election return detailing electoral expenditure if expenditure more than $200	Legislative Council candidates to lodge post-election return detailing election expenditure	None	Post-election return detailing electoral expenditure
	None	None	None	Post-election return detailing electoral expenditure
	None	None	None	None
	Post-election return detailing electoral expenditure if expenditure more than $200	None	None	Post-election return detailing electoral expenditure if expenditure more than $500

and Queensland schemes, are a significant improvement. But even they do not provide the 'real time' disclosure that is necessary for informed voting – political donations made in the months leading up to elections need not be disclosed until after the event. This limitation is of particular concern with large donations, as these are seen to involve a serious risk of corruption; this concern is heightened by the major parties' dependence on large contributions (see Chapter 3). It is only through provisions like the Queensland one to disclose gifts of $100,000 or more within 14 days, or imposing weekly reporting obligations during election time (discussed below), that this deficiency can be dealt with.

The detail of the information disclosed is also inadequate. Under current schemes, registered parties and associated entities are not legally required to accurately categorise a receipt as a 'donation' or otherwise. This system of self-declaration is a recipe for errors and under-reporting. Moreover, a list of donations received from particular types of donors (companies and trade unions, for instance) can only be extricated with a great deal of effort. This has been learnt the hard way by academics, political researchers and activists.[28]

What is perhaps the most serious loophole of the current law is the astonishing level of non-disclosure permitted by the high disclosure thresholds in the federal scheme. This is a direct consequence of the *Electoral and Referendum Amendment (Electoral Integrity and Other Measures) Act 2006* (Cth), which greatly relaxed the disclosure obligations of federally registered parties and their associated entities. These entities are now required to disclose details only of sums exceeding an indexed threshold ($10,000 when the law was enacted, and now $11,200), instead of sums of $1500 or more (as was the case under the previous law).[29]

According to Commonwealth Parliamentary Library research, the previous disclosure threshold of $1500 or more resulted in 74.7 per cent of declared total receipts being itemised over the period from the 1998–99 financial year to the 2004–05 financial year. If the threshold of $10,000 had been applied, this figure would have dropped to 64.1 per cent.[30] Updating that research, the Joint Standing Committee on Electoral Matters found that under the $10,300 threshold (which applied in 2006–07), only 52.6 per cent of the income of the ALP and Coalition parties was itemised for that year.[31] On these calculations, we have a remarkable situation: the source of nearly half the income of the major parties is unknown.

While these figures give some indication of the level of non-disclosure under the federal scheme, they may still underestimate the proportion of funds that remain undisclosed. As non-disclosure is increasingly legitimised, it is likely that parties will take greater advantage of the regulatory gaps. One gap stems from disclosure thresholds applying *separately* to each registered political party. Where the national, state and territory branches of the major political parties are *each* treated as a registered political party, this means that a major party constituted by nine branches has the cumulative benefit of nine thresholds. For example, a company can donate $11,200 to each state and territory branch of the ALP as well as to its national branch – a total of $100,800 – without the ALP having to reveal the identity of the donor. There is little doubt on this point – having such a high threshold can only mean more secret donations.

The Commonwealth's *Electoral and Referendum Amendment (Electoral Integrity and Other Measures) Act 2006* also increased the threshold at which the prohibition against anonymous donations and loans applies, from amounts greater than $1000 to amounts exceeding $10,000 (indexed). It is this increase that will perhaps most seriously compromise transparency. This change is less about public disclosure of donations and loans and more about records kept by parties: it will mean that parties can legally accept larger sums without recording details of the donor.

Take, for instance, a situation where the Liberal Party, through its nine branches, accepts anonymous donations from a single company totalling $100,800. The company then gives an additional $11,300 to each of these branches that is publicly disclosed. Under the current law, details of the entire $202,500 should be disclosed. The ability to legally accept $100,800 in anonymous donations, however, means there is no need to keep the records, the paper trail, required to enforce such an obligation. At best, this change is an invitation to poor record keeping; at worst, it is an opportunity for wholesale circumvention of the disclosure scheme.

These results of the *Electoral and Referendum Amendment (Electoral Integrity and Other Measures) Act 2006* are hardly unintended. Senator Eric Abetz, the Minister sponsoring the Act, perhaps spoke for many others in his party when he said that he hoped for 'a return to the good old days when people used to donate to the Liberal Party via lawyers' trust accounts'.[32] The Act has also produced greater secrecy in some states and territories, since the federal scheme acts as a default scheme for those without their own schemes (South Australia, Tasmania, Victoria). Moreover, as noted above, Western Australia and the Northern Territory allow state parties and associated entities to comply with the disclosure obligations under the federal scheme in lieu of adhering to the more demanding requirements of their own laws.

These shortcomings vividly illustrate Australia's 'lackadaisical law' regulating political money.[33] It is accompanied by lackadaisical attitudes. There is good evidence that the parties are not treating their disclosure obligations under the federal scheme seriously. The AEC has observed:

> The legislation's history to date can be characterised as one of only partial success. Provisions have been, and remain, such that full disclosure can be legally avoided. In short, the legislation has failed to meet its objective of full disclosure to the Australian public of the material financial transactions of political parties, candidates and others.[34]

Much of the AEC's cause for complaint is based on its view that there is a culture of evasion in some quarters. It has previously stated that 'there has been an unwillingness by some to comply with disclosure; some have sought to circumvent its intent by applying the narrowest possible interpretation of the legislation'.[35]

It could be argued that evasion of disclosure obligations is facilitated in two other ways. First, there are foreign-sourced contributions: contributions that originate from foreign addresses. As Table 2.5 indicates, the main parties did not receive many such contributions in the period 1998–99 to 2002–03. Table 2.6, which draws on analysis of AEC records by former Democrats Senator Andrew Murray, however, indicates that the amounts of these contributions have significantly increased in recent years (attributable in part to the $1 million gift to the Liberal Party by Lord Michael Ashcroft). Such contributions pose a challenge for the integrity of disclosure schemes as it is difficult for electoral commissions to ensure the accuracy of the information provided.

Second, there is the enormous amount of money being channelled through the associated entities of the major parties (as noted

TABLE 2.5: FOREIGN CONTRIBUTIONS TO PARTIES, 1998–99 TO 2002–03	
Party	Amount
ALP	$82,529
Liberal Party	$41,609
National Party	Nil
Australian Democrats	$2200
Greens	$31,573

Source: Calculated from AEC (April 2004) *Submission to the Joint Standing Committee on Electoral Matters' Inquiry into Disclosure of Donations to Political Parties and Candidates*, 26.

TABLE 2.6: FOREIGN-SOURCED CONTRIBUTIONS TO PARTIES, 1998-99 TO 2006-07	
Party	Amount
Liberal Party	$1,664,279
ALP	$475,067
Greens	$170,564
Citizens Electoral Council	$7110
Australian Democrats	$2200
Total	$2,319,220

Source: Senator Andrew Murray, *Briefing Note: Foreign Political Donations* (2008) (available at http://www.andrewmurray.org.au/documents/464/PR%20Foreign%20Political%20Donations%20February%20 2008.pdf).

in Chapter 3). The use of such entities is not necessarily motivated by an attempt to evade disclosure. For instance, parties might be using an associated entity as a vehicle for investment. The benefits of this might include the limited liability of such an entity, if incorporated, and the opportunity to have directors who have investment expertise. Also, there may be a perception that donors are more willing to contribute to an organisation that appears to be at arm's length from the party.

On the other hand, using an associated entity might be aimed at compromising transparency. Party officials may wish to avoid the formal decision-making processes of the party. While associated entities have exactly the same obligations as registered parties in most disclosure schemes, money received by such entities might not be as closely scrutinised by the media or other organisations as money directly received by the parties.

Party officials might also suspect that the electoral commissions themselves face greater difficulties in enforcing the law against associated entities. The case of the Greenfields Foundation is instructive. In 1996, the foundation was assigned a loan of $4.45 million from the Liberal Party after Ron Walker, then the Liberal Party National Treasurer and a prominent businessman, discharged the guarantee of an existing debt of the party. In 1998, the AEC required the trustees of the foundation to lodge an 'associated entity' return. It refused. The *Commonwealth Electoral Act* was then amended to give the AEC the power to inspect records of an organisation for the purpose of determining whether or not it was an associated entity. After exercising this power, the AEC formed the view that the foundation was an associated entity and again asked it to lodge an associated entity return. Under protest, the foundation eventually lodged such returns in September 1999.[36] What the Greenfields Foundation episode demonstrates is that when an organisation resists its obligations as an associated entity, electoral commissions may have to double their efforts and, in some situations, secure amendments to the law, before they can enforce the law against such an organisation.

The deficiencies of the disclosure schemes are compounded by the reluctance of parties to voluntarily disclose details of their income. In September 2005, the author, together with Dr Sally Young, a political scientist based in the University of Melbourne, sent letters to federal and state branches of the main parties seeking information regarding their finances. We sent follow-up letters in January 2006. As Table 2.7 demonstrates, most did not provide a response. Moreover, those who did overwhelmingly referred us to returns lodged with the AEC.

The federal ALP was most forthcoming in its response and provided general information as to the sources of its income, which was said to include 'membership and affiliation dues from state branches, public electoral funding, private donations and investments'. It also advised of its policy on not receiving donations from the tobacco industry and its Code of Conduct for Fundraising.[37] Further, in 2010, the ALP voluntarily disclosed amounts greater than $1000 despite the disclosure threshold being $11,200[38] (the $1000 threshold is the one proposed under the Commonwealth Electoral Amendment (Political Donations and Other Measures) Bill 2009 (Cth); see below).

While the Greens did not provide a response, their policy includes 'making public within three months all donations greater than $1500'.[39] Disclosure of some of these donations is made through the *democracy4sale* website, which is maintained by the NSW Greens.[40] In addition to listing the donations to the Greens, the website also indicates whether donors are individuals, unions or corporations. With corporate donors, there is also information about the type of company.

TABLE 2.7: RESPONSES TO REQUESTS FOR INFORMATION ON PARTY INCOME			
Letter sent to (party)	Provided a response	Response referred us to AEC	Provided additional information
ALP – ACT	✗	n/a	n/a
ALP – National	✔	✔	✔
ALP – NSW	✗	n/a	n/a
ALP – NT	✗	n/a	n/a
ALP – QLD	✗	n/a	n/a
ALP – SA	✗	n/a	n/a
ALP – TAS	✗	n/a	n/a
ALP – VIC	✗	n/a	n/a
ALP – WA	✗	n/a	n/a
Democrats – National	✔	✗	✗
Greens – National	✗	n/a	n/a
Liberal – ACT	✗	n/a	n/a
Liberal – National	✗	n/a	n/a
Liberal – NSW	✗	n/a	n/a
Liberal – QLD	✔	✔	✗
Liberal – SA	✗	n/a	n/a
Liberal – TAS	✗	n/a	n/a
Liberal – VIC	✔	✔	✗
Liberal – WA	✗	n/a	n/a
CLP – NT	✗	n/a	n/a
Nationals – National	✗	n/a	n/a
Nationals – NSW	✗	n/a	n/a
Nationals – QLD	✔	✔	✗
Nationals – SA	✔	✗	✗
Nationals – VIC	✔	✔	✗
Nationals – WA	✗	n/a	n/a

Local government disclosure schemes

Academic scholarship on Australian political finance has generally neglected local government regulation: there has not yet been a systematic inquiry into such regulation.[41] This is a glaring gap, as this level of government is probably more susceptible to corruption (see Chapter 3). Also, the list of political finance scandals at the level of local government grows longer and longer, and now includes Wollongong City Council, Greater Geelong City Council, Gold Coast City Council and the Tweed Shire Council. I will now make a (very) modest effort to address this lacuna by providing a critical analysis of local government disclosure schemes.

In Queensland, South Australia, Victoria and Western Australia, local government disclosure schemes only impose obligations on candidates.[42] The SA and Victorian schemes require post-election returns,[43] and the WA scheme requires, for the 6 months leading up to election day, that gifts are disclosed within 3 days of receipt once nominations are made (and for gifts received before nominations are disclosed, within 3 days of nominations being announced).[44] Under these schemes, the returns, which provide various details of gifts exceeding specified amounts, are lodged with the Chief Executive Officer of councils and open to public inspection.[45]

With NSW, Queensland and Tasmanian local government elections, disclosure obligations apply more broadly; they cover candidates and other political participants. In Queensland, local government candidates, third parties and donors have to lodge post-election returns with the Chief Executive Officer of the relevant council.[46] In Tasmania, candidates and other persons or groups publishing electoral advertising in local government elections have to lodge returns with the Tasmanian Electoral Commissioner.[47] In New South Wales, the biannual disclosure system (previously described) also applies to local government elections.[48]

There is little doubt that many of these schemes do not provide transparency. The schemes in Queensland, South Australia, Victoria and Western Australia do not extend to political parties. Further, all except for the NSW and Tasmanian schemes require returns to be lodged with the relevant council. This limits the accessibility of the information, as there is no agency responsible for collecting and publishing it, and public inspection probably has to occur at the council offices.

Except for the WA scheme, the lack of timeliness means that local government voters will be unaware of the finances of the candidates until well after the election. There are telling examples. The 2004 Gold Coast City Council election saw a group of candidates bankrolled by 'donors with development interests'.[49] These funds were raised by two sitting councillors, David Power and Sue Robbins, who successfully solicited money from '[m]embers of the various Gold Coast chambers of commerce ... [who were] highly receptive to the idea of supporting pro-business, "sensible" candidates'.[50] These arrangements were, however, to remain covert, and 'a concerted effort to conceal both the existence of the fund for selected candidates, and the involvement of Power and Robbins' was made.[51] The result, in the view of the Queensland Crime and Misconduct Commission, was a 'barrage of secrecy, deceit and misinformation'.[52] In a paragraph worth quoting in full, the Commission found that:

> These [Power and Robbins-selected] candidates were presented
> as totally independent candidates, funding their own campaigns.
> In fact, they had received funding through the initiative of
> two sitting councillors [David Power and Sue Robbins], and
> the funding came exclusively from parties with development
> interests. If elected, the candidates would be, consciously or
> unconsciously, beholden to Power and Robbins for that funding
> during their four-year term. If they harboured ambitions of
> running for a further term, they would be aware that their
> chances of receiving funding through Power and Robbins at the
> next election would depend on their being still viewed by Power
> and Robbins as 'like-minded' candidates.[53]

We saw a similar story unfold in relation to the 2004 Greater Geelong City Council elections. David Saunderson, a sitting councillor who was subsequently re-elected, solicited funds from six Geelong businessmen, including Frank Costa, a leading local businessman, and property development company Lascorp Development Group (Aust.) Pty Ltd,[54] with Costa and Lascorp respectively contributing to support 'higher quality candidates'[55] and a 'productive Council'.[56] Saunderson, who controlled the disbursement of these funds, channelled them to 17 candidates; six of them, including himself and current Deputy Mayor (previously Mayor), Bruce Harwood, were elected.[57] At no time during the election campaign was this financial support disclosed to the public and, indeed, there was no disclosure even after the election. Yet the penalty for these failures has been minimal: only Saunderson was convicted for failing to disclose under the *Local Government Act 1989* (Vic), and he was fined a derisory $1000.[58] This conviction does not even seem to have produced much contrition: when declaring that he would stand for re-election in the November 2008 council elections, Saunderson was quoted as saying that the people of Geelong would not benefit if the elections became embroiled in questions surrounding the funding of candidates[59] (sentiments that seem to have been shared by plenty of Geelong voters, as Saunderson was elected for another term).[60]

Like the Gold Coast City Council elected in 2004, a conflict of interest resulted from the 2004 Greater Geelong City Council[61] being bankrolled by particular business interests. The observations made by the Queensland Crime and Misconduct Commission in relation to councillors selected by Power and Robbins could apply equally to these councillors: would they not be consciously or unconsciously beholden to Saunderson and/or his business supporters during their term?

These arrangements, however, seem to have been normalised. Rather than being viewed as improper, they may, in the words of Frank Costa, be treated as a sign of a 'high quality' council with 'some good, proactive people'.[62] For Costa, councillors who accept campaign contributions need not declare this, nor excuse themselves from voting on matters affecting their financiers. In his words, 'It could be seen as an issue, [but] not by me it's not.'[63] Like the Local Government Association of Queensland's view of the conduct of Power and Robbins, this behaviour is being treated as part of a 'perfectly ordinary political process'.[64]

A new era of disclosure?

What we have seen so far is a catalogue of the weaknesses of disclosure schemes at all levels of government. The outlook for such schemes is not, however, uniformly pessimistic. Set against the problems is a growing push to improve the disclosure rules. In 2008, the federal government released the *Electoral Reform Green Paper: Donations, Funding and Expenditure*, which canvassed various options for improving the federal disclosure scheme.[65] The 2008 amendments to the Queensland and NSW disclosure schemes, which made these schemes leaders in this field, have already been mentioned. The Queensland amendments also introduced bans on political parties and candidates receiving gifts of foreign property,[66] and bans modelled on provisions of the Commonwealth Electoral Amendment (Political Donations and Other Measures) Bill 2009 (Cth) (discussed below).[67] This Bill is the most important disclosure measure proposed in recent times. If adopted, it will significantly improve the transparency of political finance in Australia.[68]

The Bill introduces a biannual disclosure system for registered parties, associated entities, donors and third parties based on a $1000 (non-indexed) threshold.[69] The threshold will not apply to political parties separately; 'related' political parties will be treated as one.[70] Lodgment periods will be shortened and penalties will be increased.[71] The Bill also proposes various bans in relation to gifts of foreign property. If enacted, it will be unlawful for:

- registered political parties and their state branches to receive such gifts;[72]
- candidates and groups of candidates to receive such gifts for specified periods;[73] and
- third parties, candidates and groups of candidates to incur political expenditure if a gift of foreign property enabled such expenditure and the donor's main purpose was to enable such persons or entities to incur political expenditure.[74]

The Bill also proposes various prohibitions relating to anonymous gifts. Subject to an exemption for certain anonymous gifts under $50,[75] it will be unlawful under these prohibitions for:

- registered political parties and their state branches to receive anonymous gifts;[76]
- candidates and groups of candidates to receive such gifts for specified periods;[77]
- associated entities to receive such gifts if the donor's main purpose was to enable the entities to incur political expenditure;[78] and
- third parties, candidates and groups of candidates to incur political expenditure if an anonymous gift enabled such expenditure.[79]

The bans relating to anonymous gifts and gifts of foreign property will be enforced in two ways: the amount involved in breaches of the bans will be payable to the Commonwealth, and breaches will also be criminal offences.[80]

Table 2.8 summarises the key differences between the current provisions and the provisions that will apply if the Bill is passed.

There is great merit to most of the measures proposed by the Bill. It will address the gaping holes in the federal scheme that result from increasingly high disclosure thresholds and the ability to split contributions across branches of a political party. It will also remove

TABLE 2.8: COMPARISON OF CURRENT PROVISIONS (COMMONWEALTH ELECTORAL ACT 1918)
WITH THOSE OF THE ELECTORAL AMENDMENT (POLITICAL DONATIONS AND OTHER MEASURES) BILL 2009 (CTH)

	Current provisions: Commonwealth Electoral Act 1918
Registered political parties	Annual return
Associated entities	• Amounts exceeding $11,200 (indexed) to be itemised • Return to be lodged 20 weeks after financial year
Candidates and groups of candidates	Post-election gift disclosure return • Amounts exceeding $11,200 (indexed) to be itemised • Return to be lodged 15 weeks after polling day Post-election election expenditure return • Return to be lodged 15 weeks after polling day
Donors	Post-election return for gifts made to candidates and groups of candidates • Any gifts received by the donor exceeding $11,200 (indexed) that were then used to make gifts to candidates or groups of candidates to be itemised • Return to be lodged 15 weeks after polling day Annual return for gifts made to registered political parties • Any gifts received by the donor exceeding $11,200 (indexed) that were then used to make gifts to registered political parties to be itemised • Return to be lodged 20 weeks after end of financial year Annual political expenditure return • Expenditure exceeding $11,200 (indexed) to be detailed • Return to be lodged 20 weeks after financial year
Third parties	Annual returns for gifts enabling political expenditure if such expenditure exceeds $11,200 (indexed) • Gifts that enabled political expenditure that exceeded $11,200 (indexed) to be itemised • Return to be lodged 20 weeks after end of financial year Annual political expenditure return if such expenditure exceeded $11,200 (indexed) • Return to be lodged 20 weeks after end of financial year
Bans on anonymous gifts	Ban on receipt of anonymous gifts exceeding $11,200 (indexed)
Ban on gifts of foreign property	None

Source: *Commonwealth Electoral Act 1918* (Cth); Electoral Amendment (Political Donations and Other Measures) Bill 2009 (Cth).

	Proposed provisions: Electoral Amendment (Political Donations and Other Measures) Bill 2009 (Cth)
	Biannual return • Amounts of $1000 or more to be itemised • Return to be lodged 8 weeks after reporting period
	Post-election gift disclosure return • Amounts of $1000 or more to be itemised • Return to be lodged 8 weeks after polling day Post-election gift disclosure return • Return to be lodged 8 weeks after polling day
	Post-election return for gifts made to candidates and groups of candidates • Any gifts received by the donor exceeding $1000 that were used by the donor to make gifts to candidates or groups of candidates to be itemised • Return to be lodged 8 weeks after polling day Biannual return for gifts made to registered political parties • Any gifts received by the donor exceeding $1000 that were then used to make gifts to registered political parties to be itemised • Returns to be lodged 8 weeks after reporting period Biannual political expenditure return • Expenditure of $1000 or more to be detailed • Return to be lodged 8 weeks after reporting period
	Biannual returns for gifts enabling political expenditure if such expenditure is $1000 • Gifts that enabled political expenditure of $1000 or more to be itemised • Return to be lodged 8 weeks after end of reporting period Biannual political expenditure return if such expenditure exceeds $1000 • Return to be lodged 8 weeks after end of reporting period
	Ban on receipt of all types of anonymous gifts except for certain anonymous gifts that are of less than $50 Ban on incurring political expenditure enabled by such anonymous gifts (excepting those of less than $50)
	Ban on receipt of foreign property Ban on incurring political expenditure enabled by gifts of foreign property

the current (nominal) prohibition against anonymous gifts and put in place a much sturdier ban. It increases the timeliness of disclosure by registered parties, associated entities, donors and third parties through biannual returns. Compliance is promoted through higher penalties.

In other respects, however, the Bill does not go far enough. It fails to propose any electoral (or political) expenditure disclosure obligations on registered political parties and their associated entities, which is an especially anomalous limitation given the obligations imposed on third parties. Further, there are no amendments that would make the disclosed information more meaningful. One way forward in this respect would be to adopt the British system of donation reports, whereby political parties are required to submit reports for all transactions considered to be donations, and the reports disclose the amount and date of such donations and identify the donor as an individual, trade union, company or other entity.[81]

Biannual returns do not provide the 'real-time disclosure' required for informed voting (as discussed earlier). There are various options here, including the Queensland requirement to disclose gifts exceeding $100,000 within 14 days, or the British requirement for weekly donation reports during election periods.[82] Another possibility worth seriously considering is that proposed by the Democratic Audit of Australia: a continuous disclosure scheme modelled on the system supervised by the New York Campaign Finance Board.[83]

In other respects, the Bill goes too far. The offences relating to gifts of foreign property are generally strict liability offences, which means that they can be committed without knowledge that the gifts were of foreign property.[84] For instance, a party official who reasonably believed that a gift was not foreign-sourced based on the information s/he had, and after making extensive inquiries, might still be caught by these offences. These provisions should be amended to allow a 'due diligence' defence.

The Bill also imposes very onerous obligations in relation to third parties. It preserves the structure of third party disclosure obligations but increases their frequency from annual to biannual, and lowers the disclosure threshold from $11,200 (indexed) to $1000. This exacerbates current problems with these obligations. First, third parties are required to detail 'political expenditure' made in any financial year if such expenditure exceeds $11,200 (indexed). 'Political expenditure' includes 'the public expression of views on an issue in an election by any means'.[85] As commentator Andrew Norton has correctly observed, this is hard to determine in advance, making it difficult to comply with the obligations.[86] Second, third parties are required to disclose gifts that 'enable' 'political expenditure' if such gift/s exceed $11,200 (indexed). This, as Norton pointed out, captures donations to third parties that are not intended to fund 'political expenditure'.[87] The Bill has missed the opportunity to improve these provisions.

Inherent limitations of disclosure schemes

This chapter began by underlining the importance of transparency of political funding in terms of protecting the integrity of representative government; in particular, its role in promoting informed voting and preventing corruption. Its central focus has been on one vital mechanism for ensuring such transparency: disclosure schemes. Lest this emphasis be misunderstood and the importance of disclosure schemes be overstated, it is important to bear in mind two inherent limitations of such schemes.

First, disclosure schemes, even if properly designed and adequately complied with, do not by themselves provide effective transparency. Effective transparency depends on the actions and conduct of the agents of disclosure: the electoral commissions, as the public authorities in charge of the schemes; the regulated community, in particular the political parties; reform-minded politicians; civil society organisations; media; and academics.[88] The role of the media is especially important,[89] but cannot be taken for granted. As Young has observed, there are various impediments to the media being an effective watchdog in relation to political finance matters ranging from inaccessibility and lack of availability of information to the financial benefits that media organisations gain from political funding, notably government advertising.[90]

Second, disclosure schemes cannot prevent all corruption. While such schemes expose details of the funding received by the parties, they do not cast light on the effects of such funding. It then becomes a matter of conjecture, in the case of corruption through graft, as to whether favourable treatment by a political party or its representative resulted from a donation. In other words, the effectiveness of funding disclosure schemes in preventing corruption through graft founders upon the difficulty of proving a causal link between preferential treatment and donations (see Chapter 3). Further, the aim of preventing corruption can be defeated by a debased political morality. As the next chapter will document, the major parties regularly run fundraisers, which are in reality a way to sell access and influence, practices that constitute a form of corruption. The negative publicity that has attended these fundraisers, however, has yet to dissuade the major parties from engaging in them. Transparency is not the same as political ethics; indeed, transparency can only work to prevent corruption when there is a bedrock of political ethics. Without such a bedrock, transparency may normalise unethical behaviour and undermine public trust in the political system.[91]

These limitations do not, of course, mean that disclosure schemes have no role in achieving the sort of transparency that can deter some graft and undue influence. However, even if 'loophole free', they should not be invested with elixir-like qualities and expected to banish graft and undue influence. Other measures, such as contribution limits (Chapter 4) and election spending limits (Chapter 7), are required as well. The mantra 'sunlight is the best disinfectant' is snappy, but it overstates the case.

Disclosure schemes and political finance research

The deficiencies of the disclosure schemes pose particular challenges for academic analysis of Australian political finance. In some cases, the schemes fail to disclose key pieces of information, such as spending in federal elections (see Chapter 7) and investment income received by political parties (see Chapter 3). In other cases, relevant information, such as the composition of party funding (the split between public and private funding; the proportions of individual, corporate and trade union contributions) (see Chapters 3 and 5), can only be extricated with a great deal of effort.

As a result, information on Australian political funding is partial. Where possible, this book uses contemporary data, and original data . Where this has not been possible, because of limitations in the publicly available information or in the resources available, the book relies on best available information (even when somewhat dated) and, occasionally, estimates.

3
PRIVATE FUNDING OF POLITICS:
DEMOCRACY FOR SALE?

This chapter continues the examination of the private funding of political parties and candidates. It begins by identifying the broad features of such funding: it is party-centred (only a small fraction of money goes directly to candidates) and it mostly comes from companies and trade unions, and as investment income.

Is such funding problematic from the perspective of democratic principles? Some, drawing support from the principle of respecting political freedoms, would say 'no': political donations are the legitimate exercise by citizens of their freedom to influence the political process through financial contributions. This is an influential view, and heavily informs the current laissez-faire approach to private political funding, where 'freedom from' state regulation prevails.

However, as I argued in Chapter 1, heavy emphasis on 'freedom from' can lead to a distorted understanding of the principle of respecting political freedoms. 'Freedom to' – in this case, the actual ability to make political donations – is of also of crucial importance, especially in light of the economic inequalities of Australian society.

There are also other important principles: protecting the integrity of representative government, promoting fairness in politics and supporting parties to discharge their functions.

This chapter evaluates private political funding in terms of respect for political freedoms, protecting the integrity of representative government, promoting fairness in politics and helping parties to discharge their functions. It then examines the relationship between political contributions and corruption. It will argue that such contributions undermine Australian politics when they give rise to corruption through graft and undue influence. The chapter then documents three ways in which private funding of political parties damages the fabric of Australia's democracy: first, through the purchase of political access and influence, a form of corruption through undue influence; second, by producing various forms of unfairness; and third, by undermining the ability of the major parties to perform their democratic functions.

Chapter 4 proposes a regulatory framework that addresses these corrosive practices and better promotes the legitimate role of private funding.

The business of giving

The private dollar holds up our political system. An analysis of the budgets of political parties for the financial years 1999–2000 to 2001–02 shows how dependent the major parties (the ALP and the Coalition parties) are on private money: more than 80 per cent of their funding comes from this source. The minor parties were slightly less dependent, with half to three-quarters of their budgets privately financed.[1] AEC analysis of financial returns made for the 2004 federal election cycle provides a similar result. For the financial years 2002–03 to 2004–05, private funding of the ALP and the Liberal Party stood at 81 per cent and 79 per cent of their total budgets respectively.[2]

There is nothing fundamentally wrong with parties being dependent on private money. Indeed, a funding base made up of many small donations would reflect a vibrant party with strong grassroots support. It would also testify to a robust democracy where many citizens engage with the political process by donating money to their preferred candidates and parties. Such a development could be a crucial antidote to the hollowing-out of the party system that has witnessed falling party membership and affiliation.

It is clear that parties are awash with big money: the budgets of major parties are in the order of millions. But for the most part, they are not made up of small sums from individual citizens; big money comes from large donations. While donations of less than $1500 were 42 per cent of the *number* of donations made to the federal political parties in 2004–05, a federal election year, they amounted to only 4 per cent of the *amount* donated. A reverse situation applied to donations of $25,000 or more: they were only 4 per cent of the *number* of donations but 48 per cent of the *amount* donated.[3] Donations of this magnitude are out of the reach of ordinary Australians. In 2009, the average annual earnings of Australian employees was $48,604.40.[4] A donation of $25,000 would be more than half of this amount.

So institutional contributions – money from corporations and trade unions – are the lion's share of party finances. All the major parties depend on corporate funding. The figures are stark: in the financial years 1999–2000 to 2001–02, the dollar amount of corporate donations received by the Liberal Party was more than 18 times the amount of individual donations received. The ratio for the National Party was slightly over 11. Even with the ALP, corporate donations are more important than either individual or trade union donations. In the 2001–02 financial year, for example, corporate donations received by the ALP were nearly 2.5 times the amount of trade union donations.[5] Of the main parties, only the Greens can plausibly claim to have a funding base grounded in individual donations.[6]

The ALP and the Liberal Party also receive a significant amount of money from their own investment activity, much of which appears to be conducted by their commercial arms (many of which seem to operate as property trusts).[7] It is difficult to find out the amount of income generated by these investment vehicles, all of which are considered 'associated entities' under the *Commonwealth Electoral Act*, but their importance can be seen in Table 3.1 below. The table reveals the revenue from associated entities, and their proportion of the total revenue of the parties. While this proportion fluctuates, the figures show the extensive use of 'associated entities' by the ALP and the Liberal Party. The lowest proportion, occurring in the financial year 2001–02, is still close to half of the parties' revenues.

Table 3.2 shows even more clearly the importance of these funding sources. It lists the prominent investment vehicles of the ALP and the Liberal Party, their total receipts for 2005–06 to 2007–08, and the amounts they gave and loaned to their associated political parties.

Private funding is predominantly channelled to political parties. Funding provided directly to candidates makes up a very small part of the total funding of political parties and candidates. Table 3.3 compares donations received by candidates standing in the 2007 federal election with donations received by the federal branches of the parties in 2007–08.

TABLE 3.1: PARTY REVENUE COMPARED WITH REVENUE RECEIVED BY ASSOCIATED ENTITIES			
	Federal election year, 2001–02 ($m)	Federal non-election year, 2002–03 ($m)	Federal non-election year, 2003–04 ($m)
Revenue received by political parties (RPP)	$147.24	$91.14	$91.93
Revenue received by associated entities (RAE)	$63.59	$80.12	$72.60
RAE as a proportion of RPP	43.19%	87.91%	78.97%
Source: Australian Electoral Commission, *Funding and Disclosure Report: Election 2004*, 19 (Table 6).			

TABLE 3.2: SELECTED INVESTMENT VEHICLES OF THE ALP AND LIBERAL PARTY, 2005–06 TO 2007–08				
Associated entity	Political party associated with	Total receipts	Amount provided to political party (all branches)	Loans provided to political party (all branches)
John Curtin House Ltd	ALP	$58,516,841	$12,447,811	$4,509,839
Labor Holdings Pty Ltd	ALP	$51,199,627	$4,499,999	NIL
Labor Resources	ALP	$3,005,933	$3,000,000	NIL
Progressive Business Association Inc.	ALP	$2,482,008	$1,441,559	NIL
Bunori Pty Ltd	LP	$6,459,195	NIL	$5,579,423
Cormack Foundation	LP	$8,900,752	NIL	$100,000
The Free Enterprise Foundation	LP	$1,020,238	$963,000	NIL
Greenfields Foundation	LP	$151,375	NIL	$11,550,000
The 500 Club (Vic.)	LP	$1,532,240	$314,280	NIL
Vapold Pty Ltd	LP	$1,767,554	$569,308	$679,585

Source: AEC Annual Returns 2005–06 to 2007–08.

There are, of course, exceptions to the rule of funding being party-centred. The most notable is probably Malcolm Turnbull, former Leader of the Opposition. Mr Turnbull has his own fund-raising organisation, Wentworth Forum. Reporting on the Forum, *The Age* revealed its various types of membership packages: for $5500 one can become a 'member', but for $55,000 one can become a 'governor'. Those taking up membership include some of the richest

TABLE 3.3: DONATIONS RECEIVED BY CANDIDATES IN THE 2007 FEDERAL ELECTION				
	ALP (Federal)	Liberal Party (Federal)	National Party (Federal)	Greens (Federal)
Donations received by candidates	$428,466	$55,100	$50,733	$100,515
Party receipts	$61,764,260	$34,662,036	$1,809,362	$1,965,185
Donations received by candidates as a proportion of party receipts	0.69%	0.16%	2.80%	5.11%

Source: AEC 2007–08 party returns and 2007 federal election candidate returns.

individuals in Australia, such as Seven Network chairman Kerry Stokes, Westfield founder Frank Lowy and Aussie Home Loans executive chairman John Symond.[8]

Corporatisation of political funding

Empirical study of corporate political contributions in Australia is only just beginning,[9] but already research reveals several features of such giving. First, only a small number of large businesses make regular political contributions. A study by political scientist Iain McMenamin of 450 large businesses showed that 47 per cent of these businesses did not make *any* payments to political parties between 1998–99 and 2004–05, and only 15 per cent of the sample made a payment to political parties *every year* during this time.[10] The study also found that the larger the business, the more likely it was to contribute, and that contributions are more likely to be made as elections approach. The study also found that it was difficult to state with any certainty which sectors were more likely to contribute.[11]

How then do businesses distribute their political money once they have decided to contribute? An analysis by law professor Ian Ramsay and others of corporate contributions made between 1995–96 and 1997–98 found that 99 per cent of these contributions went to the Coalition parties and the ALP,[12] and that '[t]he Liberal Party consistently outperformed the other parties in terms of attracting corporate donations'.[13] The McMenamin study also found that businesses principally channelled their money to the ALP and the Coalition parties. It added that:

> Australian businesses have a strong underlying ideological predilection towards the conservative coalition of Liberals and Nationals. Nonetheless, they react strongly to changing political conditions. If the ALP has the political advantage, in terms of either control of government or a lead in the polls, businesses tend to be even handed. By contrast, if the Coalition has the political advantage businesses target the vast majority of their money on the Coalition.[14]

These comments indicate that for businesses which make political contributions, ideology's significance is tempered – perhaps even rivalled – by pragmatism: *corporate money follows power.* This logic is seen in the practice of businesses hedging their bets by giving to both the ALP and the Coalition. For instance, nine of the top ten corporate donors in the financial years 1995–96 to 1997–98 gave to both the ALP and the Liberal Party; seven of them donated to the National Party as well.[15] More recently, in the 2005–06 financial year, Inghams Enterprises, ANZ and Westpac ranked among the top ten donors to both the ALP and Liberal Party federal branches.[16]

Work by political scientist Nicholas Harrigan has cast some light on the characteristics of companies that split their contributions between these parties. According to Harrigan, these contributors, bipartisan donors, are more likely to be corporations that operate in highly regulated industries, or potential defence contractors. Donors that only give to the Coalition parties, on the other hand, tend not to have these characteristics; they are more likely to have rich individuals on their boards and ties with other Coalition donors or conservative thinktanks. Perhaps ideological motivations are at play here, with contributions aimed at securing support for a business-friendly political agenda.[17]

The labour question

Trade union contributions to political parties fall into two categories: party affiliation fees and non-membership subscriptions. Party affiliation fees are fees paid by a union to a political party as a condition of taking out organisational membership of the party. Non-membership contributions are essentially political donations made by unions to support the cause or policies of a political party.

Everyone knows that the ALP is the principal recipient of trade union contributions (the Greens are beginning to receive modest amounts too). The ALP receives trade union money in the form of both affiliation fees and non-membership contributions; the Greens only receive non-membership contributions.

For the ALP, trade union money is clearly important. Table 3.4 provides two measures of the ALP's dependence on trade union money: union receipts as a percentage of the total sums received from all branches of the ALP and union receipts as a percentage of total receipts itemised by these branches. The table shows that trade union money, while significant, should not be overstated. Even at its highest proportion for the financial years 2006–07 and 2007–08, trade union money was less than one-sixth of the ALP's total income.

Table 3.5 is an attempt to divide the amounts received by all branches of the ALP for the financial year 2006–07 (a non-federal election year) and 2007–08 (a federal election year) into affiliation fees and non-membership contributions. Sums declared by trade unions as 'Other Receipts' and 'Subscriptions' are treated as affiliation fees, and sums identified as 'Donations' are treated as

TABLE 3.4: TRADE UNION CONTRIBUTIONS AS PROPORTION OF ALP INCOME, 2006–07 TO 2007–08

	2006–07	2007–08
Trade union receipts as percentage of itemised ALP receipts	13.09%	10.8%
Trade union receipts as percentage of total ALP receipts	7.52%	8.18%

Source: AEC Annual Returns (ALP), 2006–07 to 2007–08.

TABLE 3.5: BREAKDOWN OF ALP RECEIPTS: TRADE UNION AFFILIATION FEES AND NON-MEMBERSHIP CONTRIBUTIONS, 2006–07 TO 2007–08

	2006–07	2007–08
Affiliation fees	$4,066,931	$4,206,836
Affiliation fees as a percentage of trade union funding	75.44%	46.57%
Non-membership contributions	$1,323,800	$4,826,177
Non-membership contributions as a percentage of trade union funding	24.56%	53.43%
Total trade union funding	$5,390,731	$9,033,013

Source: AEC Annual Returns, 2006–07 to 2007–08.

non-membership contributions. This breakdown provides only a rough-and-ready analysis for two reasons. First, the description of sums as 'Other Receipts', 'Subscriptions' or 'Donations' is based on a system of self-classification. Second, the table only works on sums that are required to be itemised (for disclosure purposes), not on the total amounts received (see Chapter 2).[18]

Bearing these limitations in mind, Table 3.5 suggests that the balance between affiliation fees and non-membership contributions shifts according to whether or not it is a federal election year. In both 2006–07 and 2007–08, the amount received in affiliation fees was steady, at slightly over $4 million. However, the amount received in non-membership contributions nearly tripled, from $1.3 million in 2006–07 to $4.8 million in 2007–08. The effect was that non-membership subscriptions amounted to more than half the trade union money paid to the ALP in 2007–08.

We can now turn to the question of which unions pay affiliation fees and non-membership contributions to the ALP. Affiliation fees are paid to the state branches of the ALP. The decision to affiliate is, therefore, made by the state branches of the various unions. As a result, for any union some branches might be affiliated to the ALP while others are not.

An overwhelming majority of trade unions are affiliated to the ALP. Of the unions registered with various federal, state or territory industrial registrars, more than 80 per cent are affiliated to the ALP in each of these jurisdictions; the number is 100 per cent in Queensland, the Australian Capital Territory (ACT) and the Northern Territory.

In some cases, all branches of a particular union are affiliated to the ALP. The list of such unions includes the Shop, Distributive and Allied Employees Association (SDA); the Liquor Hospitality and Miscellaneous Workers Union (LHMU); the Communications, Electrical and Plumbing Union (CEPU); the Australian Services Union (ASU); the Australian Manufacturing Workers Union (AMWU); and the Transport Workers Union (TWU).

With some other unions, all but one of their branches are affiliated to the ALP. These include the Construction, Forestry, Mining and Energy Union (CFMEU); the Rail, Tram and Bus Industry Union (RTBU); the National Union of Workers (NUW); the Maritime Union of Australia (MUA); the Australian Workers Union (AWU); and the Australasian Meat Industry Employees Union (AMIEU).

There are, however, major unions that are not affiliated to the ALP. No branches of the National Tertiary Education Union (NTEU) or the Association of Professional Engineers, Scientists and Managers Australia (APESMA) are affiliated to the ALP, and only one branch of the Australian Nursing Federation (ANF) is affiliated to the ALP.[19]

Non-membership contributions by trade unions to the ALP

TABLE 3.6: TOP FIVE TRADE UNION CONTRIBUTORS TO THE ALP IN TERMS OF NON-MEMBERSHIP CONTRIBUTIONS, 2006–07 TO 2007–08			
2006–07		**2007–08**	
CEPU (including ETU)	$631,800	CEPU (including ETU)	$1,318,123
CFMEU	$192,000	LHMU	$274,000
LHMU	$180,000	CFMEU	$230,650
ETU	$120,000	AWU	$227,000
ASU	$100,000	HSU (Health Services Unit)	$176,000
Source: AEC Annual Returns, 2006–07 to 2007–08.			

TABLE 3.7: TOP FIVE TRADE UNION CONTRIBUTORS (ALL CONTRIBUTIONS) TO THE ALP, 2006–07 TO 2007–08			
2006–07		**2007–08**	
CEPU (including ETU)	$1,333 398	CEPU (including ETU)	$1,728,621
LHMU	$661,022	SDA	$1,488,591
SDA	$628,245	CFMEU	$1,339,386
CFMEU	$609,800	LHMU	$764,906
AMWU	$385,277	AMWU	$650,934
Source: AEC Annual Returns, 2006–07 to 2007–08.			

seem to be made either by state labour councils or affiliated trade unions. In the 2006–07 and 2007–08 financial years, not a single non-affiliated trade union made a non-membership contribution to the ALP.[20] Table 3.6 identifies the top five unions in terms of non-membership contributions given to the ALP by all branches (as noted earlier, trade union contributions identified as 'donations' are treated as non-membership contributions).

Table 3.7 goes beyond the amounts declared as 'donations' and lists the top five union contributors to the ALP for the financial years 2006–07 and 2007–08 based on the total amount given to the ALP by all branches of the various unions. In other words, the figures in Table 3.7 include items declared as 'donations', 'subscriptions' and 'other receipts', and thus also include membership fees.

It remains to discuss trade union funding to the Greens. In the financial years 2006–07 and 2007–08, three unions gave money to the Greens: the AMWU, the CFMEU and the ETU (Electrical Trades Union). The biggest giver was the ETU, which contributed $219,506. The CFMEU and the AMWU donated much smaller amounts: $60,000 and $30,000 respectively. Trade union funding does not form a significant part of the Greens' budget. Of the disclosed amounts, trade union funding of the Greens was 6.4 per cent for 2006–07 and 3.3 per cent for 2007–08.[21]

The question of corruption

We can begin this examination by asking: Is there a real problem of corruption with political contributions? Those answering 'no' would argue that political contributions are, in principle, legitimate. Victorian Premier John Brumby, for example, has defended political contributions from individuals and companies (even when access and influence is 'purchased') as part of a 'healthy democracy', provided there is accountability and disclosure.[22] Those answering 'no' would also draw attention to the fact that there have been only a few cases of bribery or graft – only one federal parliamentarian, Dr Andrew Theophanous, has been jailed for corruption.[23]

This, however, is no reason for complacency. Serious episodes of graft have occurred – we need only remember the WA Inc. scandals that enveloped the WA government in the 1980s and early 1990s,[24] and the police corruption uncovered by the Fitzgerald Inquiry in the 1980s, which nearly led to the jailing of then Queensland Premier Joh Bjelke-Petersen on perjury charges.[25] For those thinking that these are matters of ancient history, think of Gordon Nuttall, the former Queensland Minister convicted in 2009 of corruptly receiving secret payments from two leading Queensland businessmen.[26]

Corruption through graft is not uncommon at the local government level. In 2005, the NSW Independent Commission Against Corruption (ICAC) found two councillors of Strathfield Municipal Council and a property developer guilty of corrupt conduct because of bribes paid and received in relation to the proposed development of a car park.[27] Similar conduct occurred in relation to Wollongong City Council. In 2008, the NSW ICAC recommended that all elected council positions there be vacated on the basis that 'systemic corruption exists within the Wollongong City Council'.[28]

Various features of local government politics make it more susceptible to corruption than federal and state politics. Less intense party competition and media attention means a diminished level of scrutiny. Lax disclosure laws (see Chapter 2) allow the policing of political contributions to become a matter of self-regulation. The number of voters to be reached is fewer and there is less reliance on expensive electioneering techniques such as television advertising, so campaign costs are therefore much lower – in the order of four-digit sums. The decisions made by local councillors can, however, involve much larger amounts. Planning decisions, in particular, can affect development projects costing millions of dollars, which can give property developers a strong incentive to influence local councillors.

That being said, graft is notoriously difficult to prove.[29] Take, for example, the controversy over the appointment of Robert Gerard, a generous Liberal Party donor, to the Reserve Bank in 2005[30] or the dramatic increase in the political donations made by the Australian Wheat Board (AWB) – from nil to more than $200,000 – during the time when its wheat contracts with the Iraqi government came under close scrutiny.[31] In both cases, there was a scent of graft, and questions lingered as to whether the federal Coalition government appointed Robert Gerard because of his contributions to the Liberal Party and whether the AWB received preferential treatment because of the handsome sums it had paid to the major parties. These questions remain questions. The combination of political contributions and government actions which benefit donors always seems to raise suspicions of impropriety. But without more, they can only be suspicions. In most cases, citizens will not know whether they are looking at impropriety or innocent coincidence.

We should not necessarily lament the difficulty in proving graft: serious allegations should be subject to stringent standards of proof, not determined according to innuendo, speculation or gossip. But as we inquire further, matters become much more problematic. The problem of proof lies first with the elements that constitute the criminal offences of bribery, extortion and abuse of public office. These offences typically require a dishonest, corrupt or improper motive as well as a link between a financial contribution and specific actions (see below). Both are difficult to establish. Public officials, like the rest of us, usually act from mixed motives,[32] so there is usually an innocent explanation that can be pointed to, which can make it hard to nail down a dishonest, corrupt or improper motive. This can also complicate the task of establishing a causal link between contributions and particular government actions.[33]

Moreover, these elements will almost always be impossible to establish without a wide-ranging inquiry, and in some cases the truth would not be known in the absence of powers to compel the production of information. Two cases illustrate this. In 2003, controversy erupted over donations received by then Immigration Minister Philip Ruddock's election campaign fund from Mr Karim Kisrwani. Kisrwani, a long-time financial supporter of Ruddock and the Liberal Party, also regularly requested Ruddock to exercise his powers as Immigration Minister to intervene in unsuccessful visa applications: nearly half of these requests were successful, in that they received ministerial intervention. A Senate inquiry into the matter was established to determine whether or not there was any impropriety. The outcome of this inquiry, however, was pretty much nothing. After criticising the Immigration Department and the Minister's refusal to allow the inquiry access to the relevant case files and ministerial notebooks, the inquiry concluded that it was unable, for lack of information, to conclusively determine the connection between Kisrwani's donations and Ruddock's exercise of powers. Any connection, according to the report, was 'open to speculation'.[34]

The other example comes from Victoria and concerns the millions of dollars contributed by property developer Walker Corporation to the major parties, including a sum of $100,000 to the Victorian ALP one month before Walker Corporation won the contract to develop Kew Cottages.[35] In a report handed down in 2008, a Victorian parliamentary committee noted '[a] strong public suspicion that the nature and timing of political lobbying and donations may have had an improper influence in the awarding of the tender to develop the Kew Residential Services site' and that 'the community cannot be confident that donations made by Walker Corporation to the Australian Labor Party had no improper influence in the tender process'.[36] What is noteworthy is the tentative terms used to express the committee's views ('suspicion', 'may have had'). The reason for this was clear: lack of information. As the committee stated, 'The Committee's ability to investigate ... was significantly restricted by the less than full cooperation from the Government.'[37]

These cases illustrate the problem of proving graft and suggest another reason not to be so sanguine about such corruption. In both, the inability to prove graft (or, for that matter, to conclusively disprove it) foundered on a lack of information. This resulted from the refusal of those accused of engaging in corrupt conduct to provide full information. In some cases, the inability to prove graft points less to the absence of such conduct and more to the success of those accused in stonewalling.

The final and most important reason not to feel confident that corruption does not flow from political contributions is that graft — the receipt of private funds directly leading to political power being improperly used in favour of contributors — is only one kind of corrupt conduct. Requiring a concrete link between contributions and specific actions means we will never catch corrupt conduct where the connection between money and preference is less direct. Situations where the connection between money and preference from a public official is mediated by political parties fit badly within the concept of graft; in these situations, the gain tends to be political, not personal. Further, by insisting on a dishonest or improper motive, the law tends to neglect conduct that is corrupt by virtue of its damaging the democratic process. In other words, focusing on graft means focusing on individual corruption, and therefore ignoring institutional corruption (see Chapter 1).

Let us now reintroduce the idea of corruption through undue influence (discussed in Chapter 1): when large political contributions result in the donor securing influence simply by virtue of paying money to an elected official (or more often, the party to which the elected official belongs). Public officials who exercise their powers or make decisions by reference to such contributions are engaging in a form of corruption.[38]

Such corruption is closely bound up with notion of 'conflict of interest': undue influence results from political contributions when they create or tend to create a conflict between public duties and the financial interests of parties and public officials.[39] Unlike graft, this kind of corruption does not depend on a tight nexus between contribution and a specific action; it can occur 'not through any conscious motives or individual exchanges but [through] habitual actions and institutional routines'.[40] In other words, it may very well be, and in fact usually is, institutional corruption.

When comparing corruption through graft with corruption through undue influence, the common perception is that they lie on a continuum, with graft being much more serious than undue influence. For instance, newspaper reports most often represent the problem of corruption in the area of political contributions as one of graft. This is in itself highly debatable, and may result in a blind spot regarding other forms of corruption. Thus undue influence can soon seem permissible. As the NSW ICAC has said:

> Corruption of the system is complete, when it allows the
> payment of money for political favours, and when decisions
> by public officials can be bought. That is almost universally
> understood. Corruption of the system is well on the way, when
> it allows ... payment without obvious favour. That is not so well
> understood.[41]

The result of this lack of understanding may be a failure to fully come to grips with the real problem of corruption in Australia. At the federal and state levels, the danger of graft is contained through a mixture of laws, scrutiny and ethics. The problem of undue influence, on the other hand, pervades Australian politics at all levels. While graft cannot be said to pose a systemic threat to Australian democracy, undue influence can. As the following section will show, one of the tricks of the trade in Australian politics is the peddling of influence.

This discussion may lead us to ask questions that are the exact opposite of those we began with: Are all political contributions corrupt? Do all political contributions involve undue influence? There are some who seem to say 'yes'. Morris Iemma, for instance, when he was Premier of New South Wales, advanced a radical proposal to completely ban political contributions in favour of a system of complete public funding,[42] an option that only makes sense if all political contributions are considered illegitimate. Prominent commentator Janet Albrechtsen appears to have some sympathy with this view:

> Just as a property developer looks for a return on money paid, so
> do unions. And they get it in spades. While many corporates give
> to both sides of politics in the name of supporting democracy
> (read hedging their bets) there are no pretences here about even-
> handed, altruistic giving to support democracy. Union giving is
> an unashamed quid pro quo. It's cash for policy.[43]

What she is implying is that all political contributions involving *quid pro quo* are illegitimate.

There are grave difficulties with these views. Political contributions are legitimate from a democratic perspective because they constitute a form of political participation and a mechanism for ensuring that parties and candidates are responsive to the broader citizenry. In appropriate forms and amounts, political money can promote democratic accountability. However, this is only the case when the gift of political money constitutes an endorsement of the positions of a political party; political money should be interested or partisan money, not 'altruistic giving to support democracy'. In this sense, there is (and should) always be a certain *quid pro quo* in the giving of political contributions or 'cash for policy', in the sense that money is given to indicate approval of the party and its positions. It is misconceived to issue a blanket condemnation of such *quid pro quo*.

The problem is with the kind of *quid pro quo*. It is not the flow of private money into politics itself that is the problem; it is how this money flows. We should draw a distinction here between contributions given to support the positions of parties and those given with the 'primary aim ... to influence the candidate (or party) when in office'. According to political philosopher Dennis Thompson, the latter '[i]n its pure form ... has no function other than to translate the private desires of a contributor directly into government action ... it short-circuits the democratic process'.[44]

What are the elements of the democratic process? The answer depends on what conception of democracy one is using. Here, the perspective of deliberative democracy is particularly useful. One of the most influential theories of deliberative democracy is that advanced by Amy Gutmann and Dennis Thompson.[45] Two principles drawn from their theory are of particular relevance here. First, the publicity requirement: 'The reasons that officials and citizens give to justify political actions, and the information necessary to assess those reasons should be public.'[46] Second, the reason-giving requirement:[47] 'Deliberative democracy asks citizens and officials to justify public policy by giving reasons that can be accepted by those who are bound by it.'[48] It is crucial to note that this requirement is not satisfied simply by giving reasons. For Gutmann and Thompson, 'the practice of deliberation ... is a process of seeking, not just any reasons, but mutually justifiable reasons, and reaching a mutually binding decision on the basis of those reasons'.[49] We can perhaps frame this requirement as one to provide reasons based on the 'public interest'.

These principles can help us clarify what 'short-circuiting' the democratic process means. Applying them also helps us distinguish between legitimate and illegitimate political contributions. First, the reason-giving requirement implies that contributions that are given to express support for a party's policies, and thus some notion of the 'public interest', would be legitimate. As Thompson has explained, a political contribution given to support party policies 'directly serves a political function: its aim is to help a candidate get elected, and it works through the political process'.[50] 'Rather than bypassing the process, the contribution animates it.'[51]

On the other hand, contributions given to a political party because of self-interest, and with no (or little) regard for party's positions, work as a form of undue influence. Such donations result in 'a corrupting kind of political support [because] it bears no relation to the substance of the politics it seeks to influence'.[52]

These principles can illuminate the distinction between two types of contribution strategies: the electoral strategy, where financial support comes from donors to candidates and parties the donors agree with ideologically and want to win; and the access strategy, where contributions are given to secure access and influence after a candidate or party is elected and/or with indifference as to the policies of the party (or candidate).[53] The electoral strategy is not necessarily corrupting, but the access strategy is. When citizens, political groups, trade unions and businesses financially support candidates and parties in order to publicly back their policies, we should be slow to characterise it as corruption. When, however, they contribute in order to access and influence the party in office with little regard to its general policies, the label 'corrupt' will often be apt.

The principles help elucidate the role of party membership fees and corporate contributions in a representative democracy. First, party membership fees. The principles outlined above explain the legitimacy of such fees (and why such fees do not tend to involve corruption). The publicity requirement is met, as such fees are given with an open declaration that the individual member supports the party's ideology. Transparency also results from the mode of influence being formalised: party meetings governed by party rules are meant to be the primary mechanisms through which members influence the party's policies. Further, party members tend to be pursuing an electoral strategy, by seeking to advance their view of what is in the 'public interest' through the party, and thus putting that view to the electorate.

Is there a difference here between individual members and organisational members? To be sure, organisational members invariably wield greater influence within the party (often through powerful individuals such as trade union secretaries). Nevertheless, the points above concerning the principles of publicity and reason-giving also apply to fees paid by organisational members such as the trade union affiliates of the ALP: affiliated trade unions are required to subscribe to the ALP's constitution, policies and principles,[54] and their influence as members is exercised within party fora.[55] They too are pursuing an electoral strategy, with affiliation fees paid to secure the election of the ALP and the implementation of its policies.

These features of party and affiliation fees – transparency and the pursuit of the 'public interest' through an electoral strategy – can also apply to other political contributions. Take, for example, a large amount openly given by a business to a political party in order to secure its election: the publicity requirement is met, as is the requirement for reason-giving. Membership fees, however, have a feature that is not shared by other political contributions: they signal a deeper form of political participation. As the NSW Legislative Council Select Committee on Electoral and Political Party Funding correctly recognised, 'membership of political parties is an important means for individuals to participate in the political process'.[56] This is because it involves participation *within* political parties. As a consequence, it directly enhances the participatory function of political parties (see Chapter 1). As we will see in the next chapter, this has important implications in terms of regulating political contributions.

We can now consider the relationship between corporate contributions and corruption. The starting point is that corporations cannot and do not make donations. Under corporations law, directors and senior executives of companies are under a duty to act in good faith in the interests of shareholders.[57] When deciding to contribute to political parties, they can only comply with this duty if the company is getting something in return for the money it gives to a party. In other words, directors and managers who authorise donations with no strings attached risk breaching the law.[58] With each corporate 'donation', then, there has to be a *quid pro quo*. The character of the *quid pro quo* ranges from securing loose commitments to more tangible financial benefits.

However, as noted earlier, it is the kind of *quid pro quo* that is crucial. Coalition-only contributors, like ALP-only contributors, appear to be pursuing an electoral strategy.[59] Bipartisan contributors, on the other hand, are more often corporations involved in highly regulated industries or potential defence contractors. At one level, their pattern of giving indicates a wish to have either the ALP or the Coalition elected to office (or, more accurately, perhaps, to prevent other political parties from gaining office). Yet the apparent indifference of these businesses as to which of the major parties is elected to office suggests that an access strategy dominates. The motivations of these contributors may be close to those expressed by David Clarke, former Macquarie Bank chairman, when he said that donations were useful in making the company known to politicians and could also 'lead to direct fees and government business'.[60] If so, we should view bipartisan contributions less as evidence of being 'even-handed' and more as a sign of corruption through undue influence, and Coalition-only or ALP-only contributions, being overtly partisan, as having a *prima facie* claim to be enriching the political process.

These observations are speculative. It is unwise to draw conclusions as to motive from how corporate donors divide their contributions and their particular characteristics. Motivations are plain, however, when businesses use their money to directly buy access and influence. As the following section will explain, there can be little doubt that the sale of access and influence indicates an access strategy, a strategy that insinuates undue influence into the body politic.

Selling access and influence

The NSW Liberal Party runs a body called the 'Millennium Forum'. A testimonial from former Prime Minister John Howard describes it as 'one of Australia's premier political corporate forums' that 'provides a wealth of opportunities for the business community and political leaders at federal and state levels to meet and discuss key issues within an informal setting'.[61] 'Wealth', it seems, is the operative word. For fees ranging from $10,000 upwards, company representatives get not only '[a]n ENGAGING programme of professional corporate events and "Off the Record" briefings' (capitals in original),[62] but, in the past, also a chance to play golf with John Howard on Sydney's Bonnie Doon golf course.[63] Corporate Australia has not been reluctant to seize these opportunities. The Forum's 'sponsors' include British American Tobacco Australia, Publishing and Broadcasting Ltd, Tenix Group, major construction companies Leighton Holdings and Multiplex Constructions and key accountancy firms Deloitte and Ernst & Young.[64]

The NSW ALP has also not been shy in selling access and influence to business. For $102,000, a company can become a 'foundation partner' of the NSW ALP's 'Business Dialogue' and secure five places to events such as boardroom lunches and dinners with the Premier and state government Ministers.[65] In late 2006, a few months before the state election, the NSW ALP held a fundraising event at the Convention Centre, Darling Harbour, which was attended by nearly 1000 people. General admission cost $500 per head; attending an exclusive cocktail party with Ministers cost $15,000 for nine guests; and dining with (former) Premier Morris Iemma was priced at a hefty $45,000 per person.[66]

In Victoria, the ALP's 'Progressive Business' has been described as 'one of the most efficient money-making operations in the country'.[67] According to its website, its 'express purpose [is] building dialogue and understanding between the business community and government'. It currently offers two types of membership, corporate and small business, priced at $1550 and $990 per annum respectively. Membership entitles the company to a set number of breakfast and twilight ministerial briefings.[68] The 2009 annual Progressive Business dinner, for example, witnessed Latrobe Fertilisers, a company vigorously advocating the use of Gippsland coal mines for the production of fertiliser, paying $10,000 to the ALP so that its chairman, Allan Blood, could sit at the side of Victorian Premier John Brumby and, in Blood's words, 'ben[d] his ear'.[69]

These activities illustrate a wider set of unsavoury practices. There are other vehicles for peddling influence. For example, membership of the Liberal Party's '500 Club' will provide 'a tailored series of informal, more personally styled, early evening events', thus 'adding a new level of value for ... Club members'.[70] Party meetings are also a favoured venue for selling influence. In the lead-up to the 2004 federal election, Mark Latham, then federal ALP leader, hosted an 'It's Time' dinner at Sydney's Westin Hotel, at a cost of $10,000 per table. During the same period, the Liberal Party charged $11,000 for seats at John Howard's table as part of a fundraiser at Sydney's Wentworth Hotel that included 10-minute briefings with Ministers.[71] At the 2007 federal ALP conference, major companies including NAB, Westpac and Telstra paid $7000 per person for their representatives to be accompanied by federal ALP frontbenchers for the entire conference. Tables at the conference dinner were also sold for up to $15,000 – the price of the privilege of sitting next to shadow Ministers.[72]

Indeed, Howard was not shy in using his official residence for fundraising.[73] In June 2007, business observers paid more than $8000 each to attend a Liberal Party meeting at Kirribilli House.[74] The prize for the most successful fundraiser perhaps goes to Malcolm Turnbull, who charged $55,000 per head for a fundraising dinner to support his bid for re-election.[75] Not much seems to have changed since the election of the Rudd government, with the *Sydney Morning Herald* reporting in 2008 that a deal had been struck between the then federal ALP national secretary, Tim Gartrell, and his counterpart, the federal Liberal Party director, Brian Loughnane, to use the Great Hall and the Mural Hall of Parliament House for party fundraising purposes.[76]

With the sale of access and influence, we see the logic of the market being ruthlessly applied to political power. Demand from business for political influence is being met by supply from the major parties and their leaders. As a senior ALP figure put it, 'We use our political leadership to raise funds because they are [sic] the best product we have to sell.'[77] Like other markets, the greater the value of the product, the higher the price. Referring to ministerial lunches organised by Progressive Business, an experienced Victorian lobbyist has said: 'The cost depends on how senior the Minister is. If you want a key Minister, companies pay $10,000.'[78]

The clearest instances of access and influence being sold occur when payment is expressly exchanged for privileged access, say $10,000 for a Minister. It would be a mistake, though, to think that these are the only ways in which access and influence are being sold.

In some cases, large donations, though not directly tied to access and influence, are made to achieve the same result. Referring to $50,000 given to the Victorian ALP in 2000 by Walker Corporation, a property developer, John Hughes, the company's managing director, said:

> It does not get you access on the spot, but what it does, it allows us to support the government of that particular day, if it was (former Victorian Premier) Bracks you said. If we wished to be able to put a case at some point in the future, then one could hope that it would favourably get you that access faster than others, but it does not achieve anything. At the end of the day being able to have an appointment with somebody, to be able to put your case, does not guarantee a result.[79]

In a similar vein, Mark Fitzgibbon, former head of Clubs NSW, the peak industry body for clubs registered in New South Wales, has said of the thousands of dollars Clubs NSW donated to the NSW ALP: 'I have no doubt it had some influence ... supporting [the ALP's] fundraising helped our ability to influence people.'[80]

This process of granting and securing influence seems to be driven by the parties as much as by their corporate sponsors. In fact, there is evidence of some public officials seeking to extract rent from their positions. An example from the WA Inc. debacle involves the conduct of former WA Premier Brian Burke and his brother Terry Burke, who was then Cabinet Secretary. Referring to their conduct, the Royal Commission on WA Inc. concluded that:

> [the Burkes] were actively engaged in soliciting campaign donations from prospective corporate donors. In his approaches, the Premier was direct to the point at times of being forceful. He nominated the amounts he expected. They were far in excess of amounts previously donated in the course of campaign fundraising in this State.[81]

Those defending such practices sometimes deny that influence is being sold. According to them, all that is sold is access to political leaders, with leaders free to make up their minds on particular issues. But influence is inseparable from access.[82] Businesses that pay for 'off the record' briefings with Ministers get to meet the Ministers and, in the words of the Millennium Forum's website, secure an opportunity to 'promote issues of concern and importance' to them.[83] The website of Progressive Business used to be very up-front about what was being traded when it stated that 'Joining this influential group allows you to participate in the decision making progress [sic].'[84]

The way the corporate patrons of the ALP and Liberal Party obtain influence over party leaders can be quite subtle. Reporting on the fundraisers of Progressive Business, *The Age* journalist Michael Bachelard said:

> It's an unwritten rule that there will be no overt lobbying: businesses are there to be seen, to put a face to the name, to establish a profile in the minister's mind.[85]

Despite this, there is still value for businesses. As an executive from a property development company observed, 'It just smoothes the path to get something heard.'[86]

What is much less commented on, but perhaps even more important, is the impact of these activities on the broader political agenda. Those who are able to pay for access are in a position to highlight matters of significance to them. Ministers they can directly access will tend to pay more attention to these matters than to other issues of public interest, unless these other issues are also taken up by powerful and articulate advocates.

Clearly, businesses buying such access and influence tend not to be using this to pursue an electoral strategy – they are not donating funds to parties as an open endorsement of the parties' policies in an effort to secure their electoral success. Rather, they are largely pursuing an access strategy: money is being given to parties to secure access and influence after the parties have been elected to office.

By paying hefty fees, companies are aiming to exercise influence in non-public circumstances such as 'off the record' briefings.[87]

This is an emphatic instance of what political philosopher Michael Walzer characterises as a 'blocked exchange', where money is used to buy political power.[88] The result is corruption through undue influence: the purchase of access, and thus influence, creates a conflict between public duty and the financial interests of the party or candidate,[89] and this results in public officials giving an undue weight to the interests of their financiers when deciding matters that affect the public interest.[90]

That any eventual outcomes of the sale of access and influence are not overt or explicit makes little difference to the question of corruption through undue influence. Such corruption can still exist even when the influence is not decisive (see Chapter 1), because the structure of incentives facing parties and their leaders once a contribution has been received remain the same: their judgment may be improperly skewed towards the interests of their financiers.[91] There is thus a double injury to the democratic process: wealthy donors are unfairly privileged while the interests of ordinary citizens are sidelined. This highlights the fact that the sale of access and influence is not only corrupt, because it undermines merit-based decision-making, but is also unfair: contributors are illegitimately *empowered* in the political process while non-contributors are illegitimately *disempowered*.

Corruption through undue influence tends to take the form of institutional corruption. When access and influence are sold, the gain is principally political (not personal), as money is usually channelled to the campaign coffers of the party rather than to the purse of the individual candidate. It is also procedurally improper, as opportunities to influence the political process, often in circumstances of secrecy, are being given solely because money is being paid. Such practices also damage the democratic process by undermining the merit principle.

What's worse is how such corruption pervades Australian politics and how, in some quarters, it is perfectly normal. At the 2007 Liberal Party federal council, federal Ministers auctioned off their time for thousands of dollars: a harbour cruise with Tony Abbott, then Health Minister, fetched $10,000, while a night at the opera with Helen Coonan, then Minister for Communications, Information Technology and the Arts, cost a princely sum of $12,000, all under the council theme of 'Doing what's right for Australia'.[92]

With some companies, such practices have, in fact, become one mark of a 'real' business. As one leading Victorian business figure has observed, 'Most of the serious players in business are paying to both sides for access.'[93] Or as another business figure observed: 'You've got to be seen to be there. We do it because everyone else does it … we know it gets us access.'[94] Perhaps nobody can put it more plainly than Ashley Mason, the external affairs executive for Leighton Holdings, when he said of buying access through Progressive Business: 'It's part of the system … It's seen as part of the process.'

Some are more equal than others

In his defence of Progressive Business and its sale of access and influence, Victorian Premier John Brumby referred to his support for the 'democratic right' of people and businesses to donate.[95] There is some plausibility to this position – after all, political contributions can animate the democratic process. This perspective is, however, self-servingly selective. Not only does it gloss over the questions of corruption just discussed; it also seems to invoke a notion of a 'right' or 'freedom' that rests principally on being free from legal restrictions. It ignores the 'freedom to' make donations (see Chapter 1). It fails to acknowledge how economic inequalities render a formal freedom to donate largely meaningless for most people – the amounts involved in corporate political contributions such as those made by corporate financiers of Progressive Business are out of the reach of most Australian citizens.

These blind spots pave the way for the most damaging aspect of the peddling of influence, the idea that political power can and should be bought and sold like any other product on the market. The commodity principle is anathema to democracy. As noted in Chapter 1, at the heart of democratic principles is a commitment that each citizen has an equal status in the political process. This implies that each citizen, regardless of class and wealth, shall be treated with equal respect and concern. This is why property votes were abolished in the process of instituting the democratic franchise.

Contrast this with the logic of the market, where power equals purchasing power. This is a place where money not only talks, but is the only voice that matters. The true measure of one's worth in the market is determined by the size of one's bank balance. Any commodification of political power is a vicious assault upon Australia's democracy. While we no longer have property votes,[96] those with money have discovered other ways to translate their wealth into political power. In this context, note the following comments made by Jeff Kennett, former Liberal Premier of Victoria:

> The professionalism of selling time has risen to such a level that it has corrupted the democratic process; it corrupts the principle [that] all people are equal before the law.[97]

When applied to political power, the commodity principle also undermines the notion of the public interest. In a democracy, the calculus for the public interest gives equal weight to the concerns of each citizen. In doing so, it draws a crucial distinction between the private interests of the holders of public office and the broader interests of the community. Government property, for example, is not treated like the property of the party in power. It is held in trust on behalf of citizens and can only be used in the public interest. When he was Queensland Integrity Commissioner, Gary Crooke provided an insightful analysis of this set of issues, parts of which merit full reproduction. He observed that:

All the components of government property (whether physical, intellectual or reputational) are really no more, and no less, than the property of the community, the capital of which is held in trust by elected or appointed representatives or officials.

The term 'capital' is an amorphous one and includes all the entitlement to respect and inside knowledge that goes with holding a high position in public administration.

The trust bestowed importantly includes an obligation to deal with government property or capital only in the interests of the community. As such, it is singularly inappropriate for any person to use it for personal gain.[98]

Speaking of party fundraising, Crooke further noted that:

It seems to be a common strategy to hold a dinner or like function where entry is often by invitation, and usually at a price well beyond the cost of the provision of any food or services at the function. Often, it is openly advertised that such payment will ensure access to a Minister or other high-ranking politician.

Having regard to my reference to 'capital' and trusteeship of the same, it seems to me that questions such as the following need to be asked:

- What is being sold and who (or what entity) receives or controls the proceeds?
- Whose is it to sell, or can it appropriately be sold?
- Is what is on offer being offered on equal terms to all members of the community?
- What is the likely understanding or expectation, of the payer on the one hand, and of the reasonable member of the community on the other, of what the buyer is paying for?
- If there is a Government decision to be made, is a perception likely to arise that those interested, and not attending the function, whether competitors for a tender, or opponents to a proposal, are at a disadvantage?

Unless questions such as the above can be unequivocally answered in a way which is consonant with the integrity issues raised in the previous discussion of capital and trusteeship, it would not be appropriate to engage in, or continue this practice.[99]

This analysis suggests that the selling of access and influence involves not only corruption through undue influence and political unfairness, but also corruption through the misuse of public resources – in particular, the privileges or 'capital' of public office.

It also demonstrates why Kirribilli House, the Lodge and Parliament House should not be used for party fundraising. If political power is to be bought and sold like any other commodity, then its exercise is no longer oriented to the public interest, and it is, in fact, just like any other piece of property. It is just a small step from this to treating the national estate like the private property of the party in government, with 'those in power ... acting as if they own the trappings of office'.[100] Worryingly, this is already occurring. Federal Opposition Leader Tony Abbott has argued that holding Liberal Party fundraisers at Kirribilli House (as occurred with former Prime Minister John Howard) was entirely proper and simply a case of 'someone inviting people to a private home'.[101]

As well as increasing political unfairness among citizens and undermining the public interest, private money also creates a dramatic funding inequality among the parties. When the private money received by the main parties between 1999–2000 and 2001–02 is divided by the first preference votes they received in the 2001 federal election, a sharp cleavage emerges between the major parties and the minor parties. For each dollar of private money received per vote by the Democrats, more than $3 was received by the ALP. And for each dollar of private money received per vote by the Greens, the Liberal Party received $2. It is this unequal flow of private money that largely explains why the major parties received more than $20 per 2001 election vote, while the minor parties received less than half that amount.[102]

The imbalance stems from various sources. We saw earlier that the ALP and the Coalition have a near monopoly over corporate political money. These parties also enjoy significant income from their investments. The financial position of the ALP is further consolidated by its receipt of trade union money. Come election time, then, the playing field is far from level. Armed with larger war chests, the major parties are able to vastly outspend their competitors. The advantage secured by these parties through private funds is further amplified by inequitable state funding of parties (see Chapter 5) and incumbency benefits such as government advertising (see Chapter 6). The result is that rather than having fair elections, our electoral competitions favour the Coalition and the ALP. This highlights a circular dynamic where money follows the (greater) political power of the major parties and that power is, in turn, consolidated by such money.

The unequal flow of private money highlights how big corporations that hedge their bets by giving to the ALP and the Coalition parties rely upon a pseudo-notion of fairness. For these companies, such as Leighton Holdings, there is even-handedness, as donations are given 'in a bipartisan way'.[103] But rather than explaining away any unfairness, such bipartisanship in fact underscores the inequity of such practices. Because the major parties are the principal beneficiaries of corporate money, not only are other parties and groups placed at a financial disadvantage but their views are also sidelined in the marketplace of ideas.

There is an interesting twist to the inequality stemming from corporate money. The fact that the ALP gets corporate money *and* trade union funds has led the Liberal Party to cry foul. In the 2007 Liberal Party federal council, the party treasurer, Mark Bethwaite, criticised the fact that 'Corporate attitudes to political donations have become fixed on achieving a balance between Liberal and Labor.' He warned the business community that it:

> must realise that we do not face a level playing field at the coming election. We will need to fund-raise [to] a much more significant level than we have achieved before if we are [to be] able … to match Labor and their union bosses.[104]

There is some force to these claims: the ALP is the principal recipient of trade union money, and as I will explain in Chapter 7, there was no 'equality of arms' between the Coalition and the ALP in the 2007 federal election. But it is important to keep these claims in perspective. As was noted earlier, trade union money, even at its highest proportion, which was for the financial years 2006–07 and 2007–08, was less than one-sixth of the ALP's total income. Moreover, the inequality of arms favouring the ALP is a recent phenomenon: the position was the reverse for the previous three elections (see Chapter 8). Having lodged these caveats, it remains the case that the inequality between the ALP and the Coalition parties is significant in terms of political fairness.

Selling out the party

The health of the Australian party system suffers from the undue influence that is spawned by the sale of access and influence. As corporate financiers of the major parties increasingly call the shots, the interests and rights of citizens become sidelined. The ideal of governing in the public interest is placed in jeopardy when, as former High Court Chief Justice Gerard Brennan observed:

> The financial dependence of a political party on those whose interests can be served by the favours of government … cynically turn[s] public debate into a cloak for bartering away the public interest.[105]

The agenda-setting function of the party system is also impaired, as the policies of the major parties can be influenced by a small band of businesses.

There are other serious effects on the major parties. Their ability to effectively govern is undermined by the time consumed by fundraising.[106] Former federal Human Services Minister Joe Hockey, for instance, is reported to have complained in the Liberal Party room about the constant pressure to attend fundraisers.[107] A submission of the NSW ALP has similarly observed that:

> Under the current system, it is an unfortunate reality that Party Officials and MPs must dedicate a considerable amount of their time to fundraising efforts. This is time which could be better spent promoting progressive policies and advocating on behalf of constituents.[108]

The quality of the candidates that parties recruit may also suffer from this preoccupation with fundraising. The importance of fundraising ability in Liberal Party preselections, for instance, has been frankly acknowledged by former Treasurer Peter Costello:

> In my time in politics, the amount of time and effort put into fund-raising has exploded. Fund-raising is considered such an integral part of an MP's job that candidates for pre-selection are assessed for their fund-raising potential. A candidate who can bring in campaign funds is as highly prized as one that will bring in votes.[109]

The significance of fundraising ability can also be seen in the following instances. In the aftermath of the last federal election, one of the factors said to have enhanced Malcolm Turnbull's chances of winning leadership of the federal Liberal Party was his ability to raise money to restore the party's depleted funds.[110] The same was also said of Alan Stockdale's (successful) candidacy for presidency of the federal Liberal Party.[111] This is not to deny that Turnbull or Stockdale are worthy candidates. Rather, the point is that the calculus of merit appears to have been weighted heavily in favour of their ability to fundraise and, arguably, has reduced the attention paid to more important leadership attributes, such as their policies and ability to effectively challenge the ALP.

Fundraising practices may also lessen the ability of the major parties to act as vehicles for popular participation. Their appeal to ordinary citizens may lessen, as these practices may hollow out the meaning of party membership. As parties sell influence to moneyed interests, they also send out a signal to their rank-and-file members that the voices that will be listened to are those with large purses, rather than those who faithfully subscribe to party principles.

The role of party members is also sidelined in other ways. 'Capitalist financing' increasingly outstrips 'democratic financing' through membership subscriptions in terms of financial importance.[112] This occurs through corporate fundraising, but also through the growing reliance of the major parties on investment (discussed earlier). The federal government's *Electoral Reform Green Paper: Donations, Funding and Expenditure*, for instance, estimates that three-quarters of the major parties' private funding comes from fundraising activities, investments and debts.[113]

This 'business' model tends to centralise power within a party. It vests increasing control over fundraising in the party leadership, and that control is made more effective when the investment arrangements are opaque, with lines of accountability blurred or hidden from view. More subtly, it contributes to 'the increasing *profession-alization* of party organizations' (emphasis in original).[114] According to some commentators, the major parties are increasingly becoming electoral-professional parties,[115] in which 'a much more important role is played by professionals (the so-called experts, technicians with special knowledge)'.[116] This is occurring in the context of a small membership base.[117] The 'business' model of the party will shape what is seen as 'professional' and, consequently, the distribution of power within the party: as the ability to fundraise and manage investments is seen as key to the success of the party, party officials having these skills will gain more power within the party.[118] With growing centralisation, responsiveness to rank-and-file members decreases. ALP Senator John Faulkner has, for example, argued that, for the ALP, 'Grass-roots members are an afterthought and for many in the machine, an inconvenience.'[119] Developments such as this directly undermine the participatory function of the major parties. In addition, the bypassing of rank-and-file members saps the ability of these parties to generate new ideas and policies and weakens their claims to be representative of citizens.

Conclusion

The laissez-faire character of Australia's political funding regime is best reflected in its treatment of private political funding – in general, such funding is regulated only to the extent of being subjected to disclosure obligations. Thus we see a premium placed on 'freedom from' legal restrictions, with the right to donate (in the sense of a formal ability to make political contributions) apparently held up as the core principle.

Perhaps there was a hope that this formal freedom would give rise to a widespread practice of political donations, with the parties financially reliant on – and responsive to – a multitude of citizens. If so, this can only be described as a naive expectation. In the space vacated by state regulation, political money has imposed severe costs on Australia's democracy: corruption through undue influence pervades, through the sale of access and influence, and various forms of unfairness have resulted. Even the parties themselves have suffered, with their health undermined by preoccupation with fundraising. It is time to decisively reject the laissez-faire approach and devise more democratic regulation of private funding of Australian politics, a topic the next chapter will take up.

4

REGULATING PRIVATE MONEY

The damage inflicted on Australia's democracy by the unregulated flows of private political money has already been documented. We can now turn to the question that forms the focus of this chapter: how should such funding be regulated in order to advance democratic principles?

The chapter begins by providing a survey of current regulation of private funding. Its core message is that there needs to be an overhaul of such regulation. It argues that a range of reforms are necessary to protect the integrity of representative government, promote fairness in politics, support political parties in discharging their functions as well as respect political freedoms. Specifically, it advocates two sets of measures – one to strengthen the regulation of conflicts of interests, the other to improve the internal accountability of corporate and trade union political contributions.

The chapter also provides an extended discussion of what is commonly advanced to be *the* central measure to deal with private funding of Australian politics: contribution limits. It argues that there are compelling grounds for introducing such limits and that, if properly designed, they will not fall foul of the constitutional limitations relating to the implied freedom of political communication. It emphasises that such limits should be subject to an exemption for membership fees (including trade union affiliation fees) and, crucially, should be integrated with a reconfigured public funding system and election spending limits.

What we have now

The focus of current regulation has been on preventing corruption in the form of graft and undue influence. There have been three broad approaches. First, transparency measures or disclosure obligations (as detailed in Chapter 2). Second, offences set out in criminal law. Most jurisdictions have two main corruption-related criminal offences: bribery and abuse of public office. While there are differences in detail, the essence of the offences is largely similar. Bribery occurs when a person dishonestly or corruptly provides a benefit (or dishonestly causes a benefit to be provided) to a public official with the intention to influence the exercise of power by that official. Abuse of public office occurs when a public official exercises or fails to exercise power because of a dishonest or corrupt intention to benefit oneself or to cause detriment to another.[1] As discussed in Chapter 3, determining whether or not any of these offences are committed depends on being able to prove the intentions of the donor and the recipient.

The third approach seeks to regulate conflicts of interest. The default position is one of permissiveness – political parties, candidates and parliamentarians are free to accept contributions from any source and of any amount (subject to making the required disclosure). There are exceptions to this rule. Section 45(iii) of the *Commonwealth Constitution* provides that the seat of a federal parliamentarian is vacated when s/he 'directly or indirectly takes or agrees to take any fee or honorarium … *for services rendered in Parliament* to any person or State' (emphasis added). Similar statutory prohibitions also exist in the ACT and the Northern Territory.[2] These provisions would disqualify parliamentarians in these jurisdictions if they took political contributions in exchange for conduct within their Parliament: being paid to ask a question in Parliament, for instance.

Conflicts of interest are also regulated through the ministerial[3] and parliamentary[4] codes of conduct that exist in various jurisdictions.[5] Some of these codes ban personal gifts, including political contributions, except for those of nominal value. The Tasmanian Legislative Assembly code, for example, states that 'Members of the Assembly must not accept gifts, benefits or favours except for incidental gifts or customary hospitality of nominal value.'[6] The SA and ACT ministerial codes require that personal gifts exceeding $200 be surrendered to the government.[7]

Most codes, however, have less strict provisions. Generally, they provide broad prohibitions on gifts to avoid conflicts of interest. For instance, under its provisions dealing with gifts, the Commonwealth ministerial code states that:

> When taking decisions in or in connection with their official capacity, Ministers must do so in terms of advancing the public interest – that is, based on their best judgment of what will advance the common good of the people of Australia.[8]

The Queensland Ministerial Code is more specific:

> Ministers or ministerial staff, members of their immediate families (i.e. partners and dependant children) should not accept gifts which could give the appearance of a conflict of interest past, present or future with the duties of the Minister or a staff member, or shall not in any circumstances accept gifts involving transfer of moneys, regardless of value, (e.g. by cash or loan) other than as part of an approved assistance program.[9]

The NSW Parliamentary Code of Conduct is similar:

> Members must not accept gifts that may pose a conflict of interest
> or which might give the appearance of an attempt to improperly
> influence the Member in the exercise of his or her duties.[10]

While codes of conduct deal with *personal* contributions to parliamentarians and Ministers, there is very little regulation of contributions to *political parties* in terms of conflicts of interest, apart from the disclosure schemes (see Chapter 2).

Another way to regulate conflicts of interest is by preventing any conflict from affecting government decisions. In 2008, for example, the Victorian Parliament passed amendments banning local councillors from taking part in council proceedings when they have received more than $200 in the preceding five years from persons or entities who have a direct interest in the matters being discussed.[11] Less strict rules apply in other states and territories: local councillors are prohibited from participating in proceedings if they have a 'pecuniary interest' (NSW),[12] a 'material personal interest' (Queensland),[13] an 'interest in a matter' (SA),[14] an 'interest' (Tasmania)[15] or a 'personal or financial interest' (NT)[16] in the proceedings. These concepts have not, however, been defined to specifically include gifts or political contributions.[17]

Improving the regulation of conflicts of interest

Two sets of measures should be adopted to better manage conflicts of interest resulting from political contributions. The first involves bans on contributions when the contributor has a strong interest in governmental actions. In the United States, for instance, contributions from persons or companies with contracts with the federal government are completely banned.[18] Similar bans should be adopted in all Australian jurisdictions. The recommendation made by a Victorian parliamentary committee, that 'political parties be precluded from accepting donations from those engaged in commercial use or development of public land or other public assets',[19] should also be adopted (such a ban would be narrower than the NSW ban on political donations from property developers, which applies to development of public *and* private land).[20]

The second set of measures relates to parliamentary and ministerial codes of conduct. Two circumstances provide a strong case for adopting these codes rather than legal sanctions. The first is when the standards to be prescribed do not come in the form of precise rules, but instead call for careful judgment and sensitivity to context. Legislative ethical conduct from parliamentarians will often meet this criterion. Meredith Burgmann, former President of the NSW Legislative Council (who was deeply involved in the development of the NSW parliamentary code of conduct), described it nicely. According to her, the NSW code mainly deals with 'grey areas' because the ethical issues relating to parliamentary conduct are 'not black and white, there is this huge area in the middle'.[21]

The other circumstance is when it is considered appropriate that standards be developed and enforced principally through the political process.[22] Putting aside constitutional reasons (in particular, those relating to parliamentary privilege), a central reason for such an arrangement is that it places the responsibility for political ethics squarely where it belongs.[23] As one commentator has observed:

> the strongest argument is that the process of code development
> and regular review can provide a clarifying focus for legislators
> to reflect about their role and duties and their obligations to
> legislative democracy, a way of consolidating around principles
> the various existing injunctions about good legislative practice
> and of communicating them to a wider public.[24]

Operating in this way, 'Codes are not merely cudgels, [t]hey are lights.'[25]

However, these possible advantages can be easily subverted. An emphasis on broad provisions can lead to codes filled with 'absolutely meaningless rhetoric'.[26] Also, relying on enforcement through the political process can lead to codes with no 'bite'. As the Bowen Inquiry into conflicts of interest observed, 'Self-regulation may be abused to the point that there is no regulation at all.'[27] This could be a danger if the major parties collude in suspect behaviour or when the target is institutional corruption. Rather than illuminating such behaviour, codes can underwrite a conspiracy of silence about unethical conduct.[28]

In order to ensure that parliamentary and ministerial codes of conduct are effective in dealing with conflicts of interest stemming from political funding, there are several priorities. The first is obvious: codes should be adopted in jurisdictions where they are absent.[29] Second, the scope of conflict of interest provisions should include not only personal gifts but also gifts to political parties. Both types of financial contributions can give rise to situations where there is a conflict of interest, so there is no good reason to confine the provisions to the former. Indeed, the party-centred character of Australian political funding underscores how essential it is to bring gifts to political parties within the scope of such provisions.

Third, these broader provisions should include obligations relating to the communications between parliamentarians and Ministers and contributors to their parties. At a minimum, Ministers, shadow Ministers and their staff[30] should keep records of meetings with party contributors, as well as records of meetings with party officials discussing party contributors.[31] While there is no general requirement to make these records public, they should be accessible to the Parliamentary Ethics Commissioner, who should be authorised to make them public in certain circumstances (see below). Further, the announcement of government decisions specifically benefiting a contributor should be accompanied by a chronology of contacts between the contributor and its representatives, and the relevant Minister and his or her staff discussing the subject matter of the decision, as well as the amount of contributions made in the past five years.

Further prohibitions should be set up under these codes in relation to party fundraisers. These events, especially if they involve the sale of access and influence, can pose a serious danger. Queensland Premier Anna Bligh's ban on ALP parliamentarians attending party fundraisers[32] should be adopted in all jurisdictions with all parliamentarians, including Ministers, banned from attending party fundraisers. Such a prohibition will still allow party fundraisers to be held but will significantly reduce the risk of undue influence.

Some might see such a ban as overkill. Overdue is perhaps the more appropriate description. There should not be any equivocation on this point: these fundraisers are in reality sales of access and influence, and that is a form of corruption (see Chapter 3). It must be addressed given the expectations that the public rightly has of its elected officials, which are clearly reflected in many of the codes of conduct. The Tasmanian Legislative Assembly code of conduct, for instance, enjoins members to have 'a commitment to the highest ethical standards'.[33] Three ministerial codes variously require Ministers to demonstrate 'appropriately high standards of personal integrity' (the Commonwealth),[34] 'high standards ... in the execution of their public duties' (Queensland)[35] and 'standards of conduct of the highest order' (SA).[36]

The final, and arguably the most important, priority is to ensure that the codes of conduct are enforced.[37] At the moment, enforcement resides with the Prime Minister in the case of the Commonwealth code,[38] and the Premiers and Chief Ministers in the case of the state and territory codes.[39] Deciding whether to refer a matter to an independent authority, or whether to require a Minister to stand aside or resign, falls within the prerogative of these heads of government.

The parliamentary codes of conduct are enforced differently in different jurisdictions. In many cases, breach of a code is subject to the general power of the Parliament to discipline its members, including the power to find them in contempt of Parliament.[40] In Queensland[41] and New South Wales[42] there are parliamentary committees responsible for supervising and reviewing the codes. These states and the ACT have also set up advisory bodies. In Queensland it is the Integrity Commissioner,[43] in New South Wales it is the Parliamentary Ethics Adviser[44] and in the ACT it is the Ethics and Integrity Adviser.[45]

Two matters suggest that these arrangements are not adequate. First, while all parliamentary codes of conduct are public documents, the same cannot be said of the ministerial codes. Specific requests had to be made for the codes applying in New South Wales and Tasmania; specific inquiries also had to be made to discover the status of the planned NT code; information about the existence of a code in Victoria was difficult to come by and rather inconclusive; and it has been difficult to confirm the ongoing operation of the WA Code.[46] With secret codes and codes that operate opaquely, it is impossible to know whether or not they are being adequately policed – it is imperative that all codes are made publicly available.

The second matter concerns 'off the record' briefings (discussed in Chapter 3). In all the ministerial codes I obtained, except for the Commonwealth code, there are strict provisions requiring respect for Cabinet confidentiality.[47] In the parliamentary codes, there are often prohibitions against the use of confidential information for private purposes.[48] It is exceedingly difficult to see how 'off the record' briefings, which presumably involve disclosure of confidential information, are compatible with these provisions.

A crucial way to tighten up the enforcement of the codes would be to inject an independent element into the process by establishing a body that investigates alleged breaches of the codes. The Bowen Committee on conflicts of interest, for example, recommended that a statutory body, the Public Integrity Commission, be set up at the federal level, made up of members appointed by the Prime Minister after consultation with Opposition Leader. The primary function of this Commission would be to investigate complaints of unethical legislative behaviour, and it would table its findings before Parliament. Importantly, it would have the power to compel the production of information.[49] A variant of this is the British Parliamentary Commissioner on Standards, whose powers include the ability to investigate alleged breaches of the British parliamentary code of conduct and to report the findings to a parliamentary committee.[50]

Corporate and trade union political contributions: internal accountability

Corporate and trade union money are the key sources of private funding for the major parties (see Chapter 3). Internal accountability is an area of crucial concern for both. For trade unions, this is a question of democratic accountability.[51] At present, federal industrial legislation requires federally registered trade unions to set out rules in relation to the spending of money,[52] and to spend sums of more than $1000 only when authorised by the union's committee of management, which must be satisfied that such spending is in accordance with the rules of the union.[53] There is no requirement that such unions adopt specific rules in relation to political spending.

In some cases, unions have of their own volition adopted specific rules in relation to political spending. The rules of the AMWU, for example, require that any spending to further political objectives shall only be made from a Political Fund. The Political Fund is financed by members, and is segregated from other union money. Under the AMWU rules, members have a right to be exempted from making this contribution.[54] In most unions, however, there is no specific provision made for political spending. The rules of the CEPU (General),[55] LHMU[56] and CFMEU,[57] for example, essentially reproduce the statutory requirements and generally authorise their committees of management to make decisions in relation to spending.

These arrangements provide a notional guarantee of internal accountability, as unions are meant to have democratic elections.[58] But the guarantee is liable to be subverted by the reality of power relations. Here we confront the problem that was identified by sociologist Robert Michels almost a century ago. Michels argued that there was a tendency towards oligarchy – that is, the ruling elite in effect having control – in large organisations because of the general passivity of rank-and-file members, the elite's superior political skills and its control over finances and the means of communications. This, according to Michels, was the iron law of oligarchy.[59] Studies of trade union internal democracy, whilst identifying particular circumstances where such democracy can flourish (most importantly, the institutionalisation of organised opposition), have been similarly pessimistic.[60] These studies underscore the persistent and complex challenge of installing and maintaining internal democracy in large organisations, including unions.

Promoting internal union democracy in relation to political expenditure is not exempt from this challenge. Indeed, decisions relating to political expenditure may involve particularly serious threats to internal union democracy. The decision-making is often hidden from the gaze of ordinary union members. With decisions on industrial issues, such as wage rises, union members ordinarily need to be consulted, not least to enlist their support for the industrial claims to be made by the union. This is not the case with decisions to engage in political expenditure, through contributions to political parties or independent political spending. For unions that are affiliated to the ALP, the influence their representatives wield by virtue of their membership of the ALP – in the preselection of candidates, for instance – is also typically shrouded in secrecy. For example, in 2009, unions affiliated to the Victorian ALP were involved in a secret 'peace deal' that decided who should be preselected as ALP candidates in the upcoming federal and state elections.[61]

Also, there is a long list of union officials who have moved on to become ALP parliamentarians. Recent additions include Greg Combet, former secretary of the Australian Council of Trade Unions (ACTU), now a Minister in the Rudd Labor government, and Bill Shorten, former national secretary of the Australian Workers Union (AWU), currently a parliamentary secretary. There is of course nothing wrong in itself with these transitions. These established pathways do, however, throw up a risk that the prospect of a parliamentary career will tempt some union officials, consciously or not, to prefer either their interests or the interests of the ALP over those of their members when making decisions on political spending.

Some may also infer oligarchical decision-making in relation to these decisions from the voting record of union members. This record clearly shows that not all union members support the ALP. For example, only 63 per cent of union members from 1966 to 2004 voted for the ALP.[62] However, this figure does not necessarily provide any further evidence of oligarchical decision-making in relation to trade union political spending. Several large unions have neither affiliated nor contributed to the ALP (see Chapter 3). While further examination is required, it may be the case that the number of members in unions that are affiliated to the ALP corresponds to the number who voted for it. Moreover, it is quite rational for union members to endorse their union's decision to support the ALP in order to promote the importance of the union agenda, while deciding that overall the Coalition is better suited for government.

Turning to corporate contributors, we are still faced with the problem of internal accountability, but in a different form. It is not a question of democratic accountability or of oligarchy: commercial corporations, as plutocratic organisations, have no pretensions to democratic decision-making. As sociologists Lipset, Trow and Coleman correctly pointed out, 'Oligarchy becomes a problem only in organizations which assume as part of their public value system the absence of oligarchy, that is, democracy.'[63]

But plutocratic organisations still rely upon notions of

accountability: accountability to providers of capital. With corporate political contributions, this means accountability to shareholders. Has making these contributions been in the best interests of the shareholders? Dangers analogous to those that threaten democratic decision-making in relation to trade union political spending are also present: secrecy generally attends decision-making in relation to whether or not political contributions should be made, as they tend to be made by company boards rather than the shareholders at large. There is also the risk of managers making contributions in order to further their self-interest rather than the interest of the company.[64]

For some, the dangers are more acute given that companies tend not to be overtly political organisations. To illustrate, a senior business figure has been quoted as being uneasy with the decision of the Business Council of Australia (BCA) and Australian Chamber of Commerce and Industry to create the National Business Action Fund to fund advertisements supporting the Howard government's WorkChoices legislative program, on the basis that 'Business associations are about issues and the best interests of their members. They shouldn't be part of the political process like this.'[65] In a similar vein, the policy of the Australian Shareholders Association on political donations states that:

> Companies must operate within the legal and regulatory
> system applying in the places in which they operate. Theirs is
> an economic role – as expressed in the dictum 'The business of
> business is business' – not a political one.

Accordingly, the Australian Shareholders Association completely opposes political contributions by public companies.[66]

So there are significant challenges to internal accountability in relation to both trade union and corporate political contributions. There are good reasons to require trade unions and corporations to seek specific authorisation from their members and shareholders before making political contributions. Former Senator Andrew

Murray has recommended that they do ·this at least once every 3 years.[67] This sort of requirement has an Australian precedent in relation to trade union political expenditure: for a few years, WA trade unions were required to set up a separate fund for political spending.[68]

Another possible model is the UK rules about donations made by trade unions and companies. British trade unions are required to ballot their members every 10 years for authority to promote their political agendas. Once authorised, political expenditure by a trade union must be made from a separate political fund, and individual members must have a right to not contribute to that fund. British companies are required to seek authorisation from their shareholders every 4 years to make political donations and/or political expenditure.[69]

The case for limits on contributions

Greater restrictions on political contributions have support across the political spectrum. In a response to the Wollongong City Council scandal, former NSW Premier Morris Iemma advanced the radical proposal of completely banning political contributions in favour of a system of complete public funding.[70] Following not too far behind, his predecessor, Bob Carr, has advocated banning political contributions from organisations such as trade unions and companies and only allowing contributions from individuals. Former Leader of the Opposition Malcolm Turnbull[71] and the NSW Greens[72] have similar positions. Queensland Premier Anna Bligh has also called for a national cap on political donations of $1000 and has signalled that Queensland will act to implement such a cap by July 2010 if there is no movement on the federal front.[73] In a bipartisan report, the NSW Legislative Council Select Committee on Electoral and Political Party Funding (NSW Select Committee) recommended that there be a ban on all political donations except those by individuals, and that their contributions be limited to $1000 per political party per annum (and $1000 per independent candidate per electoral cycle).[74]

There are compelling arguments for limits on contributions such as those recommended by the NSW Select Committee. They would clearly act as a preventive measure in relation to graft. Moreover, the larger the amount of money contributed by an individual, the higher the risk of undue influence. Bans on large contributions may therefore deter corruption through undue influence (and also, as a corollary, obviate the need for bans on contributions from particular types of companies, such as property developers[75] and holders of gambling licences[76]). Such a limit could also promote fairness in politics, as it would prevent the wealthy from using their money to secure a disproportionate influence on the political process. The result is a promotion of the fair value of political freedoms, despite limiting the formal freedom to contribute.[77] This could break the hold of the commodity principle that is implicit in the sale of access and influence (see Chapter 3). Requiring parties to secure the support of a large base of small contributors would also be likely to improve performance of their participatory function.

However, there are significant objections to contribution limits.[78] First and foremost, instituting such limits would leave the parties seriously underfunded, jeopardising their continued existence (see Chapter 3). In the context of party government, this would place the system of government at risk. It is also unclear what impact the contribution limits would have on fairness among the parties. Further, contribution limits are likely to mean that parties will spend more time fundraising – they will need to persuade more individuals to part with their money. This development is likely to detract from the performance of their democratic functions (apart from the participatory function), especially if the 'arms race' between the parties continues (see Chapter 7).

These objections are not insurmountable. It is imperative that contribution limits be adopted as part of a *broad* package of reform – those who advocate contribution limits as the principal, at times the only, reform measure, often do not fully recognise the potential adverse effects of such limits. To reduce these effects, there needs to be a reconfiguration of public funding of parties and candidates, including a significant increase, to make up the shortfall resulting from limits on contributions (see Chapter 5). Such funding should provide for sustainable parties, redress any inequities that arise from contribution limits and lessen the risk of parties devoting an undue amount of time to fundraising. Also, contribution limits must be accompanied by election spending limits (see Chapter 7). The latter will staunch the demand that fuels the parties' aggressive fundraising activities.

An exemption for membership fees (including union affiliation fees)

While it recommended a ban on all but small donations by individuals, the NSW Select Committee also proposed that membership fees be exempted from the ban provided they are set at a reasonable level (as determined by the Auditor-General).[79] This position has considerable merit. As the NSW Select Committee correctly recognised, 'membership of political parties is an important means for individuals to participate in the political process'.[80] Specifically, it involves participation *within* political parties. Further, as we saw in Chapter 3, political contributions have different degrees of legitimacy, depending on whether they increase or reduce the quality of democratic deliberation, and the extent to which they meet the requirements for reason-giving and publicity. We saw in that chapter the connection between these and party membership fees (and why such fees tend not to involve corruption): the reason-giving requirement is met by party members taking out membership in order to advance their understanding of what is in the 'public interest', with a view to putting that understanding to the electorate; the publicity requirement is met through members openly declaring their support of the party's ideology and the mode of their influence being for-malised. These features of membership fees justify an exemption for membership fees. While contribution limits permit membership fees (as long as they are below the limits), an exemption would go beyond such permissiveness to encourage party membership.

Perhaps the most controversial question about any exemption for membership fees is whether it should be extended to organisational members; in particular, to trade union affiliates of the ALP. Indeed, this is shaping up as one of the most controversial issues concerning contribution limits. At the time of writing, the reform process at the federal level had reportedly stalled because of union opposition to limits that would ban trade union affiliation fees.[81]

This very much looks like unions thwarting the public interest. If political contributions are to be restricted, why should union affili-ation fees be exempt? Aren't such fees, like other political contribu-tions, paid as an attempt to influence the political process through money, and if so, shouldn't they be regulated just like any other con-tribution? As Janet Albrechtsen has argued, 'If big business is to be prevented from bankrolling political parties in return for favourable policies, surely the same rule must apply to unions.'[82]

I take a contrary view: I believe the exemption for member-ship fees should extend to organisational membership fees, including trade union affiliation fees.

Banning organisational membership fees: why we shouldn't

A ban on organisational membership fees would produce striking anomalies. Presumably, parties would still be allowed to have state and territory-based branches with intra-party transfers exempted from contribution limits. If so, collective affiliation based on geo-graphical areas will still be allowed. But if collective affiliation is permitted on this basis, why limit collective affiliation based on ideological grounds (for example, environmental groups seeking to affiliate to the Greens) or those based on occupation (for example, farmers' groups seeking to affiliate to the National Party)?

A ban on organisational membership would also detract from the participatory function of parties. In the case of the ALP, there would be a loss of the membership participation provided by trade union affiliates. However attenuated, such participation is still a form of participation. If limits applying to party contributions are enacted without limits also being placed on third parties and their spending, money may very well flow to third-party activity.[83] We could then see a preference for pressure group politics over party politics, as political groups engage in independent third-party activity rather than become members of political parties. Such a preference may favour issue politics over the broader and more inclusive forms of politics that are more likely to emerge through political parties.[84] Weakening the party system would fly in the face of one of the key principles of a democratic political finance regime: support for parties in performing their functions (see Chapter 1).

A ban on organisational membership fees (including trade union affiliation fees) would also have a severe impact on the trade union–ALP link. It would most likely weaken the relationship. Indeed this is one of the key aims of some advocates of these contribution limits: see former NSW Premier Bob Carr endorsing Morris Iemma's call for banning organisational contributions.[85] Clearly, some within the ALP are not pleased by the power wielded by 'trade union bosses' in the party, and would prefer that the ALP-union link be made illegal.

There are three main complaints bundled up in the epithet 'trade union bosses'. Let us consider them separately. The first is the claim that the presence in the party of 'trade union bosses' – or, more kindly, the influence of trade union officials within the ALP – is making the ALP unelectable or at least preventing it from becoming 'the natural party of Federal government'.[86] The issue here is that the influence of trade unions makes the ALP not properly representative of the Australian community, thereby impairing – perhaps even severely damaging – its electoral prospects.

Such views may or may not be correct. The point is whether a ban on organisational membership fees is a legitimate way of dealing with concerns regarding the electability of the ALP (or for that matter, any party). The answer is 'surely not': these are matters for the ALP and its members (both individual and organisational) to decide, not one for regulation. If it is not dealt with properly, the ballot box will let the ALP know.

There are two other complaints implied by criticisms of 'trade union bosses': one relating to internal party democracy and the other to trade union democracy. Mark Aarons, a former union official who was also an adviser to Bob Carr when he was NSW Premier, has argued that the ALP is organised in 'a most undemocratic way'[87] because affiliated trade unions through their delegates (often union secretaries) exercise 'a grossly out-of-proportion, even extraordinary, influence over policy formulation'.[88] This lack of proportion is said to arise because the level of power trade union delegates exercise within the ALP is not justified by the level of union density: how can it be right that trade unions have 50 per cent of delegates in ALP conferences when less than one-fifth of the workforce is unionised?[89]

This argument turns on a fallacious use of the term 'undemocratic'. It is true that parties have a representative function in that they, or the party system as a whole, should represent the diversity of opinion within a society (see Chapter 1). This is, however, not the same as saying that a single party should seek to represent the entire spectrum of this opinion. Not only is this practically impossible but paradoxically, parties discharge their representative function by representing different sections of society. It is the cumulative effect of such sectional representation that stamps a party system as representative in overall terms. In this context, characterising the manner in which the ALP is organised as being undemocratic simply because its membership base is not wholly representative of the Australian public is somewhat perverse.

There is nothing self-evidently 'undemocratic' about such influence. But that does not imply that the extent of union influence over the ALP is justifiable or desirable. Some, for example, might argue that such influence results in a rather partial notion of the 'public interest'. Just as the relationships between the Liberal Party and its business supporters, the National Party and agricultural producers, and the Greens and the environmental groups, are relevant considerations for the voters in deciding whether a political party adequately represents the 'public' or 'national' interest, such matters are clearly legitimate considerations for voters thinking about voting for the ALP.

There is another difficulty with characterising the manner in which the ALP is organised as undemocratic: reducing trade union influence will not necessarily revitalise the internal democracy of the ALP.[90] The party elite is made up of the parliamentary leadership, the members of Parliament and their staff,[91] the union leadership (including union delegates to state and national party conferences), and the party officials and bureaucrats. The rank and file, on the other hand, consists of the party members. Reducing the influence of the union leadership does not mean that power would flow to the rank and file. In the context of shrinking party membership within the ALP,[92] it is far more likely that power would be redistributed to others within the party elite. Where the 'party in public office', the parliamentary leadership, is already ascendant over the 'party on the ground' as well as the 'party central office',[93] it is a fair bet that the parliamentary leadership would be a key beneficiary of such a redistribution of power. A similar conclusion results when one casts an eye over power relations beyond the party. Looking at the ALP's relationship with 'class' forces, diminishing the influence of trade unions within the ALP is likely to mean a corresponding empowerment of business interests but not of the rank and file. The power of the government bureaucracy also needs to be factored in, especially when the ALP is in government: its influence is likely to increase as sources of countervailing power, such as trade unions, weaken in strength.

Underlying all this is a risk of throwing the baby out with the bath water. While it is true that the internal democracy of the ALP is undermined in some cases by trade unions because of their oligarchical tendencies (see above), the answer is not to excise trade unions from the party. Collective organisations such as trade unions play a necessary, though at times problematic, role in empowering citizens. The ambivalent character of such organisations is well captured by Michels. As noted earlier, Michels is famous for his iron law of oligarchy: 'Who says organization, says oligarchy.'[94] He is perhaps less well known for his observation that 'Organization … is the weapon of the weak in their struggle with the strong.'[95] Within the ALP, collective organisations such as trade unions allow individual members to band together to secure a voice that they would not otherwise have. While there is a risk of oligarchy within the member organisations themselves (the unions), when they function well they provide 'effective internal polyarchal controls'[96] that counter the oligarchical tendencies of the party. Severely diminishing the role of trade unions within the ALP is likely to increase the oligarchical tendencies within the party.

The other complaint in relation to 'trade union bosses' concerns trade union democracy. Aarons has argued that because 'individual unionists have no practical say in whether they are affiliated to the ALP and whether a proportion of their membership fees pay for this [and] … in how their union's votes will be cast', there is 'not a democratic expression of the union membership's wishes'.[97] This criticism, however, is misconceived. First, under any system of representative governance, most decisions are made by representatives without the direct say of their constituencies. It is this feature that distinguishes representative systems from those based on direct democracy, and this is how the Australian system of parliamentary representation is supposed to work. The key question in such contexts is not whether members have a direct say but whether the representatives are effectively accountable to their constituencies, in this case, trade union conference delegates to their members. The real problem here is one of 'union oligarchies'[98] that are insulated from effective membership control (discussed above). But a ban on organisational membership (including trade union affiliation fees) would do little to meaningfully address this problem.[99] At best, it would carve out certain decisions from the remit of trade union oligarchies while leaving the oligarchies intact.

Freedom of political association

It is essential that political finance regulation respect freedom of political association, because such freedom is crucial to the proper workings of Australian democracy. Specifically, it is necessary in order to ensure pluralism, and pluralism is required to protect the integrity of representative government and fairness in politics. This does not mean that state regulation of political associations is impermissible. There can be public interest grounds for limiting freedom of political association. Whether or not particular measures are justified will depend on the weight of the rationales, the extent to which the limitation advances such rationale/s and the severity of the limitation (see Chapter 1).

In evaluating a ban on organisational membership fees, it is convenient to begin with the last factor, the severity of the ban. Freedom of political association has several key aspects:

- the individual's right to form political associations, act through such associations and participate in the activities of these associations; and
- the association's ability to determine its membership, the rules and manner of its governance and the methods it will use to promote its objectives.[100]

Here we focus on freedom of party association, and in particular, the ability of political parties to determine their membership. Some parties, such as the Liberal Party[101] and the National Party,[102] for instance, may restrict themselves to individual memberships: they are direct parties. Others, such as the ALP[103] and the NSW Greens,[104] allow both individual membership and membership by groups: they are mixed parties. The constitution of the federal National Party also allows it to be a mixed party, as organisations can become associations of the party where there is no state branch.[105] Some parties, such as the NSW Shooters Party, fall somewhere in the middle: membership is formally restricted to individuals,[106] but close links are maintained with various groups.[107] These groups, while not members of the party, are ancillary organisations.[108] Such diversity of party structures should be respected, because it is one of the main ways in which the pluralism of Australian politics is sustained (see Chapter 1).[109]

When viewed from this perspective, the impact of a ban on organisational membership fees on the freedom of party association would be quite severe: it would mandate a particular party structure – direct parties – and while not directly banning parties that allow for organisational membership, it would generally make them unviable without public funding.[110]

The specific impact on the trade union–ALP relationship can be illustrated through the typology developed by industrial relations experts Matthew Bodah, David Coates and Steve Ludlam. According to these authors, there are two dimensions to union–party linkages – formal organisational integration and policy-making influence – and these give rise to four types of linkages:

- external lobbying – no formal organisational integration, with unions having no or little influence in party policy-making;
- internal lobbying – no formal organisation integration, but unions are regularly consulted in policy-making;
- union/party bonding – unions occupy important party positions but do not dominate party policy-making; and

- union dominance – unions occupy important party positions
  and dominate party policy-making.[111]

According to this typology, the trade union–ALP link is either the union/party bonding type or the union dominance type because of the organisational integration of trade union affiliates into the ALP. As members of state and territory branches of the ALP, affiliated trade unions are guaranteed 50 per cent representation at state and territory conferences.[112] These conferences determine state and territory branch policies and elect state party officials and delegates to national conference.[113] The latter functions as 'the supreme governing authority of the Party'[114] and elects members of the National Executive, 'the chief administrative authority' of the party.[115] A ban on organisational membership fees would make organisational integration between the ALP and unions much less viable; the menu would be restricted to the external or internal lobbying links.

Is there a compelling justification for such a severe incursion into the freedom of the ALP to organise itself as it sees fit? It is exceedingly difficult to see one. There is, first, the prima facie legitimacy of membership fees. Further, as the previous discussion has argued, the 'trade union bosses' objections are misdirected. Also, a ban on organisational membership fees would neither enhance internal party democracy nor invigorate trade union democracy. Absent an adequate rationale for limiting freedom of party association, it is hard to escape the conclusion that such a ban represents an unjustified limitation on freedom of party association.

It was such a concern that led the NSW Select Committee to include trade union affiliation fees in their exemption for membership fees.[116] The key reasons given by the six-member committee, which had only two ALP members, are worth reproducing:

> The Committee considers that membership fees should not be
> encompassed by the Committee's proposed ban on all but small

individual donations ... *Similarly, the Committee believes that trade union affiliation fees should be permissible, despite the proposed ban on union donations. To ban union affiliation fees would be to place unreasonable restrictions on party structures* (emphasis added).[117]

There are many critics of the trade union–ALP relationship: many voters believe that it casts doubt on the ability of the ALP to govern for all. Within the union movement there are members – even leaders[118] – who are strongly of the view that the relationship fails to serve their best interests, and even within the ALP the relationship does not enjoy unqualified support. Some rank-and-file members feel disenfranchised and more than a few key party officials express concern that the relationship undermines the party's ability to win public office.

This chapter has had very little, often nothing, to say on these questions. It has focused on whether there should be a ban on organisational membership fees (including trade union affiliation fees) under a regime of contribution limits. Concluding that there should be an exemption for such fees does not constitute a general defence of the trade union–ALP relationship. The point is that this relationship should not be prohibited as a matter of law. The broader question of whether this relationship is desirable or justified raises a complex range of issues, most of which fall outside the scope of this book.

One issue that does fall within the scope of this book is the unfairness that is likely to result from an exemption for membership fees including trade union affiliation fees. As will be explained in Chapter 7, there is a lack of 'equality of arms' between the ALP and the Coalition parties that results in part from the fact that the ALP receives trade union income as well as corporate money. This inequality could worsen if union affiliation fees were included in a membership fee exemption. Such unfairness should be addressed, but not through contribution limits (or removing the exemption for membership fees). Rather, as will be argued in Chapter 7, this task needs to be dealt with through election spending limits.

The implied freedom of political communication

What is perhaps the most controversial constitutional issue about contribution limits[119] is whether they are in breach of the implied freedom of political communication.

The High Court has implied a freedom of political communication from sections of the *Commonwealth Constitution* relating to representative and responsible government, specifically sections 7, 24, 64 and 128.[120] This freedom, while derived from the *Commonwealth Constitution*, also applies to state and territory legislation because discussion of matters at the level of state and territory (or local government) can bear upon the choices to be made at federal elections. According to the High Court, this inter-relationship results from the fact that we have national political parties, the financial dependence of state, territory and local governments on federal funding and 'the increasing integration of social, economic and political matters in Australia'.[121]

The current test for determining whether or not this freedom has been breached (often referred to as the *Lange* test) has two limbs:

- Does the law (of a state or federal parliament or a territory legislature) effectively burden freedom of communication about government or political matters in its terms, operation or effect?
- If it does, is the law reasonably appropriate and adapted to serve a legitimate end (in a manner) which is compatible with the constitutionally-prescribed system of representative and responsible government?[122]

Applying the first limb of the *Lange* test, it is clear that limits on political contributions do burden the freedom to communicate about government or political matters. First, making a political contribution is, in most cases, a way of communicating support for a party or candidate. Limits on contributions, therefore, affect the formal ability of citizens to communicate in this way by making contributions exceeding the limits. Second, political contributions enable parties and candidates to communicate about government and political matters, so limits on such contributions will reduce their ability to do so.

Turning to the second limb of the *Lange* test, there are two principal issues:

- Do the contribution limits serve legitimate aims that are compatible with the system of representative and responsible government prescribed by the *Commonwealth Constitution*?
- Are such limits reasonably appropriate and adapted to serve such aims in a manner compatible with that system of representative and responsible government?

On the question of legitimate aims, the key rationales of contribution limits are to lessen the risk – and the perception – of corruption through graft and undue influence. They are also aimed at promoting the fair value of political freedoms by preventing the wealthy from securing a disproportionate influence over the political process.

Reasoning from first principles, it would seem that both the anti-corruption and fair value rationales of contribution limits are compatible with the system of representative and responsible government prescribed by the *Commonwealth Constitution*. The former aim is directed at protecting the integrity of representative government. Not surprisingly, in *Australian Capital Television Pty Ltd v Commonwealth (ACTV)*, the High Court fully accepted that a ban on political broadcasting (together with the free-time regime) served a legitimate aim of lessening the risk of corruption.[123] The fair value rationale is derived from the principle of political equality (see Chapter 1), a principle that informs the system of representative government prescribed by the *Commonwealth Constitution*. In *ACTV*, for instance, then High Court Chief Justice Mason quoted with approval Harrison Moore's observation that the 'great underlying principle' of the

Commonwealth Constitution is that citizens have 'each a share, and an equal share, in political power'.[124]

It remains to be considered whether the types of contribution limits proposed are reasonably appropriate and adapted to serving these rationales. In determining this issue, the High Court provided a 'margin of appreciation'[125] or 'margin of choice'[126] as to what regulation should be adopted. The terms of the *Lange* test reflect this judicial deference: the test is whether the regulation is reasonably appropriate and adapted to serve a legitimate end, not whether it is best suited to serve this end. In particular, the *Lange* test does not require that Australian legislatures adopt regulation serving a legitimate end that involves the least burden on freedom of political communication. Two High Court judges did consider that regulation of the content of political communication would require a higher level of justification,[127] but that circumstance does not apply to contribution limits.

The deference informing the *Lange* test rests on two crucial considerations. The first concerns the proper role of Australian courts. Contrasting our implied freedom of political communication with US First Amendment jurisprudence, then High Court Chief Justice Brennan, in *Levy v Victoria*, stated that:

> Under our Constitution, the courts do not assume the power to determine that some more limited restriction than that imposed by an impugned law could suffice to achieve a legitimate purpose. The courts acknowledge the law-maker's power to determine the sufficiency of the means of achieving the legitimate purpose, reserving only a jurisdiction to determine whether the means adopted could reasonably be considered to be appropriate and adapted to the fulfilment of the purpose.[128]

This approach is, as noted by Gleeson CJ in *Coleman v Power*, based on 'the respective roles of the legislature and the judiciary in a representative democracy'.[129] Second, the concepts of representative and responsible government that inform the provisions of the

Constitution that gave rise to the implied freedom are 'descriptive of a whole spectrum of political institutions', permitting 'scope for variety' in the design of electoral institutions, including the regulation of political finance.[130]

Taking account of such deference, whether contribution limits are reasonably appropriate and adapted to serving their aims in a manner compatible with the system of representative and responsible government prescribed by the *Commonwealth Constitution* depends on a range of factors. Chief among these are 'the extent of the restriction, the nature of the interest served and the proportionality of the restriction to the interest served'.[131]

Let us turn first to the extent of the restriction. Contribution limits burden the freedom of political communication by: first, restricting the ability of citizens to communicate by making contributions above the limit; and second, reducing the income available to parties and candidates and therefore their ability to engage in political communication. The first burden is likely to be very limited. Contributions below the limits can still convey a message of support. Further, the limits only affect those who have the ability to make contributions above them. A limit of $1000 per annum (as recommended by the NSW Select Committee) would probably only affect a small number of citizens (see Chapter 3).

The more significant burden is on the ability of parties and candidates to engage in political communication. Specifically, contribution limits will reduce the private funding available to political parties. The extent of this reduction will, of course, depend on the level at which the limits are set. This burden is, however, offset by the exemption for membership fees. Parties that are successful in attracting members and supporters are likely to be able to retain, perhaps even increase, their ability to engage in political communication. Importantly, the burden placed by contribution limits is also offset by other measures recommended by this book. Public funding would compensate for the fall in private income (through the Party and Candidate Support Fund) and, in particular, would provide greater subsidies to newcomers than currently is the case (see Chapter 5). Election spending limits would limit the significance in the reduction of the overall budgets of the major parties by containing the costs of electioneering (see Chapter 7).

As for the nature of the interests being served, both the anti-corruption and fair value rationales of contribution limits go to the heart of representative and responsible government. Both rationales have great importance, especially in light of the arms race amongst the major parties (see Chapter 8).

The final consideration under this head is the proportionality of restriction to the interest served. This aspect concerns the design of the contribution limits and the extent to which they are properly tailored to anti-corruption and fair value rationales. There are compelling reasons in principle for considering these limits proportionate to their anti-corruption rationale: they do not impose a blanket ban on political contributions, but only prohibit those which are seen as producing a significant risk of corruption (that is, large contributions), and they allow exemptions for contributions (such as membership fees) where such a risk is minimal or nonexistent. Similarly, with the fair value rationale, prohibiting large contributions targets contributions which are seen as allowing wealth to have a disproportionate influence.

In conclusion, there are cogent reasons to conclude that contribution limits set at appropriate levels do not breach the implied freedom of political communication. True, they do burden that freedom, but they do so in service of the legitimate aim of preventing corruption and promoting the fair value of political freedoms. Further, there are strong arguments that they are reasonably appropriate and adapted to serve these aims because of the limited burden they involve (especially were they to be established in the context of election spending limits and increased public funding), the importance of the aims and the proportionality of the limits to the aims.

Conclusion

The previous chapter rejected the notion that political contributions necessarily corrupt the political process. It emphasised that political contributions can enhance Australia's democracy. The challenge has been how to promote the legitimate role of such contributions. The laissez-faire treatment of political contributions in Australia has failed to meet this challenge, and there has been a high price for that failure: the perception (and the reality as well) of corruption through undue influence, and the reality of political unfairness and an undermining of the health of the political parties.

This chapter has elaborated on a regulatory framework that would better promote the legitimate role of political contributions. This framework consists of three key elements: improved regulation of conflicts of interest, enhanced internal accountability of corporate and trade union political contributions, and contribution limits (with an exemption for membership fees). These measures should not be implemented alone, though; they should be integrated with measures such as a reconfiguration of public funding for political parties and candidates and election spending limits. The coming chapters will examine these measures.

5
PUBLIC FUNDING OF POLITICS

To this point, this book has been predominantly concerned with the private funding of politics. This chapter and the next will switch the focus to public funding of politics.[1] Such funding takes various forms.[2] This chapter will analyse the two principal forms of public funding of political parties and candidates: election funding and tax subsidies. It will also examine an important section of parliamentary entitlements (the benefits that accrue to those who currently hold elected office) – those that are to be used for electioneering. The next chapter will continue this examination of incumbency benefits by analysing government advertising.

With the public funding of politics, all four principles of the political finance regime considered in Chapter 1 are significant: protecting the integrity of representative government, promoting fairness in politics, supporting parties to perform their functions, and respecting political freedoms. These principles are relevant for both the rationales and the problems of such funding. In terms of rationales, all types of public funding of political parties can clearly be justified by reference to the democratic functions the parties perform. In some cases, election funding being a notable example, public funding also aims to prevent corruption, and to promote fairness in politics, including 'freedom to' engage in the political process.

Equally, public funding of electoral activity can be criticised from the perspective of these principles. There is a risk that such funding enervates political parties by reducing their need to engage with the citizenry via fundraising. Corruption through misuse of public resources is also a possibility. Such corruption is often associated with unfairness, because public funding advantages the major parties.

I have considerable sympathy for the critics of the current system of publicly funding parties and candidates. I believe current election funding schemes are both ineffectual and unfair, and in this chapter I call for their reconfiguration into Party and Candidate Support Funds. I also advocate the abolition of tax subsidies for political parties and candidates. Parliamentary entitlements, the chapter argues, can all too easily result in corruption through the misuse of public resources, and electoral unfairness. Rules governing such entitlements should be made more transparent, should more strictly regulate the use of such entitlements, and should avoid an excessive amount being provided to parliamentarians.

Election funding

All jurisdictions except South Australia, Tasmania and the Northern Territory have election funding schemes that give money to political parties and candidates after every election. As Table 5.1 indicates, these schemes usually operate by giving eligible political parties and candidates an amount calculated according to the number of first preference votes in the last election. With all but one of the schemes, political parties and candidates must have won at least 4 per cent of the first preference votes to be eligible. The NSW scheme has an additional ground of eligibility: the election of a parliamentarian.

The schemes vary according to the conditions they impose before an eligible candidate or party can receive election funding.

TABLE 5.1: ELECTION FUNDING SCHEMES				
Jurisdiction	Availability of election funding	Threshold of first preference votes	Amount per first preference vote (cents)	Conditions
CTH	✔	4%	227.999 (indexed)	Nil
NSW	✔	4% or Member elected	Determined by statutory formula	Disclosure of electoral expenditure Funding capped to disclosed electoral expenditure Compliance with disclosure obligations
QLD	✔	4%	159.596 (indexed)	Disclosure of electoral expenditure Funding capped to disclosed electoral expenditure
SA	✘			
TAS	✘			
VIC	✔	4%	146.44 (indexed)	Disclosure of electoral expenditure Funding capped to disclosed electoral expenditure
WA	✔	4%	160.267 (indexed)	Disclosure of electoral expenditure Funding capped to disclosed electoral expenditure
ACT	✔	4%	153.551	Nil
NT	✘			

Source: *Commonwealth Electoral Act 1918* (Cth) ss 294, 297, 321 (the current rate of public funding is available from the AEC website, viewed 10 February 2010: <http://www.aec.gov.au/Parties_and_Representatives/public_funding/Current_Funding_Rate.htm>); *Election Funding and Disclosures Act 1981* (NSW), Pt 5, Divs 3–4 (ss 58–68), ss 74–76, 78 (there are, in fact, two funds that provide for election funding in New South Wales, the Central Fund and the Constituency Fund: see Pt 5, Divs 3–4); *Electoral Act 1992* (Qld) s 126B, Sch – 'Election Funding and Financial Disclosure Based on Part XX of the Commonwealth Electoral Act' – ss 293–294A (the indexed value was obtained by contacting the Queensland Electoral Commission directly; this figure is updated annually and will be updated on 1 July 2010); *Electoral Act 2002* (Vic) ss 208–12, 214 (the indexed value in Victoria was obtained by contacting the Victorian Electoral Commission directly; this figure will be updated on 1 July 2010 in preparation for the 2010 State Election); *Electoral Act 1907* (WA) ss 175LB–LH (the current indexed value in WA is available from the WA Electoral Commission website, viewed 10 February 2010: <http://www.waec.wa.gov.au/pp_candidate/financial_disclosure/electoral_funding.php>); *Electoral Act 1992* (ACT) ss 207–208 (the ACT indexed value is available from the Australian Electoral Commission website:, viewed 10 February 2010: <http://www.elections.act.gov.au/parties.fadfunding.html>).

TABLE 5.2: FEDERAL ELECTION FUNDING, 1984–2007

Federal election	Amount of election funding
1984	$7,806,778
1987	$10,298,657
1990	$12,878,920
1993	$14,898,807
1996	$32,154,801
1998	$33,920,787
2001	$38,559,409
2004	$41,926,159
2007	$49,002,639

Source: Joint Standing Committee on Electoral Matters (2008) *Advisory Report on the Commonwealth Electoral Amendment (Political Donations and other Measures) Bill 2008*, 13, viewed 27 January 2010: <http://www.aph.gov.au/house/committee/em/taxlawbill%202/report/fullreport.pdf/>.

TABLE 5.3: RELIANCE OF POLITICAL PARTIES ON ELECTION FUNDING, 1999–2000 TO 2001–02

Party	Total receipts	Private funding (% of total receipts)	Public funding (% of total receipts)	Election funding (% of total receipts)
ALP	$117,273,999	81.85	18.15	13.57
Liberal Party	$95,542,648	83.61	16.39	14.57
National Party	$21,725,957	84.89	15.11	11.43
Australian Democrats	$6,667,728	56.90	43.10	38.80
Greens	$6,495,651	74.56	25.44	23.94

Source: Joo-Cheong Tham & David Grove (2004) Public Funding and Expenditure Regulation of Australian Political Parties, *Federal Law Review*, 32: 397, 401 (Table 1).

The federal and ACT schemes impose no conditions, but the other schemes require disclosure of electoral expenditure (for the relevant election) and then cap the amount of election funding that can be received to the amount of expenditure disclosed. The NSW scheme goes further, tying receipt of election funding to compliance with disclosure obligations.

In New South Wales, political parties eligible for election funding are also entitled to annual payments from the Political Education Fund,[3] which can be used for 'political education purposes'. What these purposes are is subject to determinations made by the NSW Election Funding Authority.[4] They include the posting of written materials and information.[5] A party's entitlement to money from this fund is based on the number of first preference votes it received.[6]

The election funding provided to political parties runs into millions of dollars (see Table 5.2).

Election funding is an important, but limited, source of income for political parties. Table 5.3 is based on figures from the annual returns lodged between 1999–2000 and 2001–02 (for both federal and state branches of the parties), and highlights the fact that private funding remains the key source of income. For this period, election funding made up less than one-sixth of the budgets of the ALP and the two Coalition parties. However, we see a far greater reliance on election funding by the minor parties.

Ineffectual and unfair

There are two central purposes of election funding schemes. The first is to promote fairness in politics: specifically, electoral fairness. When federal election funding was introduced, in 1983, it was directed at ensuring that 'different parties offering themselves for election have an equal opportunity to present their policies to the electorate'.[7] Such equal or fair opportunity is advanced by opening up the electoral contest to 'worthy parties and candidates [that] might not [otherwise] be able to afford the considerable sums necessary to make their policies known'.[8] In promoting electoral fairness in this way, election funding clearly enhances 'freedom to' engage in political expression. Electoral fairness is also furthered by attempting to reduce candidates' and parties' reliance on private funding for campaigns, thereby preventing a possible 'serious imbalance in campaign funding'[9] of the political parties.[10] The second purpose of election funding schemes is to protect the integrity of representative government: by lessening reliance on private funding, they seek to reduce the risk of corruption that accompanies private funding. However, the schemes fare poorly in terms of their fairness and anti-corruption rationales. Worse still, they have in fact contributed to electoral unfairness and possibly increased the risk of corruption.[11]

With the fairness rationale, we can begin by considering the effect of election funding schemes on levelling out the financial inequalities among the main parties. Table 5.4 provides an indication of this effect. It analyses how the amount of each party's funding compares with their electoral support by dividing the amount of total funding, private funding and election funding received by a party for the period 1999–2000 to 2001–02 by the number of first preference votes the party received in the 2001 federal election. This measure is used to indicate how the funding received by each party corresponds to its electoral support.

These figures reveal a dramatic funding inequality between the ALP, Liberal Party and National Party, on one hand, and the Democrats and the Greens on the other. The former received more than $20 per 2001 election vote. The Democrats and Greens, however, received around $10 per 2001 election vote. Table 5.4 indicates that this inequality is due largely to the different amounts of private money received by the parties, with the pattern of private money received per vote correlating with the pattern of total funding received per vote.

To assess the levelling effect of election funding, one measure is to note the extent to which such funding narrows the disparity in private funding per vote. Using this measure, we see that election funding has a limited levelling effect on the funding inequality among the parties. However, the effect varies significantly from party to party. For example, the effect is quite substantial in relation to the Democrats. The ALP received 3.62 times more private funding per vote than the Democrats. For the total funding (which includes electoral funding) per vote, though, it received only 2.51 times more. In contrast, the levelling effect is very modest in relation to the Greens compared with the Liberal Party: the ratio of private funding per vote was 2.19, and the ratio of total funding per vote was marginally less, at 1.95. The difference is largely because the Greens received less electoral funding because of the 4 per cent threshold.[12]

As well as having a limited levelling effect, election funding schemes can increase electoral unfairness. Funding is calculated on past electoral support, which means that established parties are very likely to enjoy a financial advantage over newer parties, as history indicates that almost all political parties take many years to gain solid electoral support. The 4 per cent threshold that applies to these schemes clearly discriminates against minor parties and newcomers.[13] Indeed, it has been argued that the current system 'reinforces the duopoly that the major parties have over political office'.[14]

Election funding might exacerbate electoral unfairness in another way too, by functioning as 'an add-on that allows the competing political parties to spend more on advertising and other electoral purposes than they would otherwise choose to do'.[15] The question here is whether or not election funding fuels increases in campaign expenditure. While there has been no analysis to give us a definitive answer yet, there is good reason to suspect this to be the case. First, there is no natural limit to campaign expenditure or, more generally, to parties' expenditure. The only real limit is the parties' budgets. So if the parties' budgets expand because of election funding, and there are no other constraints (such as election spending limits), we should

TABLE 5.4: FUNDING PER VOTE, 1999–2000 TO 2001–02				
Party	First preference votes in 2001 election	Total funding per vote	Private funding per vote	Election funding per vote
ALP	4,341,419	$27.01	$22.14	$3.67
Liberal Party	4,291,033	$22.27	$18.62	$3.25
National Party	643,924	$33.74	$28.64	$3.86
Democrats	620,248	$10.75	$6.12	$4.17
Greens	569,075	$11.41	$8.51	$2.73

Source: Tham & Grove, Public Funding and Expenditure Regulation of Australian Political Parties, 404 (Table 3). The following definitions have been used in relation to this table:

Electoral funding: Funding received from federal and state electoral commissions.

Public funding: Funding from all government bodies. This would include Electoral funding as well as payments from governmental bodies like the Australian Taxation Office.

Private Funding: Total funding minus public funding.

Total funding: The total receipts indicated on the returns minus Internal Transfers.

expect increases in campaign expenditure.[16] Furthermore, there is anecdotal evidence that broadcasters charge the parties more for political advertising.[17] This may be because election funding encourages broadcasters to do this, thus necessarily increasing campaign expenditure. If election funding does lead to increases in campaign expenditure, it indirectly sets up a barrier against newcomers, who are likely to be at the very least discouraged by these high campaign costs.

These features of the election funding schemes justify, to some extent, the fear voiced by opponents of increased public funding of political parties: that public funding will ossify the current system by generously supporting existing parties while also creating a '"vicious circle" for smaller parties which would be unable to receive funding because they had no representation and would be unable to field candidates because they lacked the necessary funding'.[18]

What then of the anti-corruption rationale of election funding schemes? The fact that election funding is not tied to any conditions or obligations relating to the receipt of private funding makes a mockery of this rationale. It is fanciful, for example, to suggest that election funding acts as an antidote to the unsavoury fundraising practices of political parties (see Chapter 3). Indeed, the problems of election funding might, in fact, go beyond ineffectiveness. If it were true that electoral funding inflates campaign costs, such funding could then perversely increase reliance on private funding as parties seek more donations to meet their perceived expenditure needs. So, far from 'purifying' the political process by reducing the reliance of political parties on large donations and thus insulating them from the risk and perception of corruption,[19] election funding might be a corrupting element.

There are two other criticisms of election funding schemes to consider. First, these schemes are said to sap the vitality of political parties by reducing their need to have members, or engage with members and the broader citizenry in order to raise funds.[20] The risk here is that election funding detracts from the participatory function of political parties. It is not easy to evaluate this claim, at least partly because there has not been any proper inquiry into the connection between election funding (or public funding more generally) and the vitality of Australian political parties. This much, however, can be said: current election funding schemes do little to enhance the participatory function of political parties. This will be revisited shortly.

Second, election funding schemes are said to pose a danger of corruption through the misuse of public resources. This has come to the fore with claims of 'profiteering' from such schemes. The most prominent instance has been with candidates associated with Pauline Hanson, former leader of the One Nation Party. These candidates received almost $200,000 in election funding in relation to the 2007 federal election but only spent $35,427 on campaigning: the implication is that the difference was 'pocketed' by Hanson.[21]

In response to the issue of 'profiteering', the Commonwealth Electoral Amendment (Political Donations and other Measures) Bill

2008 seeks to bring the federal election funding arrangements in line with other schemes by limiting the amount of such funding to 'electoral expenditure' incurred by the eligible party or candidate. In its report on the Bill, the Joint Standing Committee on Electoral Matters supported the central thrust of this amendment but agreed with the suggestion of the Democratic Audit of Australia that the definition of 'electoral expenditure' should be broadened to include rental of campaign premises, employment of campaign staff and office administration.

The Democratic Audit position is sensible but does not go far enough. Whilst it would be corruption through the misuse of public resources if election funding were used for the private purposes of a candidate, there is little ground for crying foul when such funding is used for party activities other than campaigning (e.g. party administration costs) (see below). True, the original rationale of the federal election funding scheme was to promote the electoral function of political parties, but it is time for fuller recognition of the fact that parties have other functions, all of which should also be adequately resourced through state funding. As will be argued below, such recognition will come about by moving from election funding schemes to Party and Candidate Support Funds.

Party and Candidate Support Funds

Public funding can play a vital role in democratising Australia's political finance regime. If contribution limits are imposed, such funding will be necessary to (partly) make up for the shortfall in party income (see Chapter 4). Public funding will also directly support parties in discharging their functions – remember, healthy and well-resourced political parties are central to the functioning of Australia's democracy (see Chapter 1). Public funding will also wean parties off large political contributions, thereby lessening the risk of corruption. Most importantly, perhaps, public funding is, as John

Rawls has recognised, an important way to promote the fair value of political freedoms,[22] in particular greater electoral fairness.

There are, however, significant faults with current election funding schemes: their ability to promote electoral fairness is limited, as noted above. There is also no evidence to suggest that they have reduced reliance on private funding or lessened the risk of corruption through graft and undue influence (indeed, there is good argument to the contrary). Further, such schemes do little to enhance the participatory function of parties; they may even detract from it.

Some of these problems cannot be addressed through changes to election funding schemes alone. Election spending limits (as advocated in Chapter 7) are necessary in order to deal with the increase in campaign expenditure that may result from providing public funding. Other deficiencies would be better dealt with through other regulatory measures. Lessening dependence on private funding may be achieved by making receipt of election funding contingent upon various conditions, but is more effectively achieved through contribution limits (as proposed in Chapter 4).

Alongside these measures, there should be significant changes to election funding schemes. The schemes should be more expressly directed at promoting the functions of parties (including but going beyond their electoral function). Rather than being seen as election funding schemes, they should be regarded as Party and Candidate Support Funds. These funds should have three components. The first, election funding payments, would replicate the payments made under current election funding schemes, but the 4 per cent threshold should be lowered (to perhaps 2 per cent).[23] To better promote electoral fairness, the payment amount should be tapered, with the rate per vote decreasing according to the number of first preference votes received. For example, 5 per cent of first preference votes could entitle a party to a payment of $2.00 per vote, the next 20 per cent would attract a payment of $1.50 per vote and votes beyond that would attract $1.00 per vote. Tapered schemes are like our progressive income tax system, with less-resourced parties helped to a greater degree.

Second, Party Support Funds should provide for annual allowances. Parties and candidates eligible for election funding payments should be eligible for these annual allowances, and parties with individual membership numbers exceeding, say, 500 should also be eligible. The formula for calculating these allowances should use both votes received in the previous election and current membership figures. Linking annual allowances to membership figures may result in parties recruiting more members and thereby invigorating their participatory function.

Third, the Party Support Funds should include policy development grants. These could be modelled on the grants operating under the British political finance scheme.[24] Eligibility for these grants should be the same as for the annual allowances. These funds should be used to fund activities that are aimed at policy development, not electioneering. The policy development grants should encourage parties to devote more time and energy to generating new ideas and policies, thus enhancing their agenda-setting function (see Chapter 1).

Tax subsidies[25]

Under Division 30–DA of the *Income Tax Assessment Act 1997* (Cth) (*ITAA 1997*), individuals and companies are entitled to a tax deduction in respect to contributions or gifts made to political parties. Before 22 June 2006, these deductions were limited to donations of up to $100 per annum and deductions were only available to parties registered under the *Commonwealth Electoral Act 1918* (Cth). This excluded independent candidates and parties registered under state and territory legislative regimes. In 2006, amendments to the *ITAA 1997* increased the donation limit to $1500 per annum and extended deductions to parties registered under relevant state and territory legislation and independent candidates.[26]

The take-up rate of these deductions appears to be relatively low. The Explanatory Memorandum to Schedule 1 of the Tax Laws Amendment (2008 Measures No. 1) Bill 2008, a Bill that sought to remove these deductions, indicates that the Bill would result in savings of $31.4 million over 3 years.[27] It can, therefore, be inferred that around $10 million per annum is claimed through these tax deductions.

Three distinct aims may justify such subsidies. Tax deductions may be said to:

- encourage small contributions, which may diversify the funding base of parties and, therefore, reduce the influence of 'big money';
- promote political participation through increased party membership; and
- help ensure that parties are adequately funded.

All three aims are integral to the democratic functions of political parties.

Measured against these three aims, however, tax subsidies are both inefficient and inequitable. They are inefficient because neither a small contribution – say $100 or less – nor party membership is a condition for tax deductibility. The eligibility net for tax deduction is cast too wide, as it includes large contributions. Another cause of inefficiency is that the money provided from the public purse goes to taxpayers rather than to the parties[28] – if these provisions are meant to help ensure that parties are adequately funded, they do so in a rather indirect and limited fashion. There may also be another inefficiency: such a system places the incentive to make contributions and take out membership on the taxpayer, not on the parties themselves. A system of public subsidy that relies more directly on strengthening incentives for parties may be more effective.

These tax subsidies are also inequitable on several counts. They discriminate against those who do not have to pay tax: job seekers,[29] retirees without income, full-time parents and students not engaged in paid work who make small contributions or take out party membership are denied the benefit of the current system. This leads to a broader point: any system of tax relief tends to benefit the wealthier sections of society.[30] Though there is no data to indicate which taxpayers have made use of the tax subsidies under the *ITAA 1997*, the Canadian experience of using tax relief to encourage political contributions is instructive. Canadian federal law provides for a Political Contribution Tax Credit (PCTC). Under this scheme, individuals and corporations can deduct a portion of their political contributions from their tax liability. The deductible amounts are based on a sliding scale as depicted in Table 5.5 below.

In her analysis of the impact of the PCTC, Young, while acknowledging that the scheme may encourage small contributions, observed its unfair operation. Drawing upon a breakdown of tax data for 2000 (the scheme then provided slightly different amounts of tax credits from the current one), she said:

> The almost half of all Canadian tax filers whose income falls
> into the lowest bracket comprise only 10 percent of all PCTC
> claimants, while the 3 percent of tax filers in the highest
> bracket make 18 percent of all claims. The pattern is even more
> skewed when one compares the value of the tax credit for low
> and high income earners, as the latter are prone to make large

TABLE 5.5: CANADIAN POLITICAL CONTRIBUTION TAX CREDIT	
Amount of contribution	Tax credit
C$0 to C$100	75% of contribution For example C$75 credit for C$100 contribution
C$101 to C$550	C$75 + 50% of amount of contribution exceeding C$100 For example C$275 credit for C$500 contribution
Over C$550	The lesser of $500 or C$300 + 33.3% of amount of contribution exceeding C$550 For example C$450 credit for C$1000 contribution

Source: *Income Tax Act 1985* (Canada), s 42(2), viewed 9 February 2010: <http://www.gov.pe.ca/law/statutes/pdf/i-01.pdf>.

contributions. Despite its other merits, then, the PCTC reinforces an inequitable pattern of giving to parties and candidates.[31]

In fact, Young's observations may have greater force now. In 2000, the PCTC allowed tax credits of 75 per cent for contributions up to C$200; that limit has since been increased to C$400.[32]

A similar system of tax relief operates in the Canadian province of Quebec, but at less generous rates.[33] Nevertheless, the inequity of such a system is apparent. Data from 1997 indicates that while tax-payers earning C$20,000 or less per annum constituted 54 per cent of all taxpayers, they constituted only 15 per cent of those who claimed a credit under the Quebec system. Those earning C$50,000 or more, on the other hand, represented 43 per cent of those who claimed the credit, while only constituting 10 per cent of all taxpayers.[34]

This brief review of the Canadian evidence indicates that a system of tax relief aimed at encouraging political contributions benefits the wealthy in two ways. First, the rich are more likely to make financial contributions to parties than the less well off. In political scientist Louis Massicotte's words, such contribution is 'a rather elitist activity'.[35] Second, because the rich are more likely to make larger contributions, the amount of tax relief they can claim is correspondingly increased.[36]

Such inequity may exacerbate the unfairness of political competition. Given the lack of information regarding the use and impact of current tax deductions, it would be unwise to be too emphatic here. That said, it is likely that under a system of tax relief, inequity among citizens will translate to inequity among the parties. Parties with rich members and supporters will probably reap significant rewards from this system while the benefit to parties with poorer members and supporters may very well be marginal.

Worse, several features of the current scheme exacerbate the risk of such unfairness. Allowing deductions for donations up to $1500 per annum provides tax relief for political donations that are out of reach of ordinary Australians. Also, the current provisions allow corporations to claim tax deductions for their political contributions. This runs contrary to the aim of reducing the influence of 'big money'. Because corporate money tends to go overwhelmingly to the major parties, subsidising corporate contributions is likely to exacerbate the financial divide between the major and minor parties. The fundamental question is why public subsidy should facilitate contributions by entities that are not citizens (see Chapter 3).

There is, therefore, a compelling case for abolishing these tax deductions (and for the enactment of Schedule 1 of the Tax Laws Amendment (2008 Measures No. 1) Bill 2008 (Cth)).[37] While the aims that resulted in tax subsidies are sound, they should be pursued through other regulatory measures. Promoting the functions of parties should be advanced by establishing Party and Candidate Support Funds (see above). Annual allowances which are calculated in part according to the number of party members should encourage party membership. To encourage small contributions, a system of matching funds could be put in place. For example, for each contribution of $50 or less received per annum by candidates and registered parties, public funds of 10 per cent of the value of these contributions could be paid to the candidates and parties. It is important to stress that in addition to limiting this system to small contributions, the scheme should only involve a modest public subsidy in total. Both of these factors are necessary in order to reduce the bias towards wealthy citizens and parties.

Parliamentary entitlements

We now shift our focus to the public funding specifically provided to parliamentarians. Some questions immediately arise: Why should public funding be provided to parliamentarians? If public funding is to be provided at all, why is it not provided to all parties and candidates?

The answers to these questions lie with the distinctive duties of parliamentarians. Parliamentarians are not merely successful candidates; they are also holders of public office. Thus parliamentarians have two key duties. The first is to represent the constituents of their electorate (not just their supporters, the members of their party or their party organisation). It is this duty that informs the description of parliamentarians as the 'Member for [name of electorate]'. Second, parliamentarians have a duty to participate in the governance of their country, state or territory, notably through participation in Parliament. Such participation will embrace involvement in law-making, scrutiny of executive action and deliberation of important public issues.

Performance of these duties involves a range of activities, most of which require money and personnel. Proper performance of these duties requires a full-time commitment from parliamentarians. To avoid elected office becoming the privilege of the wealthy, adequate remuneration should be provided to parliamentarians themselves so that they can deliver on this commitment. Basic infrastructure (such as an office with adequate facilities and staff) is also necessary for the performance of these duties. Communicating with constituents is essential and some methods of doing so will require funding.

It is in recognition of the public duties of parliamentarians (and the resources that are necessary for their performance) that all jurisdictions have established parliamentary entitlements. Common entitlements include, for example, parliamentary salaries, office accommodation and facilities, travel and accommodation entitlements and the use of government vehicles.[38] Commonwealth, state and territory parliamentarians are also provided with a range of allowances. All parliamentarians are, for example, provided with an electorate allowance that, as the name suggests, is to be used to service the needs of their electorates.[39]

In most jurisdictions, responsibility for determining the amount and content of parliamentary entitlements principally rests with independent remuneration tribunals. In four of the states and territories – South Australia, Tasmania, Western Australia and the ACT – responsibility lies solely with such tribunals.[40] In New South Wales, the salary of parliamentarians is pegged by statute to that of members of the Commonwealth House of Representatives;[41] the salary of NT parliamentarians is tied to the salary of NT public servants.[42] Other than salaries, parliamentary entitlements in New South Wales and the Northern Territory are determined by their remuneration tribunals.[43]

These remuneration tribunals have considerable discretion in determining what parliamentary entitlements are available and their amounts. The tribunals in Tasmania, Western Australia and the Northern Territory operate without any statutory principles to guide their decision-making. In other jurisdictions, there are broad guiding principles. In determining entitlements available to NSW parliamentarians, the NSW Remuneration Tribunal has to follow two principles: entitlements are 'to be provided for the purpose of facilitating the efficient performance of the parliamentary duties of members or recognised office holders'; and 'parliamentary duties of members and recognised office holders include participation in the activities of recognised political parties'.[44] Similarly, in determining the allowances to be paid to SA parliamentarians, the SA Remuneration Tribunal is to 'have regard not only to their parliamentary duties but also to … their duty to be actively involved in community affairs' and 'their duty to represent and assist their constituents in dealings with governmental and other public agencies and authorities'.[45]

There are three jurisdictions where remuneration tribunals do not have the primary responsibility for determining these entitlements. In Queensland, the salary of parliamentarians is pegged to that provided to members of the Commonwealth House of Representatives.[46] There is no specific statute (or regulations) setting out the entitlements provided to these parliamentarians. Rather, these entitlements are provided under the various appropriation statutes, with their administration governed by an executive document, the Member Entitlements' Handbook issued by the Executive Council.[47] Under these arrangements, the Queensland Parliament and the Executive determine the entitlements conferred upon Queensland parliamentarians.

The salary of Victorian parliamentarians is also pegged by statute to that of members of the Commonwealth House of Representatives.[48] These parliamentarians are also provided with a residential allowance, a travelling allowance, an electorate allowance and an electorate office allowance at rates prescribed by regulations.[49] The Governor in Council can also make regulations with respect to 'the provision of any article, motor vehicle, equipment or service to members'.[50] Leaving the determination of entitlements and their amounts to regulations essentially means that the government of the day will be making those decisions.

What seems to be the most complicated framework governing parliamentary entitlements is that of the Commonwealth. This framework is made up of five separate pieces of legislation. The salary and electorate allowance of Commonwealth parliamentarians are provided for under the *Remuneration and Allowances Act 1990* (Cth).[51] Various other entitlements are provided for under the *Parliamentary Entitlements Act 1990* (Cth) – office accommodation, postage allowance and travel entitlements.[52] The regulations for this statute authorise other entitlements,[53] notably a printing and communications entitlement.[54] Finally, there are various allowances determined by the Commonwealth Remuneration Tribunal under the *Parliamentary Allowances Act 1952* (Cth) and the *Remuneration Tribunal Act 1973* (Cth).[55] There are no specific principles prescribed to guide the Tribunal's determinations.

Promoting corruption and unfairness?

While parliamentary entitlements have, at their base, a compelling justification, they also carry two risks: corruption through the misuse of public resources, and electoral unfairness (see Chapter 1). Corruption through the misuse of public resources occurs when entitlements are used for a purpose other than the performance of parliamentary duties: for example, for the personal benefit of parliamentarians or to advance the electoral position of parliamentarians or their parties. In the latter situation, corruption through the misuse of public resources goes hand in hand with electoral unfairness.[56] The danger of such unfairness is inherent in the provision of parliamentary entitlements, as they are provided to parliamentarians but not to their unelected competitors. Furthermore, parliamentary activities are often inseparable from campaign activities.[57] The result is that various parliamentary entitlements (for example, the provision of office, staff and electorate allowances) could be used to resource the campaigns of parliamentarians; to the detriment of their unelected rivals.

This is not an insignificant risk. There are examples of parliamentary entitlements having been used for campaign purposes. The NSW ICAC, for instance, found in 2003 that Malcolm Jones, while a member of the NSW Legislative Council, engaged in corrupt conduct by improperly directing a parliamentary staff officer to engage in recruitment drives.[58] In Victoria, a largely ignored aspect of the controversy surrounding Brimbank City Council (which resulted in the entire council being dismissed by the Victorian government in 2009) was Victorian MP George Seitz using his electorate allowance to fund the election campaigns of ALP local council candidates.[59] At the Commonwealth level, printing and communication allowances have been used to resource the election campaigns of federal parliamentarians (see below), a development that has coincided with a trend to use parliamentarians' office accommodation and facilities during election periods.[60]

Corruption through the misuse of public resources can take the form of individual corruption. Take, for example, a parliamentarian using travel entitlements to fund a holiday. In this situation, the gain to the parliamentarian is both personal and undeserved. When there is misuse of public resources involving electoral unfairness, it tends to take the form of institutional corruption. The gain that is secured in such cases is political, not personal, as it is aimed at boosting the electoral position of the parliamentarian (or his or her party), and the use of public resources is procedurally improper because of its illegitimate purpose and this purpose clearly damages the democratic process by promoting electoral unfairness.

The dangers of these types of corruption and unfairness could be addressed by following these three principles:

- Principle 1: The rules governing parliamentary entitlements should be accessible and transparent;
- Principle 2: The rules should clearly limit the use of parliamentary entitlements to the discharge of parliamentary duties; and
- Principle 3: The amount of parliamentary entitlements should not confer an unfair electoral advantage upon parliamentarians.[61]

The rationale for Principles 1 and 2 is clear. Principle 3 recognises that, as parliamentary activities are sometimes inseparable from campaign activities, Principle 2 is insufficient to prevent electoral unfairness.

Let us now evaluate the current arrangements governing parliamentary entitlements against these principles.

Principle 1: The rules governing parliamentary entitlements should be accessible and transparent.

The rules are contained in legislation and the determinations of the Remuneration Tribunals. They are also included in various handbooks issued to parliamentarians. The legislation and determinations are clearly accessible and transparent but the same cannot be said of the handbooks. Remarkably, in all cases except for Queensland, these handbooks are not publicly available. In the ACT, New South Wales, the Northern Territory, South Australia, Tasmania and Victoria, these handbooks were supplied upon request. Requests for the WA and Commonwealth handbooks were denied (there is a proposal for the Commonwealth handbook to be made publicly available in 2010).[62]

Moreover, in relation to Commonwealth parliamentary entitlements, this principle has been breached through the development of opaque conventions which are arguably in breach of formal legal rules. In 2009, the Auditor-General handed down a comprehensive report on parliamentary entitlements that found that their use was influenced by two documents developed by the then federal government, '31 Statements' and '42 Questions and Answers', which purported to capture accepted practices.[63] These documents, as the Auditor-General observed, were 'not made public'.[64] Moreover, legal advice received by the Auditor-General indicated that these documents were not consistent with the statutory provisions governing the printing entitlement, resulting in the entitlement being frequently used in breach of its conditions.[65]

Principle 2: The rules should clearly limit the use of parliamentary entitlements to the discharge of parliamentary duties.

This principle suggests four elements:

- a general policy that parliamentary entitlements only be used for parliamentary duties;
- a clear elaboration or definition of such duties;
- a general prohibition of the use of entitlements for electioneering; and
- specific rules elaborating on this prohibition.

Table 5.6 evaluates the various jurisdictions against these requirements. Table 5.6 shows that most jurisdictions — seven out of nine

TABLE 5.6: RULES RESTRICTING THE USE OF PARLIAMENTARY ENTITLEMENTS	Cth	NSW	Qld	SA	Tas	Vic	WA	ACT	NT
All entitlements to be used for parliamentary duties	✗	✔	✗	✗	✗	✗	✗	✔	✗
Definition/ elaboration of parliamentary duties	✗	✔	✗	✗	✗	✗	✗	✔	✗
General prohibition of any use for electioneering or campaigning	✗	✔	✗	✗	✗	✗	✗	✔	✗
Specific rules preventing particular uses for electioneering	✗	✔	✗	✗	✗	✗	✗	✔	✗

Source: *Remuneration and Allowances Act 1990* (Cth); *Parliamentary Entitlements Act 1990* (Cth); *Parliamentary Entitlements Regulations 1997* (Cth); *Parliamentary Allowances Act 1952* (Cth); *Remuneration Tribunal Act 1973* (Cth); *Parliamentary Remuneration Act 1989* (NSW) s 3; NSW Department of Legislative Council, *Legislative Council Members' Guide*, 'Guidelines for Additional Entitlements', 33–37; NSW Department of Legislative Assembly, *Members' Handbook*, para 8.4 (both NSW Members' Guides reproduce the Guidelines of the NSW Remuneration Tribunal); Parliamentary Service of Queensland Parliament, *Members' Entitlements Handbook*; *Parliamentary Remuneration Act 1990* (SA); South Australian Legislative Council, *Handbook for Members of the Legislative Council of South Australia*; Parliamentary Salaries, *Superannuation and Allowances Act 1973* (Tas); *Parliamentary Salaries and Superannuation Act 1968* (Vic); *Parliamentary Allowances Regulations 2003* (Vic); *Salaries and Allowances Act 1975* (WA); Western Australia Salaries and Remuneration Tribunal (2009) Determination: Members of Parliament 2009 – 14 August, viewed 20 October 2009: <http://www.sat.wa.gov.au/index.cfm?event=mpItem20090814>; *Remuneration Tribunal Act 1995* (ACT) s 9(2); Legislative Assembly for the Australian Capital Territory, *Members' Guide: Guide to Services, Facilities and Entitlements for Non-Executive Members and their Staff*, 129–30; Northern Territory Legislative Assembly, *Members' Guide*, Pt 8 'Members' salaries, allowances and other entitlements'; *Assembly Members and Statutory Officers (Remuneration and Other Entitlements) Act 2006* (NT); Northern Territory Remuneration Tribunal (2008) *Report on the Entitlements of Assembly Members and Determination No. 1 of 2009*.

– do not uphold any of the elements of Principle 2. The only two jurisdictions that do are New South Wales and the ACT. ACT parliamentarians, for example, are barred from using any of their entitlements for election campaigning or other party-political activities.[66] There are also specific rules regarding the content of publications produced using these entitlements.[67]

The rules applying to NSW parliamentarians appear to most fully uphold Principle 2. These rules are based on a definition of 'parliamentary duties'. As the NSW ICAC correctly observed, '[t]he concept of "Parliamentary duties" is fundamental to preventing the misuse of Members' entitlements',[68] with 'explanation and guidance on the meaning of [this concept] ... needed because these are issues that require the exercise of judgment and the balancing of public and private responsibilities'.[69]

The *Parliamentary Remuneration Act 1989* (NSW) generally defines such duties as those that attach to the office of parliamentarians. They include duties that parliamentarians are 'ordinarily expected to undertake, including participation in the activities of recognised political parties'.[70] The NSW Parliamentary Remuneration Tribunal has also issued guidelines on the meaning of 'parliamentary duties' in relation to the use of additional entitlements.[71] In its guidelines, the tribunal has determined that these entitlements can be used for '[a]ctivities undertaken in representing the interests of constituents, but excluding activities of a direct electioneering or political campaigning nature'.[72] The tribunal then specifies various activities as falling within the scope of political campaigning: funding party membership drives, fundraising, election campaigns, preselection and the use of electorate offices and staff for election campaigns, for instance.[73] These guidelines are supplemented by additional clauses in the NSW handbook on parliamentary entitlements that distinguish between permissible and impermissible content for advertising financed by such entitlements.[74]

The 'worst practice' jurisdictions include the arrangements governing the entitlements of federal parliamentarians. There is no general policy that these entitlements only be used for parliamentarian duties, nor is there a general prohibition against their use for electioneering. For a handful of entitlements (for instance, the postage allowance), there is a requirement that they be used for 'parliamentary or electorate business (other than party business)'.[75] Despite this restriction, the entitlements remain quite malleable and can fund electioneering activities, because the legislation does not define either 'parliamentary or electorate business' or 'party business'. As a result, there is no statutory delineation between legitimate and illegitimate uses, despite calls from bodies such as the Australian National Audit Office (ANAO) for clearer definitions and guidance.[76] As a consequence of this ambiguity, a liberal view of the definition of 'parliamentary or electorate business', one that includes various forms of electioneering, has been adopted. For instance, there is a general view that it is permissible to use electorate staff to aid the re-election of incumbent parliamentarians.[77]

The arrangements governing Commonwealth parliamentary entitlements go further, officially sanctioning the use of the entitlements for electioneering and campaigning. Take the printing entitlement.[78] Prior to October 2009, the Parliamentary Entitlement Regulations 1997 (Cth) allowed the Special Minister of State to approve additional categories of printed material that could be distributed to constituents using this entitlement.[79] In 2004, approval was given by the then Minister to use this entitlement to print 'postal vote applications and other voting information'.[80] In his 2009 report on federal parliamentary entitlements, the Auditor-General found that such use of the printing entitlement had often resulted in postal vote applications being accompanied by campaign material for the party.[81] Worse, there was obvious waste: 16.5 million applications were printed in this way, 2.9 million more than the total number of voters enrolled.[82] The Auditor-General found a similar (ab)use of the printing entitlement to produce 'How to Vote' cards (included as 'other voting information'),[83] with cards sent by parliamentarians tailored to their party's election campaign strategy.[84]

In this situation, an officially sanctioned use of the printing entitlement for particular electioneering purposes (such as printing 'postal vote applications and other voting information') intermingles with an illegitimate use: electioneering. This tension is clearly illustrated by the Auditor-General's analysis of items produced by the printing entitlement in the months leading up to the 2007 federal election. The report found that 74 per cent of the analysed sample was at risk of being deemed illegitimate, principally because the content of the printed material contained 'high levels of material promoting party political interests and/or directly attacking or scorning the views, policies or actions of others, such as the policies and opinions of other parties'.[85]

In light of its findings, it is not surprising that the Auditor-General concluded that 'fundamental reform of the overall entitlements framework is needed'.[86] The Auditor-General's damning findings have not gone unheeded. In September 2009, the federal government took important steps to curb the use of the printing entitlement and the communications allowance for electioneering and campaigning. Taking effect from 1 October 2009, amendments to the Parliamentary Entitlements Regulations 1997 (Cth) merged the two allowances into one printing and communications entitlement, with a decrease in its total amount. As a result, Senators are entitled to $40,000 per year[87] and the annual entitlement for Members of the House of Representatives is $75,000 plus an amount equal to the standard rate of postage multiplied by the number of voters enrolled in their constituency.[88] The amendments further stipulated that this entitlement 'must only be used for parliamentary or electorate purposes and must not be used for party, electioneering, personal or commercial purposes'.[89] 'Electioneering' was defined as communication that explicitly:

- 'seeks support for, [or] denigrates or disparages … the election of a particular person or persons … or a particular political party or political parties';
- 'encourages a person to become a member of a particular political party, or political parties'; or
- 'solicits subscriptions or other financial support'. [90]

The Special Minister of State can no longer approve further uses of this entitlement and the entitlement cannot be used to produce how-to-vote material.[91] There are now also limits on the number of postal vote applications that can be printed using the entitlement.[92] The federal government has also committed to installing a more rigorous vetting and checking system within the Department of Finance to ensure that the entitlement is being properly used.[93]

Unfortunately, the resolve which the ALP federal government initially demonstrated in reforming the printing and communications entitlement seems to have dissipated. In December 2009, 3 months after the above changes were made, regulations changing the rules governing this entitlement were quietly tabled. The most important of these removed the prohibition on using the entitlement for 'electioneering'; this change was backdated to 1 October 2009.[94] Remember, there is a federal election due in 2010.

All this does not bode well for broader reform to federal parliamentary entitlements. The federal government has established an independent Parliamentary Entitlements Review Committee that is due to report in 2010.[95] The backtracking on the printing and communications entitlement does not inspire much confidence in its will to prevent the use of federal parliamentary entitlements for electioneering.

Principle 3: The amount of parliamentary entitlements should not confer an unfair electoral advantage upon parliamentarians.

Parliamentary entitlements provide an enormous amount of resources to parliamentarians. In 2008–09, entitlements provided to federal parliamentarians totalled $331 million;[96] the cost during the 1999–2000 financial year was $354 million.[97] To get a sense of proportion, the total combined budget for the ALP, the Coalition, the Greens and the Democrats for the three financial years of 1999–2000, 2000–01 and 2002–03 was approximately $248 million.[98] Based on reports of the Auditor-General, Sally Young has estimated that between $887,024 and $899,324 worth of parliamentary entitlements was available to each federal parliamentarian in 2002.[99]

There is a serious risk that these entitlements will provide an unfair electoral advantage to parliamentarians. As noted above, several of these entitlements can be used for electioneering. This is especially the case with the electorate allowance, a monetary entitlement provided in all jurisdictions for parliamentarians to service the needs of their constituents. Table 5.7 details the amount of electorate allowance that is provided to parliamentarians each year.

In New South Wales, parliamentarians receive a Logistical Support Allowance that can be used to pay for communication, transport, printing, stationery and office supplies. The amount ranges from $30,615 to $39,030 per year.[100] Queensland parliamentarians receive a Miscellaneous Allowance worth $29,612 per annum,[101] and their South Australian counterparts are given a Global Allowance of $17,500 per annum.[102]

TABLE 5.7: ELECTORATE ALLOWANCE PER PARLIAMENTARIAN	
Jurisdiction	Amount per year
Cth	$22,685 – $32,895
NSW	$38,975 – $80,095
Qld	$35,934 – $71,315
SA	$16,325 – $49,865
Tas	$24,000 – $40,000
Vic	$28,906 – $38,730
WA	$53,183 – $73,383
ACT	$6,900 – $8,600
NT	$29,140 – $77,030

Source: *Remuneration and Allowances Act 1990* (Cth) s 6, Sch 3, cl 2; NSW Department of Legislative Council, *Legislative Council Members' Guide*, 49; NSW Department of Legislative Assembly, *Members' Handbook*, para 5.5; Parliamentary Service of Queensland Parliament, *Members' Entitlements Handbook*, 60–61; SA Legislative Council, *Handbook for Members of the Legislative Council of South Australia*, Pt 3 'Salaries and Allowances'; Tasmanian Legislative Council (2009) *Members' Guide*, Part 12, 93; *Parliamentary Allowances Regulations 2003* (Vic) reg 15; WA Salaries and Allowances Tribunal (2009) *Determination: Members of Parliament – 2009 August 14*, viewed 9 November 2009: <http://www.sat.wa.gov.au/index.cfm?event=mpItem20090814>; Legislative Assembly for the ACT, *Members' Guide*, 120–21 (there is no specific electorate allowance for members of the ACT Legislative Assembly. These members are, however, entitled to an annual Discretionary Office allocation); Remuneration Tribunal, Northern Territory of Australia (2008) *Report on the Entitlements of Assembly Members and Determination No. 1 of 2008*, viewed 6 November 2009: <http://www.dcm.nt.gov.au/__data/assets/file/0006/43908/MLA_Report_and_Det_No_1_of_2008_28_October_2008.pdf>, Sch 3.

Even if these amounts are not specifically used for electioneering, they are likely to give incumbent parliamentarians an unfair electoral advantage because the performance of parliamentary duties is inseparable from campaigning activity. This advantage is distributed inequitably even amongst incumbent parliamentarians. At the federal level, the ALP and the Liberal Party tend to reap a disproportionate benefit because their parliamentary representation is greater than their electoral support. This can be explained by two features of Australia's electoral system.

First, House of Representatives seats are single-member electorates (unlike the Senate, where politicians are elected according to a proportional system).[103] This favours the larger parties. For example, in the 2001 federal election, the Liberal Party and ALP respectively received 37.08 per cent and 37.84 per cent of the first preference votes, while their share of seats in the House of Representatives stood at 45.3 per cent and 43.3 per cent.[104] Second, our Constitution sets the number of House of Representatives members at twice the number of Senators.[105]

To reduce this effect, the position of parties with no elected representatives needs to be 'levelled up', which itself involves a reconfiguration of the system of public funding of parties (as discussed earlier). Also, the financial resources specifically available to parliamentarians need to be 'levelled down'. At the very least, there should be an urgent review of the entitlement amounts, and when Remuneration Tribunals determine the amounts, they should be required to follow Principle 3.

Conclusion

It is very likely that public funding to Australian political parties and candidates will increase in the near future. Nathan Rees, when NSW Premier, committed to the 2011 NSW elections being conducted under 'a public funding model',[106] a commitment that his successor,

Kristina Keneally, has promised to honour.[107] If Queensland Premier Anna Bligh proceeds with her plan to impose a ban on political donations, there can be little doubt that it will be accompanied by a significant increase in public funding of Queensland political parties and candidates.

Will such (likely) increases in public funding merely entrench the position of the powerful parties? One theory regarding the Western party system, the cartel thesis advanced by political scientists Richard Katz and Peter Mair, would say yes. At the core of the thesis is the contention that the major parties act together to prevent, or at least lessen, the threat of competition from other parties. According to the thesis, this happens in two principal ways: via a public funding system that is biased in favour of major parties, and via ideological convergence (bipartisanship on important public policy issues).[108]

It is not the intent here to provide a sustained analysis of this thesis in terms of its application to the Australian party system.[109] Rather, I will focus on the claim that public funding of the major parties has facilitated their monopoly of public office: Katz has characterised the introduction of such funding as crucial, and has further contended that a cartel party system would have such subsidies as the principal source of parties' resources.[110]

To what extent do the various types of public funding examined by this chapter lend support to this thesis? The thesis clearly has force. As we have seen, various elements of the present system of public funding do favour the major parties: specifically, election funding and parliamentary entitlements that can be used for electioneering. As the next chapter will demonstrate, party-political government advertising has the same effect. However, the thesis's prediction that public funding will become the principal source of the parties' resources has yet to eventuate (there are, however, ominous signs). At the moment, major parties do not rely on public funding as their primary source of income; on the contrary, it is private funding that is the mainstay of their finances (in the form of corporate funding for all major parties, with trade union funding being an additional flow of income for the ALP) (see Chapter 3).

The cartel thesis also reminds us of the acute danger of powerful political parties using public funds to (further) rig the electoral system in their favour. Lest we think this danger is absent from the current push to increase public funding of political parties, we need only refer to comments made by an (unidentified) ALP source. According to this source, the increase in public funding is being sought because political parties across the nation 'are broke'. Commenting further, the source said:

> It's [the proposed change] being put in high-minded terms, but Labor federally is $8 million in debt, and Rudd refuses to fund-raise. State branches are also in a parlous state.[111]

The power of the cartel thesis, though considerable, should not be overstated. The thesis misleads insofar as it implies that the public funding of parties *necessarily* favours the major parties and insulates them from competition. With all the forms of public funding examined in this book, it is not providing such funding that is the problem – on the contrary, public funding has a crucial place in a democratic political finance regime – but rather lax rules and conditions that lead to unfairness. The response to public funding that unfairly favours the major parties is not, therefore, the removal of public funding; it is the proper regulation of public funding.

This leads to a broader point. The problem in the field of political finance is not public funding (as perhaps implied by the cartel thesis) or private funding per se. To characterise the debate as private versus public funding is to overlook the fact that both private and public funding have benefits and dangers. As the previous three chapters have demonstrated, the current patterns of private funding leave in their wake the danger of corruption through graft and corruption through undue influence, result in unfairness and undermine the democratic functions of political parties. In relation to public funding, this chapter has argued that election funding, tax subsidies and parliamentary entitlements increase electoral unfairness, and that the current arrangements governing parliamentary entitlements provide considerable scope for corruption through misuse of public resources. Democratising Australia's political finance regime means setting up rules, regulations and institutional arrangements that respect the roles of both public and private funding while limiting the risks that accompany each.

6
GOVERNMENT ADVERTISING: TURNING TAXES INTO SPIN [1]

Parties elected to government enjoy a range of incumbency benefits, some of which can be used for electioneering. These include the use of government appointments and grants, government media, units and consultants.[2] There are also less tangible benefits, such as the 'selling' of access and influence. It can be argued that the greater the power wielded, the more valuable that access and influence are. It follows that parties in government have more valuable commodities to 'sell' than their unelected competitors, a benefit they secure simply by virtue of being in government (see Chapter 3).

This chapter examines what, arguably, is the most important incumbency benefit for funding electoral activity: government advertising. While such advertising clearly has a legitimate role in Australian politics, there is a risk that it is too often party-political advertising. This risk relates to the principles of protecting the integrity of representative government and promoting fairness in politics: party-political advertising constitutes corruption through the misuse of public resources and increases electoral unfairness.

This chapter begins by considering this risk and whether it is possible to regulate in order to prevent (or reduce) it. It then critically examines current regulation governing government advertising. The state of such regulation should be a cause of serious concern: it is characterised by secrecy and weak mechanisms of accountability. In order to repair this situation, the chapter proposes a range of reforms, notably greater transparency in relation to government advertising and stronger government advertising guidelines.

Party-political advertising: Impossible to regulate?

There is no doubting the significance of government advertising. Australian governments are among the biggest advertisers in the country.[3] Between 1996 and 2003, Australian state and federal governments spent a total of US$14.95 per capita on advertising. Compared with the 12 countries where the government is listed among the top 10 national advertisers, Australian governments spent the most on advertising per head for that period (see Table 6.1).

According to official figures, the federal government spent over AUD$1.5 billion (in 2004–2005 prices) for the period 1991–92 to 2004–05 (see Table 6.2) on government advertising. Moreover, these figures underestimate the full amounts spent on government advertising: they are the 'media spend' (the purchase of advertising space), and do not include the costs of advertising agency services, of the production of advertising material or of any market research carried out.[4] The extent of this underestimate is probably quite significant. For instance, the *Strengthening Medicare* advertising campaign involved $15.7 million in 'media spend' but had a total campaign cost of $21.5 million.[5]

The state governments are no laggards when it comes to matching the hundreds of millions of dollars that the federal government spends on advertising. In 2006–07, the NSW government

TABLE 6.1: SPENDING ON GOVERNMENT ADVERTISING IN COUNTRIES WHERE GOVERNMENT IS LISTED AMONG THE TOP 10 NATIONAL ADVERTISERS, 1996–2003

Country	Amount spent (US$ million)	Population	Spending per head of population (in US$)
Australia (state + federal governments)	$294.10	19,731,984	$14.91
Belgium	$69.70	10,330 824	$6.74
Ireland	$19.00	3,924 023	$4.84
United Kingdom	$271.40	60,094 648	$4.51
Singapore	$13.50	4,276 788	$3.15
Spain	$58.80	40,217 413	$1.46
South Africa	$45.90	44,481 901	$1.03
Mexico	$46.60	103,718 062	$0.44
Thailand	$27.80	63,271 021	$0.43
Brazil	$68.10	182,032 604	$0.37
Peru	$2.30	27,158 869	$0.08
Paraguay	$0.41	6,036 900	$0.06

Source: See Sally Young (2006) Government and the Advantages of Office, in Sally Young and Joo-Cheong Tham (eds) *Political Finance in Australia: A Skewed and Secret System*, Democratic Audit of Australia, 81.

spent $111.7 million on advertising,[6] and the Victorian government spent an average of $143.8 million per year for the period 2002–03 to 2004–05.[7]

The vast amount of money spent on government advertising does not necessarily mean that such advertising is problematic. Indeed, government advertising clearly has a legitimate role in a representative democracy. At a general level, governments should (and need to) communicate with citizens. Laws and policies need to be publicised so citizens can organise their lives. Such publicity is necessary in order to provide justice to citizens who are bound by these laws and policies and to promote efficacy of government. It is also vital

TABLE 6.2: FEDERAL GOVERNMENT EXPENDITURES FOR ADVERTISING CAMPAIGNS OVER $10,000, 1991–92 TO 2004–05

	AUD$million (nominal amounts)	AUD$million (in 2004–05 prices)
1991–92	$48	$63
1992–93	$70	$91
1993–94	$63	$81
1994–95	$78	$100
1995–96	$85	$106
1996–97	$46	$56
1997–98	$76	$92
1998–99	$79	$96
1999–00	$211	$250
2000–01	$156	$177
2001–02	$114	$126
2002–03	$99	$106
2003–04	$143	$149
2004–05	$138	$138
TOTAL	$1406	$1525

Source: Fiona Childs (2006) Federal Government Advertising 2004–2005, *Parliamentary Library Research Note*, 2/2006–07, Parliament of Australia, Department of Parliamentary Services.

in terms of accountability, as publicity is a necessary prerequisite for public comment and criticism of government. Routine operations also require governments to engage in particular forms of communication, such as advertising job vacancies.

We can better understand the role that government advertising plays in a representative democracy by distinguishing two broad types of government advertising: 'campaign' advertising (relating to specific government programs) and 'non-campaign' advertising (such as job vacancies and public notices).[8] There is clearly a role for 'non-campaign' advertising and, in the controversies surrounding government advertising, this type of advertising has not been at issue. Though it is more susceptible to controversy, there is also a legitimate place for 'campaign' advertising. For instance, the detail of specific government programs may need to be communicated to citizens so they can access these programs. Or laws may have been passed requiring citizens to change their behaviour, and that change may be most effectively brought about by bringing the law to the attention of the public through advertising. It is also increasingly accepted that government advertising can be used as a form of social marketing, that is, used to bring about positive behaviour change (whether or not such change is legally required). The advertisements run by the Victorian Transport Accident Commission to reduce the road toll are a good example of this.[9]

So it is not surprising that millions are (legitimately) spent on 'campaign' advertising. As Table 6.3 indicates, the federal government currently spends more than $100 million a year on such advertising.

Controversy, however, arises when 'campaign' advertising is said to be party-political. Party-political advertising occurs when government advertising is aimed at improving the electoral prospects of the governing party rather than advancing legitimate causes of

TABLE 6.3: FEDERAL GOVERNMENT 'CAMPAIGN' ADVERTISING, 2004–05 TO 2008–09	
Financial year	$ million
2004–05	$70.6
2005–06	$120.5
2006–07	$170.1
2007–08	$185.3
2008–09	$130.1

Source: Commonwealth Department of Finance and Management, Asset Management Group (2009) *Campaign Advertising by Australian Government Departments and Agencies: Full Year Report 2008–09*, 46.

government. As so understood, party-political advertising involves two wrongs: corruption through the misuse of public resources, because it is principally directed at the illegitimate purpose of securing electoral advantage for the governing party, and electoral unfairness, because such resources are only available to the governing party. As with the abuse of parliamentary entitlements (see Chapter 5), corruption through misuse of public resources that involves electoral unfairness tends to take the form of institutional corruption: the gain is typically political, not personal, and the misuse is procedurally improper because it has an illegitimate purpose, a purpose that damages the democratic process by resulting in greater electoral unfairness.

Suspicions about party-political advertising have been aroused by spikes in the amount of federal government advertising in the lead-up to elections.[10] There have been a number of notable controversies. To mention a few: before the 1993 federal election, the Keating ALP government spent $3.5 million on a Medicare advertising campaign, and just before the 1996 election, it spent an additional $9.4 million on 'Working Nation' advertisements about employment.[11] In the months leading up to the 1998 federal election, the Howard Coalition government spent $14.9 million on its proposal to implement a Goods and Services Tax, a tax which was to be introduced if the Coalition were re-elected.[12]

More recently, there was heated controversy over the Howard Coalition government's 'WorkChoices' advertisements. Costing an estimated $55 million,[13] the advertisements were aired in two tranches, during July 2005 and October 2005, both before the actual legislation was introduced in the federal Parliament (which was on 2 November 2005). The advertisements included, for example, the following statements:

- 'Australia can't afford to stand still';
- 'Countries have the choice of either going forward or backwards. Marking time is not an option'; and

- WorkChoices 'will improve productivity, encourage more investment, provide a real boost to the economy and lead to more jobs and higher wages'.[14]

These controversies suggest a need for robust regulation of government advertising. Two related but distinct arguments have, however, been made against such regulation. The first is that it is impossible to regulate to prevent party-political government advertising because everything can be portrayed as party-political.[15] This objection is misconceived. It is not government advertising that is political in a broad sense that is to be regulated; it is advertising that is aimed at improving the electoral prospects of the governing party (or damaging the electoral prospects of its competitors). To be sure, much government advertising will tend to have as one of its purposes (or effects) the enhancement of the electoral prospects of the governing party. As the SA Auditor-General perceptively observed:

> A government is elected on a party political platform and, once elected, is entitled to inform the public about the implementation of that political platform. Consequently, the party which forms government may derive a collateral benefit in electoral terms from any advertising undertaken about the implementation of the policy platform on which it was elected.[16]

In such circumstances, government advertising should not be characterised as party-political and illegitimate simply because one of the purposes is boosting the electoral prospects of the governing party. A higher threshold is required and one option is to adopt the position of the SA Auditor-General: that 'where the substantial purpose was the advancement of the electoral prospects of the party in power', government advertising would be considered improper.[17]

The second argument against regulation claims that determining what is party-political advertising is highly contextual, and regulation will not be precise enough to give effective guidance.[18] This argument, however, overreaches. It is clear in some situations that a substantial purpose is to enhance the electoral prospects of the party in power (or damage those of its competitors). Government advertising that expressly advocates a vote for the party in power or directly criticises the Opposition are cases in point. The Victorian Auditor-General has identified various situations where material could be reasonably interpreted as party-political: when it includes frequent use of the name of the state Premier (for example 'the Bracks government' or 'the Bracks Labor government'), and when it attacks or scorns views of others (for example: 'Under the former Kennett Government, Melbourne's hospitals were not only surviving on the smell of an oily rag but were secretly selling off the family silver').[19]

Other situations could provide strong circumstantial evidence of party-political advertising: when government advertising takes place close to election time, for instance. Another questionable situation is when the advertising relates to policies that have not yet been adopted. Both these circumstances applied in the case of the WorkChoices campaign, lending compelling force to the following observations of the majority of the Senate Finance and Public Administration Committee:

> in the absence of enacted legislation and detailed information,
> what can the WorkChoices campaign achieve? The real purpose
> of the campaign seems to be to try to persuade the public, in
> advance of any scrutiny or debate on the substance of the reforms,
> that whatever the legislation contains it must be supported. Such
> a campaign is properly called propaganda.[20]

That said, the point remains that deciding whether or not government advertising is party-political is very difficult. The answer will depend on various factors, including: whether or not it can be justified by reference to specific informational needs; its content and timing; the amount spent; and the broader political context of such advertising. The complexity required for such judgments does not mean regulation is unworkable in practice. What it means is that there must be an emphasis on requiring governments to justify the need for the advertising they engage in, and there must be a specific onus on governments to explain why such advertising is not party-political. For instance, requiring governments to justify advertising campaigns based on specific informational needs would be one way to filter out party-political advertisements.[21]

This implies a strengthening of the broader framework of political accountability that applies to government advertising, as well as specific measures directed at preventing party-political government advertising.

Improving accountability

Parliamentary mechanisms

Broadly speaking, political accountability in this area can be effected through parliamentary and executive mechanisms. Parliamentary mechanisms can mean monitoring and controlling advertising spending prospectively, through the appropriation process, or retrospectively, after the money has been spent.

All jurisdictions require an appropriation of public money through the parliamentary process before those funds can be spent by the executive.[22] This is the way prospective accountability works. These requirements are vital in terms of democratic accountability. The relevant provisions of the *Commonwealth Constitution*, sections 81 and 83,[23] have been described by the High Court as assuring 'the people effective control of the public purse'.[24]

Though this mechanism is a crucial part of ensuring democratic accountability, it is significantly limited when it comes to government advertising. More often than not, government advertising is not specifically itemised in appropriation bills, which makes it difficult, if not impossible, for parliamentarians to evaluate whether or not money should be allocated to such advertising. This difficulty has been compounded by the move to outcome budgeting: that is, the allocating of money against outcomes rather than for the provision of particular services or activities.

The limitations of the appropriation process at the federal level were highlighted and exacerbated by the High Court's decision in *Combet v Commonwealth*.[25] The key issue in this case was whether the WorkChoices advertising was authorised by Schedule 1 of the *Appropriation Act No. 1 2005–2006 2005* (Cth) (*Appropriation Act No. 1 2005*). Schedule 1 (reproduced in Table 6.4) was based on outcome budgeting, with millions of dollars, and sometimes more than a billion dollars, allocated against broad outcomes (such as 'Higher productivity, higher pay workplaces').

By a 5–2 majority, the High Court found that Schedule 1 authorised the WorkChoices advertising. The then Chief Justice of the High Court, Murray Gleeson, as part of the majority, found that there was a rational connection between such advertising and Outcome 2. His Honour reasoned that because the Portfolio Budget Statement which informed the interpretation of Schedule 1 stipulated that

TABLE 6.4: APPROPRIATIONS (PLAIN FIGURES) LISTED IN SCHEDULE 1, EMPLOYMENT AND WORKPLACE RELATIONS PORTFOLIO OF APPROPRIATION ACT NO. 1 2005–2006 2005 (CTH), 78.

	Departmental outputs	Administered expenses	Total
Outcome 1 Efficient and effective labour market assistance	$1,235,216,000	$1,970,400 000	$3,205,616,000
Outcome 2 Higher productivity, higher pay workplaces	$140,131,000	$90,559,000	$230,690,000
Outcome 3 Increased workforce participation	$72,205,000	$560,642,000	$632,847,000
Total	$1,447,552,000	$2,621,601,000	$4,069,153,000

Source: *Appropriations Act No. 1 2005–06 2005* (Cth) Sch 1.

'providing policy advice and legislation services' met Outcome 2, it followed that informing the public and obtaining their acceptance of such legislation would also meet this outcome.[26]

The joint judgment of Justices Gummow, Hayne, Callinan and Heydon went further, concluding that there was no need for any connection between the WorkChoices expenditure and the outcomes stated in Schedule 1. According to their Honours, such expenditure was a 'departmental output'/'departmental item', not an 'administered expense'/'administered item'. In their view, 'Departmental items are not tied to outcomes; administered items are.'[27] This conclusion rested upon a comparison of section 7(2) of the *Appropriation Act No. 1 2005*, which stated that money allocated 'for a departmental item for an entity may only be applied for the departmental expenditure of the entity' and section 8(2), which provided that the amount issued for an administered item 'may only be applied for expenditure for the purpose of carrying out activities for the purpose of contributing to achieving that outcome' – a comparison that suggested to their Honours that departmental items were not tied to outcomes. A further reason for this conclusion was the note for the definition of 'departmental item', which provides as follows:

> The amounts set out opposite outcomes, under the heading
> 'Departmental Output' are 'notional'. They are not part of the
> item, and do not in any way restrict the scope of the expenditure
> authorised by the item.[28]

The dissenting judges, Justices McHugh and Kirby, concluded that there needed to be a rational connection between the advertising expenditure and the outcomes stipulated in Schedule 1. They found this connection to be absent.[29] Justice McHugh, for instance, observed that 'The advertisements provide no information, instruction, encouragement or exhortation that could lead to higher productivity or higher pay.'[30] The dissenters variously described the majority judgment as 'erroneous'[31] and 'seriously flawed'.[32]

The majority decision in the *Combet* case has been heavily criticised by commentators, with one going so far as to query whether or not it erodes fundamental constitutional principles.[33] Whatever the merits of these criticisms, it is clear that *Combet* has implications for the general appropriation process at the federal level, not just for federal government advertising. Specifically, it has brought to the fore the challenge to financial accountability that can arise with outcome budgeting.[34] The problem here is not outcome budgeting itself, but the practice of describing outcomes in vague terms. This was clearly brought out by former Senator Andrew Murray in his report to the federal ALP government, *Review of Operation Sunlight: Overhauling Budgetary Transparency*. In this report, former Senator Murray observed that 'many agencies have formulated broad and potentially meaningless outcome descriptions that counter the Parliament's ability to understand, assess, monitor and approve Government expenditure'.[35] In a stinging criticism, he said:

> In the worst cases you have to wonder at the attitude that
> encourages useless and generalised outcome descriptions, and
> then ties large appropriations to them, consequently allowing
> for such wide ministerial and bureaucratic discretion that
> accountability loses any meaning. Such latitude, especially if
> rubber-stamped by a supine or Executive-dominated Parliament,
> can result in legitimacy being confirmed simply because the law
> does not prohibit such practice.[36]

There are promising signs that some of the deficiencies associated with outcome budgeting will be addressed by the federal ALP government. Its policy document, *Operation Sunlight: Enhancing Budget Transparency*,[37] criticises current practices on the basis that '[s]ome outcomes are so broad and general as to be virtually meaningless for the Budget accounting purposes leading taxpayers to only guess what billions of dollars are being spent on',[38] giving as an example the hundreds of millions of dollars allocated to the Department of Employment and Workplace Relations for 'Higher pay, higher productivity'.[39] In that document, the ALP government commits to a range of measures to tighten up the outcomes budget framework, in particular: making outcomes as detailed as possible; requiring agencies to include in their annual reports the outcomes of their funding; and instigating a systematic evaluation of results against targets that will be undertaken by the Department of Finance and Deregulation and subject to a performance audit by the Australian National Audit Office (ANAO).[40]

If implemented effectively – and that could be the key challenge[41] – these changes will enhance financial accountability in relation to federal government expenditure including spending on federal government advertising. They may not, however, provide for specific scrutiny of such advertising. More detailed budget outcomes does not mean, and will not result in, itemisation of government advertising. So when it comes to government advertising there are clear limits to the possibility of effective prospective financial accountability through the appropriations process.

These limitations do not apply to retrospective accountability: when parliaments hold the executive accountable for the money it has spent on advertising. There are various mechanisms to secure this kind of accountability. Parliaments in all jurisdictions have public accounts committees that can scrutinise this spending.[42] The effectiveness of the committees will depend on a range of factors: the willingness and vigour of the members for the task, their knowledge and expertise, and the resources they are given.

Most important among those resources is the information the committees are provided with and, in particular, whether or not detailed information about government advertising is publicly disclosed. Drawing upon the practices of the Canadian government, the Senate Finance and Public Administration Committee has produced an extremely useful set of recommendations for what it considers an adequate disclosure regime in relation to government advertising. The central elements are listed in Table 6.5.

TABLE 6.5: KEY RECOMMENDATIONS MADE BY THE SENATE FINANCE AND PUBLIC ADMINISTRATION COMMITTEE	
Recommendation 10	An annual report should be published by the Department of Prime Minister and Cabinet providing: • a total figure for government expenditure on advertising activities; • total figures, listed by agency, for expenditure on advertising activities; • figures for expenditure on media placement by type; • figures for expenditure on media placement by month; and • detailed information about major campaigns, including a statement of the objectives of the campaign, the target audience, a detailed breakdown of media placement, evaluation of the campaign including information about the methodology used and the measurable results, and a breakdown of the costs into 'production', 'media placement' and 'evaluative research'.
Recommendation 11	Annual reports of each government agency to provide: • a total figure for the agency's advertising expenditure; and • a consolidated figure for the cost for each campaign managed by that agency.
Recommendation 12	Annual reports of each government agency to provide: • a total figure for departmental expenditure on public opinion research; • a breakdown of the type of research, including the expenditure on research for advertising as a percentage of total research costs; • highlights of key research projects; and • a listing of research firms used by business volume.
Source: Senate Finance and Public Administration References Committee (2005) *Government Advertising and Accountability*, paras 7.94–7.96.	

When evaluated against these recommendations, all jurisdictions fall short. Remarkably, only New South Wales and Tasmania provide specific information on government advertising.[43] In the other jurisdictions, retrospective parliamentary accountability can operate only in theory, and is undermined by a paucity of information.

Even with the NSW and Tasmanian governments, the disclosure leaves much to be desired. The Tasmanian government only requires each government agency to 'publish details of the purchase' of advertising 'on both the Tenders website and in their annual report' for advertising campaigns costing more than $50,000.[44] Campaigns that cost more than $50,000 must be pre-tested and evaluated upon completion, but these results are 'forwarded to the Director

– Communications Policy', and not disclosed to the public.[45] The guidelines for the NSW government only require that the Department of Commerce release information regarding the total advertising media expenditure. As is the case in the federal context, noted above, this obligation does not extend to expenditure on other aspects of government advertising, such as consultancies and the production of advertising material; nor does it require detailed information on the government advertising campaigns to be disclosed. The guidelines also contain this weak exhortation:

> Agencies are also *encouraged* to publish information about their
> advertising programs on their websites. Information may include
> advertising rationale, objectives, costs and outcome (emphasis
> added).[46]

These arrangements fall short of the Senate recommendations, and do not implement the recommendation of the NSW Auditor-General that agencies publish information on their websites about campaigns, including total cost, justification, audience and campaign objectives.[47]

Without a question, the jurisdiction that currently provides for 'best practice' in this area is the Commonwealth. For some time, Commonwealth government departments have been required to attach information to their annual reports detailing the amounts they paid to advertising agencies, market research organisations, polling organisations, direct mail organisations and media advertising organisations for amounts exceeding an indexed threshold.[48] In 2008–09, the indexed threshold stood at $10,900.[49] In 2009, the Commonwealth government significantly supplemented this reporting obligation by releasing biannual reports on advertising campaigns. The two reports that have been released so far disclose the total amount spent on Commonwealth government advertising, identify campaigns costing more than $250,000, detail the expenditure involved in these campaigns in the categories of media placement, market research, advertising production and public relations, and provide brief explanations of the objectives of the campaigns.[50]

These reports clearly enhance transparency in relation to Commonwealth government advertising. Specifically, they go a long way towards implementing Recommendation 10 of the Senate Finance and Public Administration Committee's report on government advertising. They nevertheless fail to implement the committee's recommendations in key respects. Recommendation 12 is only implemented to the extent that the total amount spent on public opinion research is documented. Even the stipulation that there be detailed information about major campaigns (Recommendation 10) has only been partially implemented. In particular, the reports do not provide full information on the campaigns' target audiences and do not include an evaluation of each campaign, including information about the methodology used and the measurable results (see Table 6.5).

Executive mechanisms

We can see now that parliamentary accountability, in both its prospective and retrospective forms, *can* play a crucial role in addressing the risk of party-political government advertising. There are, however, serious limitations to these processes. With prospective parliamentary accountability through the appropriation bill process, government advertising is not itemised, preventing focused scrutiny. With retrospective parliamentary accountability, there is also lack of the specific information that would allow meaningful scrutiny. Further, both forms of parliamentary accountability are unable to deal with the content of government advertising *before* it appears. This brings us to the importance of executive accountability, specifically through guidelines on government advertising.

All jurisdictions have guidelines on government advertising. With the exception of the ACT, these guidelines exist by virtue of executive arrangements. By virtue of the *Government Agencies*

(Campaign Advertising) Act 2009 (ACT), the ACT government advertising guidelines take the form of legislative instruments (this means they can be disallowed by the Legislative Assembly).[51]

The real question about these guidelines concerns their content. This can be evaluated according to five principles. The first three, drawn from various reports of parliamentary committees and Auditors-General on government advertising, are about the material presented through government advertising:

- Principle 1: Material should be relevant to government responsibilities;
- Principle 2: Material should be presented in an objective, fair and accessible manner; and
- Principle 3: Material should not be directed at promoting party-political interests.

The fourth principle (which is also sourced from the reports above) states that material should be produced and distributed in an efficient, effective and relevant manner, with due regard to accountability.[52]

The final principle concerns regular independent scrutiny. This is essential if these guidelines are to be effectively implemented. Judging by the NSW and Victorian experience, leaving the implementation of the guidelines to government departments is unlikely to provide a secure basis for effective implementation. Both the NSW and Victorian guidelines operate without regular independent scrutiny. In a recent assessment of eight advertising campaigns, the Victorian Auditor-General found that six – three-quarters of them – did not comply with the guidelines.[53] The NSW Auditor-General's 2009 report on government advertising also found a serious problem of compliance with the NSW guidelines. This report examined four advertising campaigns:

- NSW Public Sector Cadetship campaign and the Investing in a Better Future campaign, both conducted by the Department of Premier and Cabinet; and

- Winter 2009 (Influenza) campaign and the Tobacco legislation change (Smoking in Cars with Kids) campaign, both undertaken by NSW Health.

While the report concluded that the two NSW Health advertising campaigns complied with the guidelines, it did not find the same in relation to the other two campaigns. In particular, it found that the Cadetship campaign featured a photograph of the Premier, which meant that a reasonable person may well see the campaign as serving party-political interests, and that the $1.9 million budget for the Better Future campaign may have been excessive.[54]

Table 6.6 provides a summary evaluation of the various guidelines. It reveals a disturbing situation: only the Commonwealth guidelines can be said to have met all the principles; the other guidelines fail to meet two or more of them. All jurisdictions expressly provide for Principle 1 (material should be relevant to government responsibilities). Some jurisdictions elaborate: the NT and Queensland guidelines require an identified information need; the NT guidelines require that the target recipients be clearly identified; and the Commonwealth guidelines state that only policies 'underpinned by legislative authority, appropriation of the Parliament, or a Cabinet Decision which is intended to be implemented during the current Parliament, should be subject to an advertising campaign'.[55]

In relation to Principle 2 (material should be presented in an objective, fair and accessible manner), only half of the guidelines expressly provide for this. The Commonwealth guidelines and those of four other jurisdictions also require that the content in government advertising be substantiated; the Commonwealth and ACT guidelines are the only ones that state that material in government advertising should distinguish fact from opinion.

All the guidelines adopt Principle 3 (material should not be directed at promoting party-political interests). Others go further, prohibiting advertising that mentions the party of government by name or ridicules or disparages another political party or group. In four jurisdictions, the government advertising guidelines provide for a prohibition on (certain) pre-election advertising. The Victorian and WA guidelines state that government advertising is generally prohibited when the government is in caretaker mode, and the ACT, NSW and Queensland guidelines provide for longer bans.

It is remarkable that only three jurisdictions, the ACT, Commonwealth and South Australia, have guidelines that expressly adopt Principle 4 (material in government advertising should be produced and distributed in an efficient, effective and relevant manner with due regard to accountability).

Equally remarkable is the fact that only the ACT and Commonwealth guidelines provide for Principle 5 (regular independent scrutiny). As a result of the *Government Agencies (Campaign Advertising) Act 2009* (ACT), ACT government advertising campaigns likely to cost more than $40,000 must be reviewed by the Campaign Advertising Reviewer, an independent statutory officer, and government agencies are generally prohibited from engaging in such campaigns unless the Reviewer has certified that the campaign has complied with the Act and the guidelines issued under it.[56] Previously, the Commonwealth guidelines required the Auditor-General to write a report for the Minister, for all advertising campaigns with an expenditure of more than $250,000, regarding the campaign's compliance with the guidelines.[57] In March 2010 the government adopted a recommendation made by Dr Allan Hawke, a former head of several government departments, that the Auditor-General be removed from the process of reviewing government advertisements before their launch. There were strong protestations from the Auditor-General. Under these changes, an Independent Communications Committee made up of former senior public servants will now carry out the review.[58] This change preserves regular independent scrutiny, but it remains to be seen whether or not it maintains 'the same level of rigour and discipline' as occurred when the Auditor-General was responsible for the reviews.[59]

The position is, of course, far worse in the jurisdictions where there is no regular independent scrutiny. The absence of such scrutiny is perhaps the most serious of the deficiencies, as it allows doubt as to whether or not the guidelines are being effectively implemented.

Conclusion

Of the various dangers posed by political funding to the integrity of Australian politics, the risk of party-political government advertising clearly ranks as one of the most serious – Graeme Orr has evocatively described it as 'not so much the elephant in the corner, but the elephant criss-crossing the room'.[60] The amounts involved in government advertising run to hundreds of millions of dollars, and that money is only available to the party/ies in government. Using it for partisan promotion is a serious breach of democratic principles: it constitutes corruption through the misuse of public resources and electoral unfairness. A central thesis of this chapter is that this risk can, and should, be properly regulated through a robust framework of accountability.

Rather than providing such a framework, current regulation shrouds government advertising in secrecy and makes only a lukewarm attempt at accountability. Prospective parliamentary accountability through the appropriation process is hampered by the practice of outcome budgeting, and retrospective parliamentary accountability is not meaningful in many jurisdictions due to a lack of adequate information. Executive accountability is undermined by weak government advertising guidelines. Such shortcomings need to be addressed if the principles of protecting the integrity of representative government and fairness in politics are to be properly respected.

TABLE 6.6: GOVERNMENT ADVERTISING GUIDELINES

	CTH	ACT	NSW
Principle 1: Material relevant to government responsibilities			
General	✔	✔	✔
Identified information need	✘	✘	✘
Target recipients clearly identified	✘	✘	✘
Require legislation or Cabinet decision for program being advertised	✔	✘	✘
Principle 2: Fair and objective presentation			
General	✔	✔	✔
Distinguishing fact from opinion	✔	✔	✘
Content to be substantiated	✔	✘	✔
Principle 3: Prohibition of party-political advertisements			
General	✔	✔	✔
Specific prohibition on mentioning party in government by name etc	✔	✘	✔
Prohibition on pre-election advertising	✘	37 days ending before polling day	2 months before a state election
Principle 4: Cost-effective and efficient			
General	✔	✔	✘
Principle 5: Independent scrutiny			
General	✔	✔	✘

Source: Australian Government, Department of Finance and Deregulation (June 2008) *Guidelines on Campaign Advertising by Australian Government Departments and Agencies*, paras 3, 6, 12–22 (incl. Guidelines 2–4), viewed 29 January 2010: <http://www.finance.gov.au/advertising/docs/guidelines_on_campaign_advertising.pdf> (It should be noted that the Cabinet Secretary can exempt a campaign from compliance with the guidelines on the grounds of 'a national emergency, extreme urgency or other extraordinary reasons the Cabinet Secretary considers appropriate'. Such exemption must, however, be notified to the Auditor-General and recorded in Parliament: *Guidelines on Campaign Advertising by Australian Government Departments and Agencies*, para 7); ACT Government (2006) *Branding Guidelines*, viewed 11 June 2009: <http://www.scripts.act.gov.au/ACTGOVlogo/index.html>; *Government Agencies (Campaign Advertising) Act 2009* (ACT); NSW Government, Department of Services, Technology and Administration for NSW Government (December 2009) *NSW Government Advertising Guidelines*, 2, 3, 5, 6, viewed 29 January 2010: <http://www.services.nsw.gov.au/advertising/pdf/NSWGovernmentAdvertisingGuidelines.pdf>; NT Government (January 2008) *Guidelines for Public Information Programs Funded by Government Agencies*, 1–2; Queensland Government, Department of Premier and Cabinet, *Queensland Government Advertising Code of Conduct*, viewed 31 March 2009: <http://www.premiers.qld.gov.au/policy/

	NT	QLD	SA	TAS	VIC	WA
	✔	✔	✔	✔	✔	✔
	✔	✔	✗	✗	✗	✗
	✔	✗	✗	✗	✗	✗
	✗	✗	✗	✗	✗	✗
	✗	✗	✔	✗	✔	✔
	✗	✗	✗	✗	✗	✗
	✗	✗	✔	✗	✔	✔
	✔	✔	✔	✔	✔	✔
	✔	✗	✔	✗	✔	✔
	✗	Within 6 months of a state election	✗	✗	When government in caretaker mode	When government in caretaker mode
	✗	✗	✔	✗	✗	✗
	✗	✗	✗	✗	✗	✗

Advertising_Code_of_Conduct/>; Government of South Australia (March 2009) *Advertising Policies and Guidelines*, 5, 6, 14, viewed 29 January 2010: <http://www.premcab.sa.gov.au/pdf/gosa_advertising_guidelines_032009.pdf>; State Government of Tasmania, Department of Premier and Cabinet, *Whole of Government Communications Policy*, Pt 4, paras 4.1.5, 4.1.7, pp. 5, 10, 13, viewed 29 January 2010: <http://www.communications.tas.gov.au/__data/assets/pdf_file/0009/43866/CURRENT_WoGCommsPolicy_V8_July2008_web.pdf>; Victorian Government, Department of Premier and Cabinet (2009) *Guidelines for Victorian Government Advertising and Communications*, viewed 23 June 2009: <http://www.dpc.vic.gov.au/CA256D800027B102/Lookup/AdvertisingandCommunicationsGuidelines_December2009_PDF/$file/Advertising%20and%20Communications%20Guidelines%20Dec09%5B1%5D.pdf>; Government of Western Australia, Department of Premier and Cabinet (April 2009) *Guidelines for Government of Western Australia Advertising and Communications*, viewed 29 January 2010: <http://www.mediadecisionsomd.com.au/Uploads/Downloads/GuidelinesforGovernmentofWesternAustraliaAdvertisingandCommunications.pdf>.

7
REGULATING ELECTION CAMPAIGN SPENDING

The earlier chapters have examined the funding received by political parties and candidates, with Chapters 2 to 4 dealing with private funding and Chapters 5 and 6 devoted to public funding. The previous two chapters reveal that there is no sharp divide between funding and spending. Parliamentary entitlements and government advertising, for example, constitute both funding and expenditure and, when used (illegitimately) for electioneering, represent a form of election campaign spending. It is such spending that gives substance to claims that there is now a 'permanent' election campaign.

This chapter focuses on expenditure by political parties, candidates and third parties in the lead-up to elections. Even if we agree that parties are engaged in a 'permanent' election campaign, election campaign spending (more narrowly understood) retains a particular significance – after all, it occurs immediately before elections, when the minds of citizens are most focused on voting decisions. The principle of fairness in politics, specifically, electoral fairness, is directly implicated here.

There is also a close and direct connection between election campaign spending and political fundraising, as such fundraising is principally aimed at financing election campaigns. This connection means that patterns of election campaign spending profoundly shape patterns of fundraising; demand for campaign funds drives the supply of political money. The problems related to fundraising – corruption through undue influence, various species of unfairness and the undermining of the health of political parties – cannot, therefore, be fully understood and addressed without factoring in election campaign spending (see Chapter 3).

This chapter begins by examining the patterns of election campaign spending. The next two sections consider the implications these patterns have for Australia's democracy. The rest of the chapter makes a case for regulating such expenditure through election spending limits, and offers some preliminary observations on the design of such limits.

'Arms races'

In analysing patterns of election campaign spending there is a threshold difficulty: the availability of data. This difficulty does not significantly apply to spending by candidates and third parties – under the *Commonwealth Electoral Act*, candidates are required to disclose their electoral expenditure and third parties are required to disclose their political expenditure. Rather, the difficulty lies with the election campaign spending of federally registered political parties. When the federal funding and disclosure scheme was introduced in 1984, these parties were required to lodge returns specifying the amount of such spending . However, this requirement was abolished after the 1996 federal election and has not been reinstated. As a result, the federal election spending of such parties has to be inferred from their total spending (see Chapter 2).

Despite these limitations, we can still identify various features of election campaign spending in Australia. First, the funding and spending of political parties and candidates both occur primarily through party organisations rather than directly through candidates (see Chapter 3). Two measures indicate how candidate election spending pales in comparison with party election spending. The first relates to the number of candidates who have lodged returns disclosing independent electoral expenditure: those who have not lodged returns are essentially declaring that they have not engaged in independent electoral expenditure exceeding $10,500 for that election.[1] Table 7.1 shows, in relation to the 2007 federal election, that most candidates of the major parties did not lodge these returns.

The second indicator is a comparison of candidate election spending with party election spending. As noted above, there is no specific data for party election spending so the total expenditure of the various parties for the financial year 2007–08 has been used as a proxy. These figures strongly suggest that the ALP and the Liberal Party conduct highly centralised election campaigns: less than 1 per cent of the spending was independent candidate spending. For the National Party and the Greens, a greater proportion of spending is candidate spending, but the share is still quite low.

Another feature of election campaign spending of the major parties is that it has been steadily increasing (in relation to federal elections) for more than two decades (that is, since disclosure returns at the federal level were introduced). As noted above, for elections held between 1984 and 1996, political parties were required to disclose their electoral expenditure. According to Australian Electoral Commission (AEC) analysis of this data, the amounts disclosed by all branches of the ALP and the Liberal Party increased in real terms by approximately 60 per cent and 45 per cent respectively in this period.[2] The AEC's calculations reveal even more dramatic increases for the national branches of these parties, with the election spending of the federal branches of the ALP and the Liberal Party increasing by approximately 116 per cent and 136 per cent

TABLE 7.1: CANDIDATE V PARTY ELECTION SPENDING FOR THE 2007 FEDERAL ELECTION				
	ALP	Liberal Party	National Party	Greens
Total number of candidates	172	157	38	141
Number of Candidate Returns lodged	13	13	5	20
Candidate election spending	$326,680	$157,577	$256,661	$102,976
Party expenditure for 2007–08 financial year	$60,850,361	$35,590,845	$2,168,372	$1,996,044
Candidate election spending as % of total party spending	0.54%	0.44%	11.84%	5.16%

Source: AEC Annual Returns 2007–08 and Candidate Election Returns for the 2007 federal election, available from AEC Annual Returns webpage, viewed 29 January 2010: <http://periodicdisclosures.aec.gov.au/>.

respectively between the 1984 and 2004 federal elections.[3]

Similar conclusions can be drawn by looking at the electoral expenditure in Victoria and, to a lesser extent, New South Wales. Table 7.2 shows how the total payments (in nominal terms) of the Victorian branches of the ALP and the Liberal Party have increased in the financial years which have had a state election. Again, the figures do not precisely indicate the amount spent on the Victorian elections, as they include non-election spending.

Table 7.3 is based on the electoral expenditure returns lodged by NSW political parties for the previous three state elections. These returns give us more precise data. The situation here does not correlate closely with that for federal and state elections in Victoria, as it cannot be said that the electoral expenditure of both the ALP and the Liberal Party increased during this period. In fact, the spending of the Liberal Party has fluctuated greatly. The spending of the ALP and the National Party has, however, steadily increased during this time. More importantly, total electoral spending of the main NSW

TABLE 7.2: TOTAL PAYMENTS OF ALP (VICTORIAN BRANCH) AND LIBERAL PARTY (VICTORIAN DIVISION)

Financial year	ALP (Victorian Branch)	Liberal Party (Victorian Division)
2006–07 (state election year)	$15,152,874	$12,873,133
2002–03 (state election year)	$9,862,006	$12,697,762
1999–2000 (state election year)	$6,745,974	$10,101,732

Source: AEC Annual Returns. The last three state elections were held on 18 September 1999, 30 November 2002 and 25 November 2006; see Victorian Electoral Commission State Election Results webpage, viewed 30 May 2007: <http://www.vec.vic.gov.au/stateresults.html>.

TABLE 7.3: TOTAL ELECTORAL EXPENDITURE FOR 1999, 2003, 2007 NSW STATE ELECTIONS

Party	1999 state election	2003 state election	2007 state election
ALP (NSW)	$6,972,749	$11,387,667	$16,819,116
Liberal Party (NSW)	$5,690,699	$3,081,051	$5,283,867
National Party (NSW)	$1,190,242	$1,276,798	$1,719, 898
Greens (NSW)	$165, 743	$547,974	$467,162
Christian Democratic Party (Fred Nile Group)	$336,595	$458,275	$436,194
Shooters Party[1]	$201,846	$401,971	$682,960
Total expenditure	$14,557, 874	$17,153,736	$25,409,197

Sources: NSW Electoral Commission, *Legislative Council Results for 1999 and 2003 State Elections*. For 1999 state election results, see NSW Electoral Commission, viewed 16 January 2008: <http://www.elections.nsw.gov.au/state_government_elections/election_results/legislative_council_results/1999_legislative_council_results>. For 2003 state election results, see NSW Electoral Commission, viewed 16 January 2008:<http://www.elections.nsw.gov.au/state_government_elections/election_results/legislative_council_results/2003_legislative_council_results>; Election Funding Authority (NSW), *Summaries of Political Contributions Received and Electoral Expenditure Incurred by Parties that endorsed a Group or by Independent Groups at Legislative Councils 1999 and 2003*, viewed 5 February 2008: <http://www.efa.nsw.gov.au/__data/assets/pdf_file/0010/30142/2000schedc.pdf> and <http://www.efa.nsw.gov.au/_._data/assets/pdf_file/0015/30138/2003SummaryPartiesGroups.pdf>; Election Funding Authority (NSW), Summary of Political *Contributions Received and Electoral Expenditure Incurred by Parties (Election: 2007 NSW State General Election)*, viewed 24 May 2009: <http://www.efa.nsw.gov.au/__data/assets/pdf_file/0020/48116/Parties_Summary_Published_080204.pdf>.

1 The Shooters Party was identified as 'John Tingle – The Shooters Party' in the 1999 State Election Summary.

political parties (in nominal terms) has increased dramatically: the amount spent in the 2007 state election was 74.5 per cent more than that spent in the 1999 state election.

Another conclusion that can be drawn from the available data is that there has been a recent increase in expenditure by third parties in federal elections. In the 2004 federal election, spending by political parties dominated: the parties spent $37.4 million on election advertising, and third parties spent only $4.4 million.[4]

Table 7.4 attempts to gauge the position in relation to the 2007 federal election. It should be noted, first, that the data in the various columns is not strictly comparable. The figures in the column relating to federal major parties are derived from the total spending made by federal branches of the ALP, Coalition parties and the Greens (which is not restricted to election spending), but the third party figures in the next column are restricted to political expenditure made in 2007–08 (see Chapter 2). This lack of comparability may not, however, be a great issue, since it can be reasonably assumed that the lion's share of the federal major party expenditure in a financial year leading up to a federal election comprises election spending.

Table 7.4 indicates that third party spending for the 2007 federal election was about half of federal major party expenditure. At slightly more than $50 million, it was nearly 12 times the amount third parties spent on election advertising for the 2004 federal election.

At times, these increases in election campaign spending are described as giving rise to an 'arms race'.[5] This is not entirely correct. Each electoral cycle produces an arms race, with parties needing to build up their resources for the next election campaign. These rolling arms races are inherent in regular elections and drive much of party fundraising. So even when the level of election campaign spending does not increase, there is still an arms race.[6] What spending increases point to is what we might call an intensifying arms race, as the parties have to amass increasingly large war-chests for their election campaigns.

TABLE 7.4: MAJOR PARTY V THIRD PARTY EXPENDITURE IN 2007 FEDERAL ELECTION

	Federal major party expenditure (2007–08)	Third party expenditure	Combined expenditure
Amount	$100,605,622.15	$50,592,204.89	$151,197,827.04
Group expenditure as % of total expenditure	66.5%	33.5%	100%

Source: AEC Annual Returns 2007–08 and Third Party Returns for 2007–08.

FIGURE 7.1: POLITICAL (ELECTION) ADVERTISING IN $ MILLIONS, 1974–2004

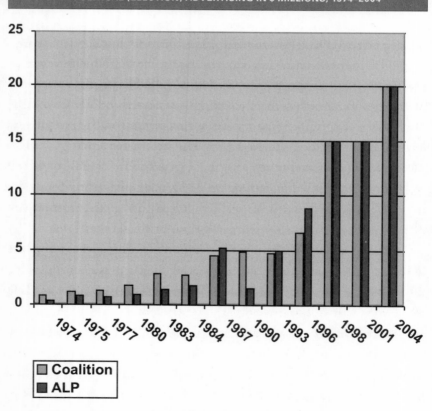

Source: Sally Young (2006) Party Expenditure, in Sally Young and Joo-Cheong Tham, *Political Finance in Australia: A Skewed and Secret System*, Democratic Audit of Australia, Canberra, Figure 5.1.

While there are various factors explaining the increases in election spending, ranging from reduced volunteer labour because of (shrinking) party membership to more capital-intensive campaign techniques,[7] a clear contributor is spending on political advertising. Figure 7.1 illustrates the growth in spending on political advertising. It is based on disclosure returns for elections for 1974–96 and, from 1996 on, data from media monitoring companies which estimate how much the parties are spending during each election. Although the latter are only estimates, they are one of the only contemporary sources available to determine election advertising spending – the obligation on media companies to lodge returns was abolished in 1998.

Buying elections?

As election campaign spending increases, concerns grow that such spending distorts election outcomes. In its strongest form, the argument is that money can buy elections, so to the biggest spender go the spoils of office. If correct, this would be a clear subversion of democratic process, with elections determined not by open deliberation in which citizens can fairly participate, but by the amount of money that is spent. If this were the case, we would have grave reason to suspect that the trappings of democracy merely conceal a plutocracy.

The proposition that 'campaign expenditure buys votes' is, however, untenable.[8] For instance, the biggest spenders on political broadcasting for the federal elections running from 1974 to 1996 only won half of these contests.[9] The flaw in this proposition is its assumption of the overriding significance of campaign spending in voting behaviour. Such behaviour is, on the contrary, shaped by a complex set of factors. There are long-term factors: cultural (a history of loyalty to a particular party), demographic (different voting behaviour between older and younger citizens) and class-based (low-income versus high-income citizens). There are also short-term factors, including the impact of election campaigns.[10] Moreover, the impact of election campaigns is not solely determined by the amount of money spent, as 'money is only one of several kinds of campaign resources'.[11] Further, all these factors interact in complicated ways, with their respective weight varying not only in different electoral systems but also from election to election.

Not surprisingly, then, there is a complex relationship between campaign expenditure and voter support[12] or, put differently, between 'spending and electoral payoffs'.[13] Given the complexity and variability of this relationship, it is perhaps unsurprising that the academic literature has reported mixed findings on the effect of campaign spending on voting behaviour. The focus of that research has been on the impact of relative campaign spending – the amount spent by a party compared with its competitors – on voter support. Much of the overseas research has concluded that increases in relative spending have a positive impact on a party or candidate's share of the vote. This was a key finding of analyses of the 1981[14] and 2005[15] New Zealand elections, and also of recent Canadian elections.[16] Extensive investigation into the impact of constituency-level campaigning in British general elections has also arrived at the same conclusion.[17] Academic research is, however, not of one voice on this issue, with several studies of British general elections casting doubt on the existence of any positive correlation between increased campaign spending and voter support.[18]

Another finding reported by much of the literature is that the electoral value of campaign spending varies according to whether the candidate is a challenger or an incumbent. Some studies of American and British elections have concluded that such spending is of greater value to a challenger candidate.[19] Similarly, an analysis of the 2005 New Zealand election concluded that the key beneficiaries of increased spending during this election were the smaller parties.[20] Research on recent Canadian elections has, however, drawn the apparently opposite conclusion: that incumbent candidates benefited more from expenditure than challengers.[21] Various US studies have qualified the proposition that challenger spending is of more value, by contending that while such spending is more effective than incumbent spending when the total absolute amount was low, it was subject to diminishing returns, and that incumbent candidates spent larger amounts more profitably.[22]

Given that the effect of campaign spending on voter support depends on the type of electoral system, the most important research for us is that on Australian elections. Only a relatively small body of research has been undertaken on this topic, all of it by academic geographer James Forrest.[23] Forrest has analysed the NSW state elections of 1984, 1988, 1991 and 1995, and the 1990 federal election. At the risk of some oversimplification, the following conclusions can be drawn from these studies. All the studies concluded that an increase in spending relative to that by competitors resulted in more votes. The effect of spending in increasing voter support, while significant, was modest given other factors that influence voting behaviour (including industry, demographic and employment factors). This was especially so in elections where support for major parties was volatile.[24] Moreover, how money was spent was as important as how much was spent.[25] The impact of the spending also varied according to the target groups. According to Forrest:

> different aspects of media activity impact differently on each. Wavering ... voters more actively use the election campaign to determine how to vote, and for these subsets campaign advertising in its widest sense has an important persuading role. For the committed voter, partisanship is the dominant influence.[26]

A level playing field?

On the best available research, we can conclude that in Australian elections, an increase in relative election spending tends to result in more votes. The impact of such spending, however, is likely to ripple out into more areas than voter support. While research has yet to determine the exact relationship between election spending and political debate, patterns of election spending may influence the boundaries and content of political debate (which issues are on the public agenda and which are not, which topics become prominent and which fall by the wayside). If so, the amount of election spending can influence election outcomes in terms of both voter support and the character of the contest. This possibility gives rise to a risk of unfair elections.

The question of unfairness in elections can be more specifically analysed. Chapter 1 identified key dimensions of electoral fairness: open access to electoral contests; fair rivalry among competing candidates and parties (including an absence of a serious imbalance between major and minor parties and some degree of 'equality of arms' between the major parties); and fairness between parties and candidates on the one hand, and third parties on the other.

Determining whether these principles are met is not a straightforward task. It involves comparative judgments admitting questions of degree. The criteria of fairness are also far from precise: what does 'open access' or 'serious imbalance' actually mean?[27] That said, these principles and their criteria are not meaningless either: as the following discussion will show, their meaning can be elaborated upon by a close consideration of actual patterns of election campaign spending.

Open access to electoral contests requires at least that the sums involved in engaging in a meaningful campaign should not deter candidates or parties that enjoy significant support in the electorate. There are clearly challenges in meeting this principle in Australia – millions of dollars need to be raised by a party for a meaningful national campaign, and hundreds of thousands of dollars for a state campaign. These amounts will generally pose a barrier to newcomers, as most would not have ready access to the level of resources that established political parties have. While this barrier stems from the (ineradicable) fact that national and state election campaigns must reach out to thousands of voters, it is exacerbated by any increase in the amounts that are necessary for a meaningful election campaign.

As noted earlier, fair rivalry among the competing parties implies an absence of a serious imbalance among them. Any notion of imbalance clearly depends on a conception of the appropriate balance among the parties. One way to understand 'appropriate balance' is through the idea of 'barometer equality',[28] the notion that, all other things being equal, parties and candidates should spend amounts of money commensurate to the public support they enjoy.

Table 7.5 attempts to assess whether there is a serious imbalance among major and minor parties in federal elections according to this idea of 'barometer equality'. The measure it uses is the amount of election spending per first preference vote secured in the *previous* election, as a crude indicator of the public support of the parties in that election. As there is no specific data on election campaign spending, total expenditure by all branches of the parties for a financial year in which a federal election was held has been used as a proxy.

According to the notion of 'barometer equality' adopted by Table 7.5, there is good reason to conclude that, with the exception of the 2001 federal election, there is a serious imbalance between the minor parties (the Democrats and Greens) and the major parties (the ALP and the Coalition parties).

What about 'equality of arms' among the major parties in federal elections? Table 7.6 shows ALP election spending as a proportion of Coalition election spending. Again, the figures for total payments made in a financial year in which a federal election was held have been used as proxies. We can see from this table that for the past four federal elections, there has not been 'equality of arms' between the ALP and the Coalition.

Fairness in electoral contests is also determined by the amount and pattern of third party expenditure. There are two aspects of fairness in such spending: first, fairness between the parties and

TABLE 7.5: ELECTION SPENDING PER FIRST PREFERENCE VOTE FOR PREVIOUS ELECTION

Party	1998 federal election	2001 federal election	2004 federal election	2007 federal election
ALP[1]	$7.15	$6.63	$7.59	$12.86
Coalition[2]	$6.35	$7.73	$8.31	$8.16
Greens	$3.49	$6.73	$5.72	$4.41
Democrats	$1.93	$3.60	$0.77	$1.88

Source: AEC Annual Returns 1998–99, 2001–02, 2004–05, 2007–08; AEC Election Results 1996, 1998, 2001, 2004.
1 ALP figures in these two tables include Country Labor (abbreviated in AEC election voting data as 'CLR').
2 Coalition' figures in these two tables include the Liberal Party, the National Party (including the Liberal/National joint Senate ticket) and the Country Liberal Party.

TABLE 7.6: ALP ELECTION SPENDING AS A PERCENTAGE OF COALITION ELECTION SPENDING FOR FEDERAL ELECTIONS: 1998, 2001, 2004 AND 2007

	1998	2001	2004	2007
ALP spend as % of Coalition spend	92.4%	85.9%	82.6%	124.7%

Source: AEC Annual Returns 1998–99, 2001–02, 2004–05, 2007–08.

TABLE 7.7: THIRD PARTY POLITICAL EXPENDITURE FOR 2007 FEDERAL ELECTION CATEGORISED ACCORDING TO TYPE OF THIRD PARTY

	Total expenditure	% of total third party expenditure
Business	$16,357,543	32.3
Trade unions	$27,040,514	53.4
Other groups	$6,881,569	13.6
Individuals	$312,579	0.6
Total	$50,592,205	100.0

Source: AEC Annual Returns 2007–08.

candidates on one hand, and third parties on the other; and, second, fair rivalry among the parties and candidates. With the first aspect, political parties and candidates have a privileged role during election time because they are standing for election. As noted in Chapter 1, this implies that their role should not be swamped by third parties: in particular, by third parties being able to outspend political parties and candidates. While third party expenditure clearly increased in the previous federal election, third parties are not outspending political parties and candidates: they spend only slightly more than half what the federal branches of the major parties spend (see Table 7.4).

Third party expenditure can also impact upon fair rivalry among political parties and candidates, as such expenditure can be directed towards supporting or opposing particular political parties. A full examination of how such expenditure has been used to support or oppose Australia's political parties is beyond the scope of this book. We can, however, get a very rough sense of what happens by dividing the amount of third party expenditure according to the type of third party: that is, whether it was a business, trade union, individual or group (other than a business or trade union). Table 7.7 does this in relation to third party expenditure for the 2007 federal election. For that election, trade unions were the biggest spenders, with more than half of the third party expenditure. Business groups came in second, with nearly a third of the total third party expenditure.

In the context of an election fought on industrial relations issues, we can make a crude assumption that business spending would have favoured the Coalition and its WorkChoices regime, while trade union spending, mostly carried on through the ACTU's Your Rights at Work campaign,[29] favoured the ALP through its opposition to this regime. Could we then say that the relatively greater trade union spending tipped the balance unfairly in favour of the ALP and, therefore, further undermined 'equality of arms' between the ALP and the Coalition? It is true that the trade union campaign worked in the ALP's favour, but this does not mean that it worsened the problem in relation to 'equality of arms'. This principle relates to fairness in the resources of the major parties as they compete for electoral support. It does not require the major parties to *have* equal support; that would clearly be contrary to the idea of a competition. The principle of 'equality of arms' requires evaluation of the position of the major parties themselves, not the position of the major parties *together with* their supporters. The number of supporters a major party has and the intensity of the campaigning carried out by these supporters are more an indicator of the success of the party in gathering support than a factor counting towards unfairness.

Could it, however, be said that the trade union campaign, specifically the Your Rights at Work campaign, was an ALP campaign or, that the ACTU, in more colloquial terms, was a 'front group' for the ALP? There is, of course, good reason to suspect this because of trade union affiliation to the ALP (see Chapter 3). There is, however, strong countervailing evidence. True, there was clearly co-operation between Your Rights at Work and the ALP, but this does not yield the conclusion that the campaign was *controlled or directed* by the ALP. This is not least because the Your Rights at Work campaign contemplated issuing how to vote cards that did not endorse a vote for the ALP because of dissatisfaction with the ALP's industrial relations policy.[30]

The argument so far has been built upon complex concepts and various calculations. This thicket of figures and abstraction should not obscure – indeed, the argument depends on it – the central conclusion of this analysis: current patterns of federal election spending have meant increasingly unfair elections. Such spending has placed limits on open access to elections, resulted in a serious imbalance between the major and minor parties and compromised 'equality of arms' among the major parties.

Such unfairness also has significant implications for the principle of respecting political freedoms: in particular, freedom of political expression, because election spending is largely directed at political communication, notably through advertisements. Respect for freedom of political expression requires both 'freedom from' state regulation and 'freedom to' engage in political expression (see Chapter 1). 'Freedom from' clearly prevails in Australia, with virtually no legal restrictions on the ability of parties, candidates and third parties to engage in election campaign spending in order to promote their positions (see below). The patterns of such spending, however, have undermined 'freedom to' or, put differently, the fair value of freedom of political expression, specifically that of new parties and candidates, minor parties and, to a lesser extent, the Coalition.

The case for election spending limits

A range of measures could be adopted to tackle this unfairness. The position of newcomers and minor parties needs to be levelled *up* to knock down the barriers to open access and the imbalance between minor and major parties. This task largely falls to public funding (see Chapter 5). Also, the spending of the major parties, in particular the ALP, needs to be levelled *down*. This will help address problems relating to open access and the imbalance between minor and major parties and also those concerning 'equality of arms' among the major parties. A key measure in levelling down is election spending limits. Such regulation is the focus of the rest of this chapter.

Currently, the only election spending limits in Australia are those that apply to elections for the Tasmanian Legislative Council. These limits ban persons and entities other than Legislative Council candidates and their agents from spending money in order to promote or secure the election of a candidate.[31] They also limit the amount that can be spent by Legislative Council candidates (and their agents). In 2009, the limit was $12,000 (it increases by $500 each year).[32]

At the federal level, and in all other states and territories, there are no overall limits on the election spending of parties or candidates. This was not always the case. For a long time there were expenditure limits on candidate spending in Australia. They were in place at the federal level for 80 years and were also common at the state level, including in Victoria, South Australia and Western Australia. However, these limits were removed in 1980.[33] An attempt in 1991 to restrict campaign spending through a ban on political advertising, together with a 'free-time' regime, came unstuck after being ruled constitutionally invalid by the High Court (see below).

There are compelling reasons to reinstate election spending limits, particularly at the federal level. The fairness rationale has already been alluded to. As Eric Roozendaal, former general secretary of the NSW ALP and current NSW Treasurer, has argued, 'caps need to be placed on campaign spending [for] the purpose of achieving a fairer political process'.[34] This rationale was implicit in the justification that Senator Dick O'Connor gave more than a century ago for the candidate expenditure limits included in the original *Commonwealth Electoral Act*:

> If we wish to secure a true reflex of the opinions of the electors,
> we must have … a system which will not allow the choice of the
> electors to be handicapped for no other reason than the inability
> of a candidate to find the enormous amount of money required to
> enable him [sic] to compete with other candidates.[35]

There are clear connections between the fairness rationale and election spending limits: if properly designed, spending limits will facilitate access to electoral contests by reducing the costs of campaigns, thereby increasing the competitiveness of these contests; they will help redress the imbalance between the minor and major parties; and they will contain departures from 'equality of arms' among the major parties.

Research on New Zealand and Canadian spending limits supports these arguments. Academics Ron Johnston and Chris Pattie have argued that:

> In New Zealand, the low spending limits for candidates in the
> MMP electorate contest clearly do ... [make] it possible for the
> smaller parties' candidates in the MMP electorates contests to
> campaign as intensively as those representing the two larger
> parties [Labour and National], without having to raise large sums.
> This clearly acts as a substantial constraint on those two larger
> parties, whose candidates are generally able to outspend their
> opponents and in many places to obtain sufficient money to come
> close to the expenditure maximum.[36]

Similarly, research on the Canadian spending limits has concluded
that these measures mostly affect incumbent candidates, and that
higher limits correlated with lower electoral turnout (voting is vol-
untary in Canada, not 'compulsory', as it is in Australia), less close
races and fewer candidates running.[37]

The other rationale for regulating political spending concerns
its relationship to fundraising. While research into this relationship
is virtually nonexistent, we can assume a tight relationship between
the demand for funds and the supply of funds.[38] Notwithstanding the
complicated effect of election campaign spending on voter support,
what is crucial is that parties and candidates *believe* increased spending
has a positive effect on voter support (or at least not a negative effect).
It is this perception that fuels the need to engage in more intensive
fundraising. Fundraising practices such as the 'sale' of access, in turn,
undermine the ability of political parties to perform their legitimate
functions. The NSW Select Committee on Electoral and Political
Party Funding captured these problems in lucid terms:

> The Committee is concerned about escalating spending levels,
> and in particular the extensive use of political advertising. The
> Committee does not consider this escalation to be healthy or
> sustainable. It increases pressure on parties and candidates to
> engage in more fundraising, thus taking time from their other
> representative and policy functions ... The increased reliance on

private funding also fosters strong ties between politicians and donors, giving rise to perceptions of undue influence.[39]

What this suggests is that there is a separate case for regulating spending in order to tackle corruption. The anti-corruption rationale for spending limits[40] argues that they can act as prophylactics by containing increases in campaign expenditure and, therefore, the need for parties to seek larger and larger donations.[41] If effective, the limits would also reduce the time spent by the parties on fundraising and allow them to devote more time to their other functions (see Chapter 1). The prophylactic function can operate if limits are set at the present levels of campaign expenditure. If such limits are not set, future increases in campaign expenditure would lead political parties, in the absence of more generous public funding, to seek extra and/or larger donations. This pressure would increase the risk of corruption that arises with political donations.

Spending limits can also perform a remedial function, as there is cause to suspect that today's high spending levels carry an increased risk of corruption. If so, spending limits should decrease the risk of graft and undue influence.

Election spending limits will also help ensure that other regulatory measures work more effectively. Increased public funding – as opposed to private funding – of political parties and candidates, as recommended in Chapter 5, raises a serious danger of inflating campaign expenditure, a risk which can be dealt with by election spending limits.

Election spending limits make the operation of contribution limits more effective in two ways. First, Chapter 4 recommended that these limits be subject to an exemption for membership fees, including trade union affiliation fees. This exemption, as was conceded, would be likely to increase the ALP's funding advantage over the Coalition. Election spending limits would prevent the ALP from being able to *use* this funding advantage.

Second, as noted in Chapter 4, contribution limits would significantly reduce the private income of the major parties, and thus reduce their 'freedom to' engage in political expression. Election spending limits can go some way to ameliorating this impact. As philosopher John Rawls has correctly observed, the public arena is a finite and 'limited space',[42] so what matters in terms of political deliberation is the *relative* capacity of citizens and their groups to engage in political expression. This is especially true in relation to electoral contests. For instance, whether or not the Coalition can match the level of ALP spending is more important than the actual amounts being spent. By capping the maximum amount that any party can spend, election spending limits at least contain the costs of an 'adequate' campaign for the major parties. If set at a level lower than present campaign expenditure, such limits would also reduce these costs. Thus, if election spending limits were enacted alongside contribution limits, the adverse impact of the latter on 'freedom to' could be significantly contained by the former.

There are therefore cogent reasons for election spending limits. Nevertheless, various arguments have been made against them. It might be said that rather than having election spending limits, there should be a ban on political advertising like the one enacted by the *Political Broadcasts and Political Disclosures Act 1991* (Cth). While the High Court found this ban constitutionally invalid in the *ACTV* case (discussed below), that decision does not rule out a different ban, one that addresses the concerns raised by the High Court.

However, there are good reasons for not having a ban on political advertising. For one thing, if the ban were enacted without spending limits, it would fail to capture key items of election spending, such as direct mail, opinion polling and consultancies. However, even if the ban *were* enacted with spending limits, there are reasons for not proceeding with it. Principally, the aims of a ban are similar to those that underlie election spending limits: the fairness and anti-corruption rationales. Aside from the different scope of the two, a ban, by its nature, involves a much more severe limitation of freedom of political communication. There is little justification for such limitation if spending limits can effectively achieve the same two goals.

There are two other arguments against election spending limits. One is that expenditure limits are 'unenforceable'[43] or 'unworkable'. This argument is usually predicated on Australia's experience with expenditure limits.[44] Arguments based on 'unenforceability' or 'unworkability', however, typically suffer from vagueness. In Australia, this argument, as it relates to campaign expenditure limits, appears to be a proxy for two other more specific arguments: that '[a]ny limits set would quickly become obsolete',[45] and that such limits would be susceptible to non-compliance.[46]

It is possible to quickly dispense with the first argument. The problem with obsolescence can be dealt with by automatic indexation of limits plus periodic reviews. As to the question of non-compliance, it is useful at the outset to make some general observations concerning the challenges faced by the enforcement of political finance regulation. Certainly, all laws are vulnerable to non-compliance, and political finance regulation is no exception. The degree of compliance will depend on various factors. First, it will depend on the willingness of the parties to comply. This, in turn, will be shaped by their views of the legitimacy of the regulation process and their self-interest in compliance. The latter cuts both ways. For example, breaching expenditure limits might secure the culpable party a competitive advantage through increased expenditure, but this needs to be balanced against the risk of being found out and the resulting opprobrium. Weak laws without adequate enforcement or penalties invite weak compliance.

The extent of compliance will also depend on methods available to the parties to evade their obligations. The effectiveness of political finance laws invariably rubs up against the 'front organisation' problem. This problem arises when a party sets up entities that are legally separate from the party but can still be controlled by that party. Political finance laws will be undermined if parties channel their funds and expenditure to these entities and these entities fall outside the regulatory net or are subject to less demanding obligations. The answer to this problem is to adopt the fairly robust approach towards 'front organisations' found in the *Commonwealth Electoral Act*. The definition of 'associated entity' is broad, and the scheme treats 'associated entities' as if they were registered political parties by subjecting both to identical obligations[47] (see Chapter 2).

Third parties create a separate issue for political finance laws. The challenge is not that the laws allow parties to evade their obligations simply because third parties are, by definition, not appendages of the parties. Political finance laws that do not deal adequately with third parties risk not evasion but irrelevance. For instance, if there was substantial third party electoral activity, a regulatory framework that centred on parties and associated entities would, in many ways, miss the mark by failing to regulate key political actors. This is not an insurmountable problem though. It can be easily dealt with by extending regulation to third parties (discussed below).

The above circumstances demonstrate that political finance regulation, like many other kinds of regulation, will *always* face an enforcement gap. But to treat that as fatal to any proposal to regulate party finance would be to give up on such regulation. Equally, one should not decide not to impose expenditure limits simply because the problem of enforcement would arise there too. The key issue is whether or not there is something peculiar to such limits that make them particularly vulnerable to non-compliance. It is this that is hard to make out. On its face, the regulation of political expenditure would be easier to enforce than regulation of political funding because a large proportion of such expenditure is spent on visible activity such as advertising and broadcasting. Further, the parties themselves have incentives to monitor each others' spending.

Finally, there is the argument that election spending limits constitute an unjustified interference with freedom of political communication.[48] This argument must be taken seriously, not only because it poses a question of principle but also because in Australia, a statute which unjustifiably infringes the constitutional freedom of political communication will be unconstitutional. These questions will be taken up in the following section.

Freedom of political expression and the *Commonwealth Constitution*

As noted in Chapter 4, the High Court has implied a freedom of political communication from sections of the *Commonwealth Constitution* relating to representative and responsible government, specifically sections 7, 24, 64 and 128.[49] The current test for determining whether this freedom has been breached (often referred to as the *Lange* test) has two limbs:

- Does the law (of a state or federal parliament or a territory legislature) effectively burden freedom of communication about government or political matters either in its terms, operation or effect?

- If the law effectively burdens that freedom, is the law reasonably appropriate and adapted to serve a legitimate end [in a manner] which is compatible with the prescribed system of representative and responsible government?[50]

At the outset, it is important to clear up a possible misunderstanding: the view that the High Court's decision in *Australian Capital Television Pty Ltd v Commonwealth*[51] (*ACTV*) stands in the way of regulating election spending. What follows is an extended treatment of this decision and its implications for regulating election spending.

The provisions challenged in that case were found in Part IIID of the *Broadcasting Act 1942* (Cth). These provisions, which were added into the principal statute by the *Political Broadcasts and Political Disclosures Act 1991* (Cth), had several key elements. Foremost, they prohibited political advertising on radio and television during federal, state, territory and local government elections. However, exceptions were made for various types of broadcasts, including policy launches, news and current affairs programs. Alongside the ban on political advertising was a scheme that provided 'free' broadcasting time to political parties. While allocated by the Australian Broadcasting Tribunal, 90 per cent of the time was reserved to parties represented in the previous Parliament that were contesting the current election.

In a 5–2 decision, the High Court struck down the legislation for breaching the implied freedom of political communication. All the judges accepted that there were legitimate objectives underlying the legislation, but the majority did not regard the scheme as pursuing these objectives in a constitutionally appropriate manner. In his leading judgment, Chief Justice Mason focused on what he saw as the discriminatory aspects of the legislation. Speaking of the ban on political advertising, Chief Justice Mason said:

> Pt IIID severely restricts freedom of communication in relation to the political process, particularly the electoral process, in such a way as to discriminate against potential participants in that process. The sweeping prohibitions against broadcasting directly exclude potential participants in the electoral process from access to an extremely important mode of communication with the electorate. Actual and potential participants include not only the candidates and established political parties but also the electors, individuals, groups and bodies who wish to present their views to the community.[52]

The 'free-time' scheme, according to Mason CJ, was similarly defective, as it 'discriminate[d] against new and independent candidates'.[53]

While welcomed by some academic commentators as reflecting a concern for freedom of political speech, the *ACTV* decision has also had its share of detractors. While recognising that the invalid scheme was far from perfect, some critics have argued that it still improved the fairness of Australian elections. Political scientist David Tucker, for instance, has contended that 'it is difficult to maintain that the proposed changes would have made the system of electoral competition more unfair than it is now'.[54] Fastening upon the established parties bias of the 'free-time' scheme, law academic Sarah Joseph has similarly argued that:

> It is true that Division 3 [of Part IIID: 'Free election broadcasting time'] effectively guaranteed that the little remaining broadcast advertising would be dominated by established political elites. However, statistics indicate that newer political parties use *less than* 10% of broadcast political advertising space. Therefore, Division 3 largely improved broadcast access for non-incumbents, while Part IIID as a whole removed the advantage gained by wealthy parties able to engage in saturation advertising.[55]

This outcome led Joseph to conclude that 'the High Court majority essentially reinforced the entrenched power of wealthy political elites and their corporate backers by giving them a constitutional "right" to drown out the voices of less wealthy political players'.[56] For Tucker, what seems at first glance to be a general defence of freedom of political expression is in fact much more partisan, with 'the judges who support the majority in *Australian Capital Television* ... more concerned to protect the right of wealthy citizens, corporations and lobby groups to distort the system of communications'.[57] All this seems to stem from the High Court's neglect of the context in which the legislation was introduced and its passing over of crucial questions such as 'who is doing all the speaking, how they are doing it, how much they are paying for it and what effect it is having upon the democratic system which free speech is designed to protect'.[58]

Deeper concerns have also been expressed about the High Court's decision. The act of implying the freedom itself has been criticised,[59] as has the High Court majority's rejection of the conception of democracy and freedom of political communication advanced by the legislature. As Tucker[60] and Campbell[61] both noted,

the Commonwealth Parliament was aiming to improve the democratic process, so the *ACTV* decision is not a case of the High Court
majority upholding democratic principles against a self-serving Parliament, but rather a case of disagreement between the legislative and
judicial branches as to which conception of democratic principles
should prevail.[62]

These criticisms are also relevant to the debate about the consti-
tutionality of election spending limits. They clearly suggest that the
outcome of the *ACTV* case was far from inevitable. A differently
constituted High Court might very well follow Justice Brennan,
who, in dissent, accepted that there was an implied freedom of political communication, but nevertheless found that the scheme was not
invalid, as it was 'comfortably proportionate to the important objects
which it seeks to obtain ... ensuring an open and equal democracy'.[63]
Indeed, in 2008, the UK House of Lords upheld a ban on political
advertising that was much more severe than the scheme challenged
in the *ACTV* case as being compatible with the free speech guarantee of the *Human Rights Act 1998* (UK).[64]

In any event, neither the *ACTV* decision nor an implied freedom
of political communication prohibits regulation of political communication, in particular election campaign spending. As constitutional
law expert George Williams has correctly observed, while the High
Court struck down the ban challenged in *ACTV*, 'the Court did
not indicate that other schemes regulating political advertising will
also be unconstitutional'.[65] On the contrary, in the *ACTV* case even
judges in the majority were of the view that restrictions on political communication may still be constitutional. For instance, Chief
Justice Mason, after accepting that there were legitimate concerns
regarding corruption and the advantage of being wealthy (in terms
of political debate), stated:

> Given the existence of these shortcomings or possible
> shortcomings in the political process, it may well be that some

restrictions on the broadcasting of political advertisements and messages could be justified, notwithstanding that the impact of the restrictions would be to impair freedom of communication to some extent. In other words, a comparison or balancing of the public interest in freedom of communication and the public interest in the integrity of the political process might well justify some burdens on freedom of communication.[66]

More fundamentally, perhaps, the regulation of political communication is not prohibited by the *Lange* test. In *Coleman v Power,* Justice McHugh explained one of the key reasons for this:

> Communications on political and governmental matters are part of the system of representative and responsible government, and they may be regulated in ways that enhance or protect communication of those matters. Regulations that have that effect do not detract from the freedom. On the contrary, they enhance it.[67]

In brief, the raison d'être of the implied freedom itself permits regulation of political communication in order to enhance political communication.

Having cleared up this possible misunderstanding, we can now proceed to specifically analyse election spending limits. With the first limb of the *Lange* test, it is clear that such limits burden the freedom to communicate about government or political matters because election spending is principally devoted to political communication, notably radio, television and newspaper advertisements.

In relation to the second limb of the *Lange* test and the question of legitimate aims, election spending limits are animated by two central purposes: to prevent corruption and the risk of corruption, and to promote fairness in elections (see earlier). Both the anti-corruption and fairness rationales are likely to be considered legitimate aims under the *Lange* test. The anti-corruption rationale is directed at protecting the integrity of representative government; in *ACTV,*

Chief Justice Mason accepted the aim of the legislation as legitimate:

> to safeguard the integrity of the political system by reducing, if
> not eliminating, pressure on political parties and candidates to
> raise substantial sums of money in order to engage in political
> campaigning on television and radio, a pressure which renders
> them vulnerable to corruption and to undue influence by those
> who donate to political campaign funds.[68]

In relation to the fairness rationale, both Chief Justice Mason and
Justice McHugh in *ACTV* accepted the objective of promoting a
'level playing field' in elections as a legitimate aim.[69] This conclusion
is perhaps unsurprising from the perspective of first principles. A key
element of the system of representative government prescribed by the
Commonwealth Constitution is that members of the federal Parliament
be 'directly chosen' by the people of the Commonwealth.[70] In *Lange*,
the High Court variously characterised this element as requiring a
'true choice', 'with an opportunity to gain an appreciation of the
available alternatives' or as mandating a 'free and informed choice as
electors'.[71] This was a key step towards implying freedom of political
communication, the reasoning being that there could not be such
choice if electors were not able to obtain information relevant to
their voting decisions.[72]

Promoting fair elections is similarly all about supporting 'true'
or 'informed' choice. Lessening the risk of those with more money
dominating elections through their spending allows other parties
and candidates to present their policies and positions. In the words
of Justice Brennan in *ACTV*, the promoting of fair elections seeks
'to reduce the untoward advantage of wealth in the formation of
political opinion'[73]. In accordance with the sentiments expressed by
Justice McHugh in *Coleman v Power*, the fairness rationale in this
respect, while indeed 'burdening' or regulating political communication, is aimed at enhancing such communication.

To sum up the argument so far: election spending limits do place a burden on freedom of political communication, but do so in pursuit of the legitimate aims of preventing corruption, or the perception of corruption, and promoting fairness in elections. The final question under the *Lange* test remains: are these limits reasonably appropriate and adapted to serve such aims? This question cannot be answered in the abstract. Much will depend upon the design of the limits,[74] a matter that will be taken up in the following discussion.

The design of spending limits

There is a range of ways to configure election spending limits so that they lessen the risk of corruption, promote electoral fairness, and ensure that political expression enjoys meaningful 'freedom from' regulation so as to conform to constitutional restrictions. The key aspects of such limits are:

- the political communication/s they apply to;
- the period they apply for;
- the amounts they are set at;
- the political participants covered by the limits (for example, political parties, candidates, third parties);
- the relative severity of the limits as they apply to different types of participants; and
- the interaction of the limits with other regulatory measures directed at the same ends.

In designing election spending limits for Australian elections, we will first examine the spending limits that exist in Canada, New Zealand and the United Kingdom (see Table 7.8).

If election spending limits are to apply to federal elections, they should apply for a period long enough to capture the majority of the campaigning. Bearing this in mind, the Canadian system of applying limits upon the issuing of writs, for example, may seem too short. A period of 6 months before the day of polling would seem to be a minimum period. It should also be noted that the absence of fixed-term federal elections is not a bar to the workability of spending limits, though it does make it more difficult. All three of these countries do not have fixed-term elections.[75]

In terms of spending covered, the categories of expenditure now required to be disclosed under the *Commonwealth Electoral Act* as 'political expenditure' are, in my view, too broad. The narrower definition of 'electoral expenditure' should be preferred (see discussion in Chapter 2). Another good template is the definition of 'campaign expenditure' used in the United Kingdom's *Political Parties, Elections and Referendum Act 1998*. There are two parts to this definition: spending falls within this definition if it comes within one or more of the eight categories of expenditure *and* if it is aimed at promoting or procuring electoral success for the party (or candidate) or directed at enhancing the standing of the party (or candidate).[76] This definition has the virtue of ensuring that the spending is related to the electoral success of a candidate and/or party and specifying categories of expenditure, allowing for greater ease of compliance.

The level of the limit should be further investigated. At the very least, the national limit should not be higher than the largest amount currently spent by a single party. Moreover, election spending limits should be imposed at a national and constituency level and at a state level, to address the question of spending for Senate elections. In terms of the limit to be set at state and constituency level, the Canadian approach is appealing. Under the *Canada Elections Act 2000*, the limit is calculated according to the number of electors, but the amount allocated per elector decreases as the number of electors increases. Under the current provisions, C$2.07 is allocated for each of the first 15,000 electors, C$1.04 for each of the next 10,000 electors and then C$0.52 each for the remaining electors. The amount allocated for each elector also increases (according to a formula) for districts with lower population density.[77]

As well as election spending limits for political parties, their

TABLE 7.8: ELECTION SPENDING LIMITS IN CANADA, NEW ZEALAND AND THE UNITED KINGDOM

	Period limits apply for	Spending covered
Canada		
Parties	'Election period': the period beginning with the issue of the writ and ending on polling day	'Election expenses': costs incurred to directly promote or oppose a registered political party, its leader or its candidate during an 'election period'
Candidates		
New Zealand		
Parties	'Regulated period': generally 3 months before polling day or the period starting from 1 January of election year, whichever is longer	'Election expenses': costs incurred in producing party advertisements
Candidates		'Election expenses': costs incurred in producing candidate advertisements
United Kingdom		
Parties	One year before polling day	'Campaign expenditure': expenditure aimed at promoting or procuring electoral success for the party or directed at enhancing the standing of the party (expenses are 'campaign expenditure' if they fall within one of the eight separate categories of expenses listed in Part I, Schedule 8 of the PPERA: party political broadcasts, advertising, unsolicited material, manifestos and other documents, market research, press conferences and dealings with the media, transport and rallies and other events)
Candidates	No specific period laid down, applies after individual becomes a candidate	'Election expenses': generally all expenses used for the purposes of the candidate's election

Source: *Canada Elections Act 2000* (c. 9) ss 2, 407, 422, 440–441; Elections Canada (2006) *Report of the Chief Electoral Officer of Canada on the 39th General Election of January 23, 2006*, 94; *Electoral Finance Act 2007* (NZ) ss 4, 72(1)–(2), 76, 94(1)–(2), 98; *Political Parties, Elections and Referendum Act 2000* (UK) s 79, Sch 9, cl 3; UK Electoral Commission (2006) *Election 2005: Campaign spending*, 13; *Representation of People Act 1983* (UK) ss 76, 90ZA; UK Electoral Commission, *Election 2005: Campaign spending*, 30.

	Level of limits
	Based on the number of electors for the electoral district in which a party has fielded a candidate (for the 2006 general election, the maximum stood at C$18.3 million)
	Based on the number of electors in an electoral district, with limits varying among districts, and with adjustments for geographically large districts and increases in limits proportionately reducing with the number of electors (for the 2006 general election, the average limit was C$81,159)
	NZ$1 million plus NZ$20,000 per electoral district contested
	NZ$20,000 per candidate
	Generally based on number of seats with £30,000 per seat (for the 2005 general election, parties contesting all UK seats were subject to a limit of £18.84 million)
	Varies for each constituency, with formula taking into account the size and nature of the constituency (for the 2005 general election, the limit for country and borough/burgh constituencies were respectively £7150 plus 7p per elector and £7150 plus 5p per elector)

'associated entities' and candidates, there should also be limits on third party election spending. The first reason relates to preserving the integrity of the limits applied to parties, their 'associated entities' and candidates. Without third party limits, political parties and candidates may be able to use front groups to engage in spending that would otherwise be prohibited. The other reason concerns fairness to those who are standing for office. Limiting candidate and party spending without limiting third party spending means that parties are at a disadvantage in relation to third parties. This turns on its head the principle that parties and candidates should have a privileged role in election contests and so clearly undermines the party system.[78]

Here we see some of the interplay between the fairness and anti-corruption rationales of spending limits. The latter applies with great force to parties and candidates as they are seeking to become public office-holders. But emphasising the anti-corruption rationale without full regard to the fairness rationale may lead to limits being applied only to political parties and candidates. Such a lopsided approach would leave parties and candidates less at risk of corruption but also much less able to perform their role in elections.

Are such limits, however, likely to be unconstitutional because they breach the implied freedom of political communication? In a report to the NSW government, law academic Anne Twomey concluded in the affirmative: 'If [expenditure] limits are imposed on third parties, there is a high risk of constitutional invalidity.'[79] The report does not, however, properly substantiate this conclusion. Its discussion of the topic of third party expenditure limits primarily comprises descriptions of third party limits in Canada, New Zealand and the United Kingdom, plus discussion of some of the cases challenging these limits.[80] Why such description results in a conclusion that these limits are fraught with a 'high risk of constitutional invalidity' is unclear. First, there is no attempt to draw out why such decisions are relevant to Australia's implied freedom of political communication, a weakness that is especially notable in light of the caution some High Court judges have strongly urged in using overseas jurisprudence for this purpose.[81] Second, the decisions in all three of these countries have not removed the limits: some cases have struck down the limits for being too low,[82] others have upheld differently designed limits.[83]

Given that third party spending limits are not necessarily unconstitutional in Australia, we can now turn to the design of such limits. Table 7.9 documents the main features of these limits as they exist in Canada, New Zealand and the United Kingdom. Australian third party limits should follow these examples, first, by requiring third parties to register should they wish to spend above a certain amount (say $10,000) in the 6 months before polling day. In common with these other countries, third party limits should be set lower than political party limits. Australian federal elections are (and should be) primarily contests among rival political parties. Third parties have a legitimate role in these contests, but they should not be allowed to swamp the contesting political parties by outspending them. On the other hand, the level should not be set so low as to preclude meaningful participation by third parties. The period and the spending covered by third party limits should be identical to those applying to parties and candidates.

Conclusion

The patterns of election campaign spending are of vital importance to Australia's democracy. They shape the fairness of electoral contests and determine the extent to which such elections can be judged to be 'free and fair'. There is also an intimate relationship between election campaign spending and party fundraising. This means that patterns of election campaign spending have significant implications for protecting the integrity of government – specifically preventing corruption – and promoting the democratic functions of political parties.

TABLE 7.9: THIRD PARTY SPENDING LIMITS IN CANADA, NEW ZEALAND AND THE UNITED KINGDOM

	Requirement to register	Period limits apply for
Canada	Required to register if have incurred more than C$500 in election advertising expenses	'Election period': beginning with issue of the writ and ending on polling day
New Zealand	Obligation to register if spend more than NZ$12,000 nationally or NZ$1000 in relation to an individual candidate	'Regulated period': generally 3 months before date of poll or period from 1 January of election year, whichever is longer
United Kingdom	Required to register if wanting to spend more than £10,000 (England) or £5000 (Scotland, Wales and Northern Ireland)	One year before date of poll

Source: *Canada Elections Act 2000* (c. 9) ss 2, 349–50, 353; Elections Canada, *Report of the Chief Electoral Officer of Canada on the 39th General Election of January 23, 2006*, 95; *Electoral Finance Act 2007* (NZ) ss 4, 5(1), 63(3)(d), 118; *Political Parties, Elections and Referendum Act 2000* (UK) ss 85, 88, 94(1), 94(3)–(5), Sch 10, c 3(2)–(3).

As this chapter has documented, a striking feature of election campaign spending in Australia, especially at the federal level, is the intensifying arms races it seems to produce. This has not only resulted in various forms of electoral unfairness, but has also contributed to unsavoury fundraising practices (see Chapter 3). The blame for this can be partly attributed to an over-emphasis on 'freedom from' state regulation. This imbalance should be corrected, and one of the chapter's principal arguments — its most important — is that enacting election spending limits would help do that. The justification for such limits arises at two levels. First, there are the fairness and anti-corruption rationales. Second, such limits are a necessary complement if contribution limits and increased public funding are adopted. Together, these two justifications amount to a compelling case for election spending limits.

Spending covered	Level of limits
Election advertising expenses	For 2006 general election, C$172,050 for a national campaign and C$3441 for an electoral district
'Election advertisement': any form of words that can be reasonably regarded as encouraging or persuading voters to vote or not to vote for a party or candidate (including material that describes a candidate or party by reference to views etc held or not held by the candidate or party)	Registered third parties can spend up to NZ$120,000 nationally or NZ$4000 in relation to an individual candidate
'Controlled expenditure': spending on publicly available material and that can be reasonably regarded as intended to promote or procure electoral success for a party or a candidate	Registered third parties: 'recognised third parties' can spend up to £793,500 (England), £108,000 (Scotland), £60,000 (Wales) and £27,000 (Northern Ireland)

8
LOBBYING

There is a fundamental link between lobbying and political money.[1] In most cases, lobbying is funded political activity: commercial lobbyists are paid hefty fees for their services, and when businesses, employer associations, trade unions and their councils, and other NGOs engage in lobbying, they do so principally through the efforts of their paid workers. This much is clear: when money flows into politics, one of its main channels is lobbying.

Lobbying and political contributions to parties and candidates can thus be seen simply as different means of using money to achieve the same overall objective – influencing the exercise of political power. This is vividly illustrated by the pervasive practice of making political contributions to secure lobbying opportunities (see Chapter 3).

It is also illustrated by various case studies which reveal how lobbying, together with large political contributions, can be a key element of a multi-faceted and structured campaign by businesses to secure political influence. There is, for example, the engagement as a lobbyist of Graham Richardson, a former Keating Labor Minister, by property developer Walker Corporation. According to John Hughes, managing director of Walker Corporation, Richardson 'facilitated' a change in the contract between the company and the Victorian government to develop Melbourne's Kew Cottages in a manner favourable to the company. In fact, Hughes has been publicly quoted as saying that until Richardson was involved, Walker Corporation had come up against a 'wall' in its requests to the Victorian government.[2] As well as engaging Richardson, Walker also made large donations to the major parties, including $100,000 to the Victorian ALP a month before the company won the contract to develop Kew Cottages.[3] The motivation for these 'donations' was made clear by Hughes in testimony to a Victorian parliamentary inquiry: from his perspective, the donations and employment of Richardson as a lobbyist were simply different ways to further the company's interests (see Chapter 3).

The report of the WA Corruption and Crime Commission on the development of Smiths Beach in Western Australia also highlights the use of lobbying and political contributions to advance a business's commercial interests. In this report, the Commission documented how Canal Rocks Ltd sought to have its proposal to build a tourist and residential development on Smiths Beach proceed despite widespread public opposition. It funded candidates for the Busselton Council who were seen as sympathetic to the proposal, and it also engaged Brian Burke, the former WA Labor Premier notorious for presiding over the WA Inc. debacle,[4] and Julian Grill, a former Minister in the Burke government, to act on its behalf.[5]

The controversies surrounding Burke and Grill have, in fact, resulted in lobbying attracting increasing opprobrium. The lobbying activities of Burke and Grill have resulted in several findings of misconduct against high-level public servants and in criminal charges being laid.[6] The Burke and Grill controversies have also given rise to a push for greater regulation of lobbying, with the previous ALP WA government banning Ministers from meeting with Burke and Grill[7] and introducing a register of lobbyists; the federal ALP government has also introduced a register of lobbyists (see below). Indeed, a number of commentators have named the fallout from the Burke and Grill affair as a key factor in voters ejecting the WA ALP from office in 2008.[8]

There is a danger, however, in considering all lobbying as inherently suspect. If lobbying is defined as any 'attempt to influence (legislators, etc) in the formulation of policy',[9] as one dictionary defines it, it embraces a wide range of activities, many of which, in the words of the NSW ICAC, are 'part of the healthy democratic process'.[10] Take, for example, a pensioner complaining to her local parliamentarian, or public campaigns aimed at supporting or opposing particular laws such as the ACTU's Your Rights at Work campaign and the Business Council of Australia's (BCA's) advertising in support of the WorkChoices industrial laws.[11] Such activities are 'part of the healthy democratic process' because the principle of democratic accountability insists there be meaningful freedom to influence the process of government. This must include meaningful freedom to lobby.

As the British Neill Committee on Standards on Public Life recognised, 'The democratic right to make representations to government – to have access to the policy-making process – is fundamental to the proper conduct of public life and the development of sound policy.'[12] Similarly, in one of its reports into the activities of Burke and Grill, the WA Corruption and Crime Commission emphasised that:

> The right to influence government decisions is a fundamental
> tenet underpinning our system of government and a form of
> political participation that helps make 'the wheels of government'
> turn. When managed according to 'the public interest', lobbying
> has not only a legitimate but also an important role to play in the
> democratic process.[13]

The 'important' role of lobbying lies in the benefit it can bring to the process of democratic deliberation and accountability. Lobbying can enrich this process by allowing citizens a voice in public decision-making, which in turn can improve the quality of information used to make such decisions. Specifically, lobbying can provide policy information, such as technical expertise and political information (information on the electoral consequences of particular policies).[14]

Arguably, lobbying plays an increasingly significant role as political parties' role as the central agents for aggregating interests and setting the policy agenda declines.[15] In this context, interest groups and issue movements[16] become more important vehicles for political participation and democratic accountability.[17] Lobbying correspondingly increases in significance as these organisations grow both in number and in terms of the scope of their role, because it is one of the key political tools of such organisations.[18]

There is little reason then to presume lobbying guilty until proven innocent. On the other hand, we should not treat all kinds of lobbying as appropriate. A more nuanced approach is called for: one that draws out '[w]hat constitutes proper influence on government'[19] and, in particular, makes 'a clear distinction between legitimate lobbying, which forms part of the democratic process and can provide important information to decision-makers, and inappropriate lobbying which is intended to or can have the effect of undermining the integrity of decision-making processes'.[20] As the WA Corruption and Crime Commission rightly noted:

> The challenge … is to ensure that access to government is available to all groups, and that decision-making processes are balanced, open and focussed on benefiting the whole society to capture the knowledge, skills and experience and co-operation of various interest groups while addressing the public interest.[21]

Three key principles of a democratic political finance regime are of particular importance in distinguishing between legitimate and illegitimate lobbying: respecting political freedoms (including the freedom to influence the political process through lobbying), protecting the integrity of government (and preventing corruption), and promoting fairness in politics (see Chapter 1). Lobbying that breaches one or more of these principles will be illegitimate: that is, when it involves processes that are not open (situations involving secrecy), when it is not focused on addressing the public interest (situations involving corruption and misconduct), and when it undermines the principle of access to government by all groups (situations involving unfair access and influence). These situations will be examined in turn.

Secrecy

The problem of secrecy[22] is neatly captured by the title of a recent primer on lobbying in Australia, political scientist John Warhurst's *Behind Closed Doors*.[23] Lobbying can be shrouded in secrecy in various ways. In some cases, the fact and details are never known – many of the informal meetings that leading politicians have with captains of industry such as Rupert Murdoch would fall into this category. In other situations, the fact of lobbying is known but not its details. This category would include lobbying through the 'purchase' of access and influence: in particular, 'off the record' briefings. This category would also include some of the informal meetings between ALP leaders and trade union officials, including those with leaders of ALP trade union affiliates (see Chapter 3). A third type of secret lobbying occurs when the fact and details of lobbying are not known at the time the law or policy is being made but are exposed later. An example is the successful lobbying by the 'greenhouse mafia' of the Howard government. The influence of this group, which Clive Hamilton has described as 'a cabal of powerful fossil-fuel lobbyists representing the very corporations whose commercial interests would be most affected by any move to reduce Australia's greenhouse gas emissions',[24] was not known when the Howard government's greenhouse policies were being developed but came to light some time later.[25]

The types of secrecy above concern the extent to which such

activities are known to the general public. There is another kind of secrecy: the withholding of information from public officials who are being lobbied. This is a particular concern in relation to commercial lobbyists and their clients, as these lobbyists could misrepresent or keep secret the identity of their clients when they are engaging in lobbying.[26]

We can see from these situations that the problem of secrecy mostly relates to direct lobbying, that is, close communication with policy-makers. It is much less an issue with indirect lobbying – strategies geared towards influencing public opinion and thus shaping the opinions of those in power.[27] This kind of advocacy takes place in public, so the fact that it is occurring and its arguments are out in the open. One example is the advertising campaign run by Victorian anti-abortionist groups opposing the government's proposal to legalise abortion in the first 6 months of pregnancy.[28] This was clearly lobbying, but its aim was to influence general opinion, so it had to be undertaken publicly. This is not to say, however, that no secrecy is involved in any indirect lobbying: there can be secrecy in relation to who is funding the indirect lobbying. 'Astroturfing' campaigns, for instance, raise particular concerns – these are campaigns that are organised and planned by organisations but conducted in a way that creates the impression that they are spontaneous 'grassroots' campaigns.

The difficulties associated with secret lobbying are reasonably obvious. Secret lobbying undermines the integrity of representative government. There are two central principles here: the principle of accountability and the principle of acting in the public interest. At the heart of these notions is the requirement of justification: public officials should openly explain their actions, their reasons for acting and the process of decision-making. It is through this process of justification that citizens are able to judge the performance of these officials. When reasons for acting (such as the influence of particular lobbyists) are kept secret, or when there are clandestine practices of making law and policy, the ability of citizens to judge public officials and to hold them accountable is impaired and distorted (see Chapter 1).

Second, lobbying practices that are kept secret are likely to undermine the health of political parties. In many cases, lobbying occurs outside party structures and is kept secret from the party rank and file. In other words, a parallel process of policy development exists, one that is outside the meaningful control of party members. Because this process involves leaders of the parties, it also tends to further centralise the power of party leadership. In short, secret lobbying threatens to undermine the ability of the parties to properly discharge their participatory and agenda-setting functions (see Chapter 1).

There are two other ways in which secret lobbying threatens the public interest: it raises the spectre of corruption and misconduct as those who engage in such conduct generally seek to conceal their behaviour; and it involves unfair access to, and influence on, the political process. Both aspects of secret lobbying were present with the efforts of former WA Minister John Bowler to conceal his contact with Brian Burke and Julian Grill. In its report into this matter, the WA Corruption and Crime Commission found that Bowler, 'in an attempt to hide his contact and communication as a Minister with Mr Grill and Mr Burke':

- asked Mr Burke not to send emails to his Ministerial email address because he believed that they could be the subject of Freedom of Information (FOI) requests;
- confirmed to Mr Grill that he did not want Mr Grill to send information to him by email, suggested it be sent by fax, and agreed to a suggestion that the client send it direct;
- asked Mr Grill not to officially request meetings with him at his office, but said that he would meet him, and Mr Burke, at Mr Grill's residence;
- organised on several occasions to attend either Mr Grill's

residence or a venue other than his office to discuss issues relating to clients of Mr Grill and Mr Burke;

- stopped Mr Grill from discussing a client (Echelon Mining) on the phone and arranged to meet Mr Grill at his residence;
- asked Mr Grill not to attend a meeting he (Mr Bowler) was having with representatives of a company, Croesus Mining, which was Mr Grill's client;
- said to Mr Grill that if he wanted to discuss anything he should phone him (Mr Bowler) and invite him for afternoon tea;
- instructed Mr Corrigan (his chief of staff) not to log correspondence from Mr Grill or Mr Burke on the correspondence system; and
- instructed administrative staff not to email messages about phone calls from Mr Grill or Mr Burke but to write them on a piece of paper.[29]

According to the Commission, 'there was a political dimension to Mr Bowler's desire to keep secret his contacts with Mr Grill and Mr Burke' in that 'evidence of this in the hands of the opposition or the media, or of some of his party colleagues, could be used to damage him politically, and Mr Bowler was at pains to avoid this'.[30]

Such concealment, in the opinion of the Commission, constituted misconduct under the *Corruption and Crime Commission Act 2003* (WA).[31] The reasons for its conclusion make clear the link between secrecy, on the one hand, and corruption, misconduct and unfair access on the other. In the words of the Commission:

> these clandestine arrangements gave at the very least the appearance of opportunity to Mr Grill and Mr Burke (and hence their clients) to influence Mr Bowler in a way that would not come to the knowledge of the Premier, the Cabinet or the Parliament. In the circumstances, that constituted *the performance of his functions in a manner that was not honest*. Nor was it *impartial*. The arrangements *favoured Mr Grill and Mr Burke (and their clients)*

over persons who did not have that type of access to him (emphasis
added).[32]

All these problems – corruption, misconduct and unfair access – are
not restricted to situations involving covert lobbying; they can occur
even in the light of publicity.

Corruption and misconduct

The lobbying activities of Burke and Grill make it clear that lobbying can threaten the integrity of government by leading to corruption and misconduct. They suggest that there are several groups
that can engage in corruption and misconduct as a result of lobbying.
Administrative lobbying, that is, lobbying of public servants,[33] may
result in such conduct. For instance, the WA Corruption and Crime
Commission found that Dr Neale Fong, as Director General of the
WA Department of Health, had engaged in serious misconduct by
disclosing a confidential matter concerning an investigation into a
Department of Health employee to Burke.[34] Political lobbying,[35]
of elected officials themselves, can also result in such conduct. For
example, the WA Corruption and Crime Commission made findings
of misconduct against three Busselton Shire Councillors in its report
on the Smiths Beach development, an episode that also involved the
lobbying efforts of Burke and Grill.[36] Finally, lobbyists and their clients can also engage in corruption and misconduct.

Judging whether or not individuals in these groups have engaged
in corruption and misconduct as a result of lobbying depends on what
standards of integrity apply. The content of these standards depends
on the nature of the position or occupation held. We therefore need
now to examine the standards of integrity that apply to public officials and then the standards that apply to private sector actors (the
lobbyists and the clients).

With public officials – elected officials and government employees

– the standards are exacting, as they are under a 'constitutional obligation to act in the public interest'.[37] This obligation has both positive and negative attributes. According to the British Nolan report on Standards in Public Life, the former would mean displaying various attributes including selflessness, objectivity and honesty.[38] The Australian statutes governing anti-corruption commissions,[39] on the other hand, identify what does *not* constitute acting in a public interest by variously defining 'corrupt conduct' or 'misconduct' as including 'dishonest or partial exercise of public functions', and any 'breach of public trust' that involves a criminal offence, disciplinary offence or reasonable grounds for dismissal.[40]

In the context of lobbying, these positive and negative aspects of acting in the public interest can perhaps be boiled down to the central principle of merit-based decision-making (see Chapter 1). As the WA Corruption and Crime Commission noted in its Smiths Beach report, 'To protect the public interest, decision making must be impartial, aimed at the common good, uninfluenced by personal interest and avoid abuse of privilege.'[41] Its NSW counterpart has similarly emphasised that:

> Public officials will be lobbied. How should they respond? If
> they are decision-makers, the answer is simple. They base their
> decision on the merits. The identity of the lobbyist is irrelevant.
> At least, that is the way it should be.[42]

This rules out 'an attempt, or perceived attempt, improperly to influence a public official's impartial decision-making' through lobbying.[43] Such 'inappropriate lobbying' includes situations where the decision-maker has given 'undertakings to an interested party prior to considering all information relevant to their decision',[44] and where the decision-maker is successfully lobbied to take into account 'factors irrelevant to the merits of the matter under consideration'.[45]

Also ruled out are 'conflict of interest' situations such as the receipt of payments from lobbyists or their clients.[46] More generally, conflicts of interest may arise whenever parliamentarians are engaged in secondary employment, that is, employment in addition to their parliamentary duties.[47] Real questions are raised, for example, by former Deputy Prime Minister Mark Vaile taking up a paid consultancy, whilst a parliamentarian, in a company he dealt with while he was Trade Minister in the Howard government.[48]

Similar risks might arise in situations of post-separation employment, that is, 'where a public official leaves the public sector and obtains employment in the private sector'.[49] As the NSW ICAC rightly notes, 'Conflicts of interest are at the centre of many of the post-separation employment problems.'[50] First, the prospect of future employment can give rise to these conflicts: public officials may modify their conduct, by going 'soft' on their responsibilities or, generally, making decisions favourable to prospective private sector employers, in order to improve their employment prospects.[51] Conflicts might also arise when public officials are lobbied by former colleagues or superiors: it is the prior (and possibly ongoing) association that can compromise impartial decision-making. Both dangers are clearly present when former public officials take up or intend to take up jobs as lobbyists; they are most clearly present 'if a former government minister obtains work as a political lobbyist, particularly if that work involves contact with his or her former department, colleagues, or staff'.[52]

Post-separation employment resulting in public officials being lobbied by their former colleagues or superiors reminds us that conflicts of interest do not have to be financial in character; they also arise where there is a close association between the decision-maker and the lobbyist. The report of the WA Corruption and Crime Commission in relation to the Smiths Beach development is illustrative here. In this report, the Commission found that Norm Marlborough had engaged in misconduct because, when he was WA Minister for Small Business, he agreed with Burke's request to appoint a particular individual to a statutory agency even though he had no knowledge of her suitability.[53] Marlborough's actions, according to the Commission, seemed to be 'driven by his close friendship with Mr Burke'.[54] In this episode, misconduct – the prejudgment – occurred as a result of a close association with an interested party.

Corruption and misconduct can also occur when public officials 'disclos[e] confidential information to a lobbyist'.[55] This is a misuse of information or material acquired during the course of public duties. This conduct is considered to be corrupt conduct or misconduct under various states' law if it involves a criminal offence, disciplinary offence or reasonable grounds for dismissal.[56] The case of Dr Fong and Brian Burke is a vivid illustration of this type of conduct[57] (see above).

The lobbying activities of Brian Burke on behalf of Urban Pacific Ltd, a company that was part of the Macquarie Group, is another example of unauthorised disclosure of confidential information. Urban Pacific was the developer of 504 hectares of land at Whitby, on the outskirts of Perth, and wanted the land to be rezoned so that it could be used for residential development.[58] Acting on behalf of Urban Pacific, Burke contacted Gary Stokes, then Deputy Director-General of the Department of Infrastructure and Resources, the department responsible for land development in Western Australia. In the course of this contact, Stokes – who at times was Acting Director-General of the Department – provided Burke with two confidential letters. When passing one of these to the WA Project Director of Urban Pacific, David Cecele, Burke said – the phone call was intercepted – 'It's worth my life if it gets out.'[59]

According to the Commission, 'Stokes deliberately provided Mr Burke and Mr Grill with information without authorisation which he knew could be of commercial value to them and their clients.'[60] He did so because he 'believed the lobbyists were able to influence [WA Minister] Mr Bowler to advance Mr Stokes' career'.[61] It was these circumstances that led the Commission to conclude that Stokes had engaged in serious misconduct[62] and to recommend that he be prosecuted under the WA Criminal Code.[63] Both Stokes and Burke have been charged in relation to this unauthorised disclosure of information and are due to face trial in August 2010.[64]

In some cases, standards of integrity apply differently to elected officials as distinct from public servants. For public servants, the electoral prospects of any particular candidate or party are generally not a relevant consideration in their decision-making. The position is, however, quite different for elected officials. Elected officials should of course be responsive to concerns of citizens as a matter of democratic accountability – a principal way in which they are made to be responsive and accountable is through the ballot box. This kind of accountability only works if elected officials *always* take into account their electoral prospects in their decision-making. Such conduct should not be seen as corrupt; it is part of responding to the wishes of citizens. Hence, lobbying of elected officials that successfully draws their attention to the electoral consequences of particular courses of action is not in itself corrupt. It is a desirable feature of democratic politics. There can be corruption and misconduct, however, in *the manner* in which electoral prospects are taken into account. They will be legitimately taken into account only if all other relevant factors are considered and given their proper weight. If electoral prospects were the *principal* motivation for a decision, sidelining other relevant considerations,[65] that would be a breach of the merit-based principle, paving the way for corruption and misconduct.

What then of lobbyists and their clients who are in the private sector? What standards of integrity should apply to them? Some would say we should expect very little in the way of propriety. Perhaps influenced by the more restrictive provisions of its statute (discussed in Chapter 9), the WA Corruption and Crime Commission seems to have adopted this stance in one of its earlier reports into the Burke and Grill affair, when it stated that 'Lobbyists are, by their very nature, not responsible for promoting an unbiased or balanced view of the issue at hand, nor must they abide by "public sector rules".'[66]

Underlying this view seems to be a notion that private sector behaviour should not be oriented towards the public interest or bound by rules of integrity. Fortunately, the WA Commission seems to have moved away from this view by laying corruption charges against Burke and Grill.[67]

The better view is to recognise 'the public significance of private sector corruption'.[68] As political scientist Barry Hindess correctly observes, 'private sector attempts to shape the regulatory environment can have significant effects on the conduct of politics'.[69] Also, private sector behaviour is a clear culprit when there is corruption and misconduct by public officials resulting from lobbying; that much is made clear by the Burke and Grill affair. The very real possibility of private sector agents engaging in corruption and misconduct explains why the NSW and Queensland anti-corruption statutes expressly capture such conduct. In these statutes, conduct in/directly leading to 'corrupt conduct' and 'misconduct' by public officials, whether that conduct was by public officials or private persons, is deemed to be 'corrupt conduct' and 'misconduct'.[70]

The need for robust standards of integrity applying to lobbyists is also made clear in the NSW and WA Lobbyists Codes of Conduct, both of which have the following in their preamble:

> Lobbyists can enhance the strength of our democracy by assisting individuals and organisations with advice on public policy processes and facilitating contact with relevant Government Representatives.
>
> In performing this role, there is a public expectation that lobbyists will be individuals of strong moral calibre who operate *according to the highest standards of professional conduct* (emphasis added).[71]

What standards of integrity should apply to lobbyists and their clients? The standards laid down in the federal Lobbying Code of Conduct, the Canadian Lobbyists' Code of Conduct and the code developed by the British Association of Professional Political Consultants suggest the following principles:

- honesty in relation to clients and public decision-makers;[72]
- transparency in representations to public decision-makers, including full disclosure of the identity of client and reasons for lobbying; [73]
- accuracy in representations made, including a positive obligation to ensure truth of statements and a prohibition on misleading statements;[74]
- avoiding conflicts of interest (e.g. elected representatives acting as lobbyists in their own jurisdictions) including a strict separation between lobbying and political party activities;[75]
- respect for confidentiality of information;[76] and
- avoiding improper influence on public decision-makers including a prohibition on gifts to public decision-makers that could be interpreted as an attempt to influence the decision-maker.[77]

When there is departure from these principles, we should be unafraid to characterise it as a form of corruption or misconduct.

Unfair access and influence

The problem of unfair access and influence in relation to lobbying is well captured by the following statements by the NSW ICAC:

> The problem arises when the lobbyist is someone who claims to have privileged access to decision-makers, or to be able to bring political influence to bear. The use of such privilege or influence is destructive of the principle of equality of opportunity upon which our democratic system is based. The purchase or sale of such privilege or influence falls well within any reasonable concept of bribery or official corruption.[78]

The underlying principles, as correctly identified by the Commission, are that:

> No public official should display favour or bias towards or against any person in the course of her official duty, even if there is no payment or return favour. Equality of opportunity, including equality of access, should be the norm.[79]

It is crucial to note that the problem of 'privileged and unfair access'[80] is not a 'victimless crime'.[81] It involves 'granting preferential access or treatment to a lobbyist *while* denying similar access requested by another party' (emphasis added).[82] As the NSW ICAC elaborates:

> One consequence is denial of the fundamental right of all citizens to equality of treatment at the hands of public officials. The more time spent on the favoured, the less there is available for others. People suffer unfairly, and the system fails, even if there was no payment. And how is the ordinary citizen who is kept waiting, or who misses out altogether, to be satisfied there was no payment?[83]

Lobbying can result in unfair access and influence in various ways. Secret lobbying, by its nature, involves such access and influence. When lobbying or the details of the lobbying are unknown, those engaged in that lobbying are able to put arguments to decision-makers that other interested parties are not in a position to counter simply because they are not aware that those arguments have been made. The same applies when details of lobbying are not known when the law or policy is being made, but are revealed later. The decisive time for influencing law or policy is when it is formulated – the die tends to be cast once such law or policy is enacted. So when the 'greenhouse mafia' secretly influenced the environmental policy of the Howard government, it enjoyed unfair leverage, as others were locked out at that crucial time.

A particular issue arises in relation to lobbying by trade union affiliates of the ALP. These organisations have considerable power within the ALP, and can exercise it legitimately or illegitimately. When their influence is exercised openly in party forums, with reasons given, and proper opportunities for debate and discussion by party members, it is legitimate (see Chapter 3). However, when trade union affiliates (or, more accurately, their leaders) reach secret 'backroom' deals with ALP leaders on questions of policy or candidates, and these deals are presented as *faits accomplis* to party members, the influence is unfair and illegitimate.

Even when there is no problem with secrecy, lobbying can still result in unfair access and influence. This would be the case if access were granted to a lobbyist on the basis of circumstances or advantages other than the merit of the lobbyist's cause, the support the cause enjoys, or the lobbyist's knowledge or expertise. The 'suspect' circumstances include situations when lobbyists wield a great deal of political power. An example is found in the WA Corruption and Crime Commission report on John Quigley and Benjamin Wyatt, both members of the WA Legislative Assembly. In this report, the Commission found that these men felt they had to cultivate Brian Burke because of his power within the ALP, to the extent of agreeing to undertake a parliamentary inquiry suggested by Burke (even though they had no intention of honouring these undertakings).[84]

Equality of access is also undermined when access is granted because of the financial power or wealth of the lobbyists. This can happen in both direct and subtle ways. The sale of access and influence are straightforward instances: the payment of thousands of dollars is aimed at securing superior lobbying opportunities. Wealth, however, also speaks in softer tones. Businesses have power both through direct contributions to parties and through ownership of the means of production, distribution and exchange. It is such power that gives rise to what noted political scientist Charles Lindblom rightly described as the 'privileged position of business'.[85] This means that businesses have tremendous power in the market *and* in the political sphere. Businesses have power in the political sphere because political representatives rely heavily on the decisions of businesses for their electoral success.[86] As Lindblom has observed, 'Businessmen cannot be left knocking at the doors of the political systems, they must be invited in.'[87]

The result is that wealthy businessmen such as Rupert Murdoch and James Packer have many more contacts in the higher echelons of government and are much more likely to be listened to than the average Australian: would an ordinary Australian have been able to share an intimate dinner with Prime Minister Kevin Rudd as Rupert Murdoch did in September 2009? Would an ordinary Australian be able to own holiday accommodation and have Prime Minister Kevin Rudd and his wife, Therese Rein, stay there, as Seven Network chairman Kerry Stokes did in October 2009?[88]

Another powerful illustration of the 'privileged position of business' was, arguably, the proposed 43 per cent increase in the number of gaming tables in Crown Casino, Melbourne. When this increase was agreed to by the Brumby Labor government, the Liberal Party spokesperson on gaming, Michael O'Brien, fiercely criticised the decision, saying it had been made after 'two phone calls from James Packer – one to the Premier, one to the Treasurer'. A few months later, however, the Liberal Party abandoned its opposition to the increase after a meeting of Packer, O'Brien, Rowen Craigie (Crown Casino's chief executive) and Ted Baillieu (Opposition Leader).[89]

The privileged access of the mega-rich also extends, although to a lesser degree, to senior executives of major corporations. For instance, Mark Ryan, Director of Corporate Affairs for Westfield, directly lobbied Graeme Wedderburn, Chief of Staff to then Premier Bob Carr, in relation to Liverpool City Council's approval of a development proposed by one of Westfield's competitors, Gazcorp Pty Ltd,[90] in a way that ordinary citizens would not have been able to do; neither would ordinary citizens have been able to lobby Treasurer Wayne Swan in relation to the application by Chinese government-owned Chinalco to purchase a share of Rio Tinto, as Don Argus, then Chairman of BHP Billiton, was able to.[91] The importance of such lobbying should not be underestimated – a study by Stephen Bell and John Warhurst found that these managers, and company directors, were responsible for the majority of 'highest level contacts'.[92]

The rich, because they are rich, are also more able to secure lobbying services, and thus access. This can operate through businesses' in-house lobbying departments, which are often called government relations or public relations departments. The Bell and Warhurst study found these played a vital role for some businesses,[93] and that larger companies are more likely to have such departments (interestingly, it also showed that companies that have lobbying departments tend also to be members of the BCA).[94] And, of course, those who are well resourced are also more able to pay the fees of commercial lobbyists and other businesses providing lobbying services. Industry sources have estimated that commercial lobbyists' fees can be up to $400 per hour with a success fee ranging from 1 to 3 per cent.[95] Not surprisingly, the national law firms that provide lobbying services tend to service major corporations.[96]

The unequal distribution of private wealth can create the conditions for unfair access and influence, but so can patterns of public funding. There is now extensive state funding of non-government organisations (NGOs). There is a legitimate foundation to such funding: NGOs can make a vital contribution to the political process because members of the public participate in them, and also because some NGOs represent the marginalised and disadvantaged, who may otherwise not be well represented, and this enhances the policy process.[97] In short, lobbying by these organisations may improve democratic politics. So it is legitimate for the public to fund such activities, especially when they would not otherwise occur because of lack of resources.

While public funding of NGO activities has a legitimate basis, such funding must be carefully directed at facilitating the empowerment of the disenfranchised. It should also avoid erecting new barriers to political access and influence: it should not entrench the position of 'insider' groups. 'Insider' groups are those recognised by government as legitimate spokespersons for specific groups or causes. They are therefore allowed to participate in dialogue with government, but there are conditions: they must abide by 'certain rules of the game' (such as staying within the boundaries of 'respectable' debate, and not criticising the government too much).[98] 'Insider' groups tend to be more influential in the policy-making process[99] than 'outsider' groups[100] and the unorganised. The difficulty here is that providing public funding is what grants a group 'insider' status. Perhaps the challenge here is to ensure that there is a diversity of insider groups, and that there are multiple opportunities for the voices of outsider groups and the unorganised to be heard.

The problem of insiders getting unfair access is compounded by the employment of former public officials as lobbyists. This brings us back to post-separation employment. We saw earlier the danger of corruption and misconduct if public officials skew their decision-making processes in order to improve their employment prospects in the private sector. This time around the danger, correctly identified by the NSW ICAC, is of unfair access and influence:

> Public officials must act fairly when providing services to the public. Problems can arise if former public officials seek to influence the work of ex-colleagues or subordinates ... Former colleagues may regard the lobbyist as an insider and grant special access and therefore give lobbyists an unfair advantage ... no public official should favour any former public official in the course of their duty and equality of access should be a feature of all official dealings.[101]

This danger is severely exacerbated by the revolving door between public officials and lobbyists. For instance, a study of nine national law firms found that a majority of the lobbyists directly employed by these firms were previously public servants.[102] The case of the 'greenhouse mafia' is illustrative. According to public commentator Clive Hamilton:

Almost all of these industry lobbyists have been plucked from the senior ranks of the Australian Public Service, where they wrote briefs and Cabinet submissions and advised ministers on energy policy. The revolving door between the bureaucracy and industry lobby groups has given the fossil-fuel industries unparalleled insight into the policy process and networks throughout Government.[103]

It is not only the public service that is a recruiting ground for lobbying firms. A study of government relations departments in large Australian firms found that a majority of these staff were either former public servants or former ministerial staff.[104] Moreover, as Warhurst observes, 'lobbying has certainly become an accepted career path after politics'.[105] The list of leading politicians who have become lobbyists or consultants after retiring from politics is long, and growing longer. It includes:

- former federal Finance Minister John Fahey, working for investment bank JP Morgan;
- former federal Environment Minister Ros Kelly, working for environment consultants Dames and Moore;
- former federal Defence Minister Peter Reith, working for defence contractor Tenix;
- former federal Health Minister Michael Wooldridge, acting as a consultant to the Royal Australian College of General Practitioners;[106]
- former ALP Opposition Leader Kim Beazley, acting as a lobbyist for Ernst & Young[107] (prior to taking up ambassadorship to the United States);
- former Queensland Premier Wayne Goss, taking up chairmanship of accounting firm Deloitte;
- former NSW Premier Bob Carr, working as a consultant for the Macquarie Group;
- former Victorian Premier Steve Bracks, working as a consultant to KPMG; and

- former WA Premier Alan Carpenter, heading up retail group Wesfarmers' public relations department.[108]

Corruption and misconduct occur in the context of public decision-making when there is departure from the principle of merit-based decision-making. There are, however, no Platonic or abstract notions of merit. The concept of merit emerges through political decision-making processes, and if those processes are distorted by unfair access and influence, notions of merit will be similarly skewed. Such distortions constitute a corruption of public decision-making. With such corruption, there can very well be a 'corrupt culture' – a culture that 'accepts corruption as part of the way things are done'.[109]

Conclusion

Lobbying is a crucial way in which money influences politics. As with political donations, this does not mean that it is inherently illegitimate. Indeed, this chapter began by emphasising the necessity and legitimacy of lobbying in Australian politics. However, this does not mean that all forms of lobbying are to be countenanced. On the contrary, lobbying crosses the bounds of democratic principles – specifically, the principles of protecting the integrity of representative government and promoting fairness in politics – when it is shrouded in secrecy, involves corruption and misconduct, or involves unfair access and influence. While no study has tried to quantify the incidence of such illegitimate lobbying (and, indeed, there are insuperable difficulties in doing so), the examples threaded through this chapter suggest that such practices are not uncommon. Far from being the life-blood of democratic politics, that sort of lobbying enervates the body politic. We need a regulatory framework that weeds out these practices, while sustaining and encouraging legitimate forms of lobbying. It is to this task that the next chapter turns.

9
REGULATING LOBBYING

There are three aims of a democratic political finance regime that are crucial in relation to lobbying: protecting the integrity of representative government, promoting fairness in politics and respecting political freedoms. These principles imply four aims for the regulation of lobbying. First, regulation should ensure that legitimate lobbying proceeds freely. Second, it should promote transparency and openness to those who are lobbied, as well as to the general public.[1] Third, it should prevent lobbying-related corruption and misconduct. Finally, it should prevent unfair access and influence.[2]

While these aims are largely uncontroversial, the means used to achieve them are not.[3] Two general approaches can be seen in regulation in Australia and overseas. The more common approach is to focus on the public decision-makers – to regulate the lobbied. The other approach concentrates on regulating the lobbyists. This chapter begins by explaining the current regulation of the lobbied and the lobbyists.

It then evaluates that regulation against the aims stated above. Here, we discover glaring weaknesses. Despite the various lobbyists' registration schemes, secret lobbying can still proceed apace: these schemes only apply to a particular group of lobbyists – commercial lobbyists – and even then they fail to provide full information about those lobbyists' activities. There is also a blasé attitude towards the risk of lobbying-related corruption and misconduct, with poor regulation of conflicts of interest and an absence of codes of conduct for lobbyists that have 'bite'. These regulatory defects increase the opportunities for lobbying involving unfair access and influence. This state of affairs throws up the real danger that legitimate forms of lobbying are edged out by their illegitimate rivals.

The lobbied

When lobbyists provide gifts to public officials who are the targets of lobbying, regulations that govern the private funding of politics come into play. They are directed principally at preventing graft and undue influence, and take several forms: they create disclosure obligations, establish corruption-related criminal offences (bribery, extortion and abuse of public office) and define and regulate conflicts of interest (see Chapter 3).

Money given by lobbyists to parliamentarians or political parties may be subject to disclosure obligations (see Chapter 2). If it is given to secure preferential treatment, the crime of bribery may have been committed. And a public official who succumbs to such inducements may have committed the offence of abuse of office. Gifts by lobbyists to Ministers and parliamentarians may also be prohibited: some codes of conduct forbid gifts that pose a conflict of interest, or are likely to do so (see Chapter 3).

Besides such regulation, various codes of conduct provide lobbying-specific regulation. The federal ministerial code of conduct, *Standards of Ministerial Ethics*, requires that Ministers, when dealing with lobbyists, establish the interests the lobbyists represent and avoid conflicts between the Ministers' public duty and private interest.[4] The federal and all state governments have also adopted lobbyists'

codes of conduct that set up registration schemes. In these jurisdictions, Ministers, ministerial staff, parliamentary secretaries and
senior public officials have to ensure that commercial lobbyists are
properly registered under these schemes.[5] Details of these schemes
are set out below.

Some codes of conduct also have provisions dealing with secondary employment, that is, employment while serving as a public
official, and post-separation employment (employment after leaving
public office). The former has more relevance to parliamentarians
than to Ministers, as ministerial positions are commonly assumed to
be full-time positions. Of the jurisdictions that have parliamentary
codes of conduct, Queensland, Tasmania, Victoria and the ACT do
not have specific provisions dealing with secondary employment.

Two codes do. The NSW code requires parliamentarians to
make disclosure in certain circumstances: when a person or entity
that is currently employing a parliamentarian, or has employed a
parliamentarian in the past 2 years, has an interest in a parliamentary debate beyond that of the general public, the parliamentarian,
when participating in the debate, has to disclose the identity of
that former or current employer and the nature of the interest.
Strangely, this obligation does not apply to voting on the subject of
the debate, or when the former employer engaged the parliamentarian when s/he was not in office (even though such engagement
might have occurred in past 2 years).[6] The other code which has
provisions relating to secondary employment is the NT code, which
provides that 'a member must not engage in any other employment
or business activity that involves a substantial commitment of time
and effort'.[7]

No parliamentary codes of conduct restrict post-separation
employment.[8] The most 'robust' regulation is the tepid approach of
the Tasmanian parliamentary code of conduct, which alerts parliamentarians to the possibility that post-separation employment may
give rise to a conflict of interest.[9]

There are now four jurisdictions – New South Wales,[10] Western Australia, the ACT and the Northern Territory – with *no* post-separation bans on former Ministers and parliamentary secretaries engaging in lobbying on matters they had official dealings with when holding such office. Table 9.1 summarises the bans. They extend for varying lengths of time. The most stringent ban applies in Queensland, through the *Integrity Act 2009* (Qld).

'Lighter touch' regulation applies to former ACT Ministers: an injunction to 'exercise care in taking up employment or business activities in the period immediately after leaving Government'.[11] The ACT code does, however, oblige former Ministers 'to ensure that preferential treatment for the new employer or the business is not obtained by the use of contacts and personal influence by the former Minister'.[12]

The federal and Queensland ministerial codes prohibit former Ministers from using information obtained in office for their personal advantage in post-separation employment if such information is not publicly available.[13] The ACT ministerial code is stricter, placing a blanket ban on the use of any confidential information gained while in office.[14]

The lobbyists

Like the lobbied, lobbyists can also be caught up by the general regulation governing private funding of politics when they give money to public officials. As noted above, disclosure obligations may apply. Moreover, as the Burke and Grill episode illustrates, lobbyists themselves can be charged with corruption-related offences (see Chapter 8).

What about lobbying-specific regulation? In comparison with regulation of the lobbied, specific regulation of lobbyists is far less common. A recent survey of lobbying regulation in developed countries, for example, concluded that 'countries with specific rules and

TABLE 9.1: POST-SEPARATION BANS ON FORMER MINISTERS AND PARLIAMENTARY SECRETARIES ENGAGING IN LOBBYING		
	Ministers	Parliamentary secretaries	Senior public service executive
Cth	Ban for 18 months after departure on lobbying on matters with which they had official dealings in last 18 months in office		Ban for 12 months after departure on lobbying on matters with which they had official dealings in last 12 months in office
NSW	None		
Qld	Ban for 2 years after departure on lobbying on matters with which they had official dealings in last 2 years in office		
SA	Ban for 2 years after departure on lobbying on matters with which they had official dealings in last 18 months in office	Ban for 1 year after departure on lobbying on matters with which they had official dealings in last year in office	Ban for 12 months after departure on lobbying on matters with which they had official dealings in last 12 months in office
Tas	Ban for 12 months after departure on lobbying on matters with which they had official dealings in last 12 months in office		
Vic	Ban for 18 months after departure on lobbying on matters with which they had official dealings in last 18 months in office	Ban for 12 months after departure on lobbying on matters with which they had official dealings in last 12 months in office	
WA	None		
ACT	None		
NT	None		

Source: Australian Government (2008) *Lobbying Code of Conduct*, cll 7.1–7.2, viewed 4 November 2008: <http://lobbyists.pmc.gov.au/lobbyistsregister/index.cfm?event=contactWithLobbyistsCode>; Australian Government, *Standards of Ministerial Ethics*, cl 2.19; *Integrity Act 2009* (Qld) s 70; Government of South Australia, Department of Premier and Cabinet Circular (2009) *Lobbyist Code of Conduct*, cl 7, viewed 7 December 2009: <http://www.premcab.sa.gov.au/pdf/circulars/pc032_lobbyist_code_of_conduct.pdf>; Tasmanian Government (2009) *Lobbying Code of Conduct*, cl 7, viewed 7 December 2009: <http://lobbyists.dpac.tas.gov.au/__data/assets/pdf_file/0020/105509/Tasmanian_Government_Lobbying_Code_of_Conduct.pdf>; Victorian Government (2009) *Professional Lobbyist Code of Conduct*, cl 7, viewed 7 December 2009: <http://www.lobbyistsregister.vic.gov.au/lobbyistsregister/documents/Vic_Gov_Professional_Lobbyist_Code_of_Conduct_Sept_2009.PDF>; *Legislative Assembly Members' Code of Conduct and Ethical Standards) Act 2008* (NT).

regulations governing the activities of lobbyists and interest groups are more the exception than the rule'.[15] The Australian experience has largely conformed to this trend until recently. In the 1980s, a lobbyists' registration scheme was briefly adopted by the federal Hawke ALP government as a result of the Combe/Ivanov affair.[16] Once elected, in 1996, the Howard government moved quickly to abandon the scheme. The controversies surrounding the lobbying activities of Burke and Grill have, however, resulted in more robust regulation that applies specifically to lobbyists, and the federal and all state governments have adopted some version of a lobbyists' code of conduct. Except for Queensland, all these codes are executive documents, with no legislative underpinning. The Queensland Parliament has codified a Lobbyist Code through the *Integrity Act 2009* (Qld).

All the codes – except the Queensland legislative code – are very similar. They can be largely described by reference to the federal Lobbying Code of Conduct. There are three key dimensions to these codes:

- who is required to register?
- what disclosure obligations apply upon registration?
- what principles of conduct must a registered lobbyist comply with?

Under the federal code, a 'lobbyist' wanting to engage in 'lobbying activities' must apply to the Secretary of the Department of Prime Minister and Cabinet to be registered on the Register of Lobbyists.[17] This provision involves complicated definitions of 'lobbyist' and 'lobbying activities'.[18] A 'lobbyist' is defined as 'any person, company or organisation who conducts lobbying activities on behalf of a third party client or whose employees conduct lobbying activities on behalf of a third party client'. 'Lobbying activities' are defined as 'communications with a Government representative in an effort to influence Government decision-making', with 'Government representatives' including federal Ministers, parliamentary secretaries, ministerial advisers, federal public servants and members of the Australian Defence Force.[19]

Significantly, there are various exclusions. The definition of 'lobbyist' does not include a long list of individuals and groups, including non-profit groups representing the interests of their members, 'individuals making representations on behalf of relatives or friends about their personal affairs', and members of professions (for example, doctors, lawyers and accountants) making 'occasional representations to the federal government incidental to the provision of professional services to their clients'.[20] 'Lobbying activities' do not include communicating 'with a Minister or Parliamentary Secretary in his or her capacity as a local Member or Senator in relation to non-ministerial responsibilities' or using 'petitions or communications of a grassroots campaign nature in an attempt to influence a Government policy or decision'.[21]

The thrust of these complex definitions is that the scheme is aimed at direct lobbying, that is, direct contact with public decision-makers, and does not cover indirect lobbying, such as public campaigns. The definitions also make clear that the obligation to register is targeted at commercial lobbyists, those who provide services to a range of clients for a fee. In-house lobbyists of companies, peak business organisations, trade unions and their councils, and other organisations will typically not be required to register. Neither will those who engage in unpaid lobbying.

Those required to register have other obligations as well. The lobbyists have to provide their business registration details, including trading names (and if the lobbyist is not a publicly listed company, the names of owners, partners or major shareholders); the names and positions of persons engaged by the lobbyist to carry out lobbying activities; and the names of the lobbyist's clients.[22] They have to update this information four times a year,[23] and also 10 business days after any change.[24] All the information provided is published on the federal Register of Lobbyists, which is a public document posted on the Department of Prime Minister and Cabinet's website.[25]

Registered lobbyists are also required to comply with the following principles. They are not to engage in corrupt, dishonest or illegal conduct, and are obliged to use 'reasonable endeavours to satisfy themselves of the truth and accuracy of information and statements' made in the course of lobbying. They are also required to avoid misrepresenting the nature of their access to government representatives, members of political parties and other public officials. Further, they are required to keep their lobbying activities separate from any personal activity conducted on behalf of a political party (for example, as a member or official of a political party).[26]

The code is administered by the secretary of the Department of Prime Minister and Cabinet. The secretary is responsible for registering lobbyists and receiving the information provided.[27] S/he also has the authority to remove a lobbyist from the register in various circumstances: the main ones are failure to provide accurate and up-to-date information and contravention of any terms of the code (including the principles of conduct).[28] The power of the secretary to register a lobbyist or remove a lobbyist from the register is subject to the direction of Cabinet Secretary, an elected official and member of Cabinet, made in 'his or her absolute discretion'.[29] The effect of non-registration or removal is severe, as 'government representatives' are prohibited from having any lobbying contact with unregistered 'lobbyists'.[30]

As noted earlier, the state lobbyists' codes bear close resemblance to the federal code. There are, however, two significant differences. First, except for the Tasmanian code, none gives an elected official the power to refuse to register a lobbyist or to remove a lobbyist from the register.[31] The Tasmanian code allows the state Premier to direct that a lobbyist's application to register be refused and that a lobbyist be removed from the register.[32] Second, in Queensland[33] and New South Wales,[34] there is now a ban on commercial lobbyists sitting on government boards.

It remains to describe the relevant provisions of the *Integrity Act 2009* (Qld). There are key similarities between these provisions and the federal and state codes. Like the other codes, the Queensland provisions establish a register for commercial lobbyists (the register is subject to the same exclusions and exemptions as the federal and state codes), with registration being a requirement for engaging in lawful lobbying, and lobbyists being required to disclose certain information upon registration.[35] As well as the legislative backing, there are other key differences: the Queensland provisions extend to lobbying of local government councillors[36] and require that when former senior government representatives are employed by the lobbyists, the date they ceased to hold public office be disclosed.[37] They also empower the Integrity Commissioner to adopt a Lobbyists' Code of Conduct (after consultation with the Commissioner's supervisory parliamentary committee).[38] Moreover, the *Integrity Act 2009* (Qld) prohibits success fees.[39]

Evaluating the current regulations

A critical principle underlying the regulation of lobbying is that legitimate lobbying proceeds freely. The opening clause of the federal and NSW lobbying codes of conduct are quite right in emphasising that 'Lobbying is a legitimate activity and an important part of the democratic process' (federal)[40] and that 'Free and open access to the institutions of government is a vital element of our democracy' (NSW).[41]

This principle does not, of course, imply freedom from all regulation. It allows for regulation to prevent illegitimate lobbying, while ensuring that the ability to engage in legitimate lobbying is not unduly impaired. This suggests two guidelines: regulation should be carefully tailored to its objectives and not impose any regulatory burden beyond what is necessary; and regulation itself should not give rise to inequities.[42]

How then does the regulation of lobbying in Australia measure up? We can examine this question in relation to the three situations of illegitimate lobbying identified in the previous chapter: secret lobbying; lobbying likely to lead to corruption and misconduct; and lobbying involving unfair access and influence.

Secret lobbying

The lobbyists' codes of conduct adopted by the federal and the state governments represent real advances in countering secret lobbying. There is now an unprecedented measure of publicity in relation to the activities of commercial lobbyists such as Burke and Grill. The public nature of the registers of lobbyists also suggests that these codes will be more effective than the code adopted by the Hawke government. However, there are still significant deficiencies. Foremost is the restricted scope of the various codes. For instance, while the preamble to the federal code states in broad terms that '[t]he *Lobbying Code of Conduct* is intended to promote trust in the integrity of government processes and ensure that contact between lobbyists and Government representatives is conducted with public expectations of *transparency, integrity and honesty*' (emphasis added),[43] the fact that its provisions are restricted to commercial lobbyists suggests a much narrower concern. This is suggested by the following comments made in a speech by Special Minister of State, Senator John Faulkner:

> In adopting the Code, the Government recognised that lobbying is a legitimate activity and part of the democratic process. However, there was a concern that Government representatives who were the target of lobbying activities were not always fully informed as to *the identity of the people who had engaged a lobbyist to speak on their behalf.* This information can be fundamental to the integrity of government decisions and should be freely available to those who are lobbied and to the wider public (emphasis added).[44]

From the perspective of countering secret lobbying, the restricted coverage of the various codes is not justifiable. As a general rule,

247

transparency should apply to all lobbyists who may be able to influence policies and laws. This includes commercial lobbyists, in-house lobbyists, staff of trade unions, businesses and NGOs that regularly engage in lobbying, and powerful individuals such as Rupert Murdoch. The exemption granted to the latter groups and individuals provides strong justification for the criticism made by Coalition Senators of the federal code's 'selective application',[45] a criticism that could be equally made of the state codes. There is also more than a grain of truth in their contention that such selective scope could encourage large companies 'to camouflage their political advocacy activities by putting former politicians — who would be exempt — on their boards for lobbying purposes'.[46] One only needs to cast an eye towards the trajectories of former politicians who have become lobbyists — it appears that most provide their lobbying services as employees of companies rather than as commercial lobbyists (see Chapter 8).

In seeking to broaden the scope of the Australian lobbying codes, lobbying regulation in Canada and the United States is a useful guide. The Canadian *Lobbyist Registration Act*[47] covers commercial lobbyists and in-house lobbyists. It extends to in-house lobbyists by requiring corporations and organisations to register under the Act if they employ one or more individuals who communicate with a public office-holder (including parliamentarians and Ministers) as a significant part of their duties.[48] Under the US federal lobbying regulation, paid lobbyists, whether commercial or in-house, are required to register with the Secretary of the Senate and Clerk of the House of Representatives when their lobbying income exceeds US$3000 per quarter or their spending on lobbying activities exceeds US$11,500 per quarter.[49]

There is another possible weakness in the federal and Tasmanian codes: the broad discretion vested in the Cabinet Secretary and the Premier, respectively, both elected officials, to refuse the registration of a lobbyist or to cancel any such registration. There does not seem to be any compelling justification for this discretion, and it is not structured by strict and clear criteria – it should be abolished.

Another limitation of the Australian codes relates to the information that the lobbyists who come within their scope have to disclose. While the codes provide essential information on the identities of the lobbyists and their clients, they do not provide any meaningful information about who is being lobbied and the subject matter of the lobbying. Again, this is in contrast with American and Canadian regulation. Under the US federal regulation, the lobbyist, upon registration, has to provide a statement of the general areas of lobbying. In addition, the lobbyist has to submit a report twice a year that lists the specific subject matter of all lobbying (including the specific executive action and Bill numbers of the legislation that was the subject of lobbying) and the federal agencies that have been contacted.[50] Under the Canadian *Lobbyist Registration Act*, registered lobbyists and corporations and organisations with in-house lobbyists must provide information about themselves, plus the name of each government department lobbied, the source and amount of government funding received, and the subject matters of lobbying (including information on specific policies and Bills).[51] Similar obligations should be added to the Australian codes.

These obligations should also be paralleled by an obligation to publish, at regular intervals, specific information on meetings between lobbyists and government representatives, including the name of the lobbyist/s, dates of contact, meeting attendees and a summary of issues discussed. This has been recommended by a NSW parliamentary committee[52] and the NSW ICAC,[53] as well as by various British committees on standards in public life.[54] In 2009, the British government also committed to publishing the list of ministerial meetings with interest groups online on a quarterly basis.[55]

Further, Ministers should publish a list of all meetings held with lobbyists relating to a Bill when that Bill is tabled. Ministers should also be required to publish the list of such meetings when they

announce government policy and decisions, if there has been lobbying related to such decisions. These disclosure obligations would
be an important counter-check to the information supplied by lobbyists under the codes of conduct and would also provide information crucial to properly debating Bills and government policies.

Lobbying involving corruption and misconduct

The transparency measures recommended above would also have a
beneficial impact on lobbying that leads to corruption and misconduct (by public officials or lobbyists and their clients). There are
other measures that should also be adopted to lessen the risk of such
lobbying. While the corruption-related criminal offences are adequate to capture egregious conduct by public officials, there needs to
be better regulation of conflicts of interest – especially in the areas of
secondary employment and post-separation employment.

It is quite remarkable that the regulation of secondary employment in relation to parliamentarians is virtually nonexistent. At the
very least, parliamentarians should be required to disclose details of
secondary employment that may give rise to a conflict of interest
whenever they are participating in parliamentary proceedings,
whether by way of voting or making a speech. Another 'minimum'
measure is to ban the receipt of income for providing services in
Parliament, such as voting or advocating for a particular legislative
measure in exchange for money, or receiving 'cash for questions'.[56]
As noted in Chapter 3, there is a constitutional prohibition on such
receipts at the federal level and comparable statutory prohibitions in
the ACT and the Northern Territory. Such prohibitions should be
put in place in all jurisdictions.

Indeed, serious consideration should be given to a prohibition on
parliamentarians receiving income that exceeds a certain (modest)
amount from secondary employment. This would prevent possible
conflicts of interest, and constitute recognition that representing
constituents is a duty that demands full-time energy and attention. If

the argument against this (a highly contested one) is that the income of parliamentarians is inadequate, then increase their remuneration. Indirect measures such as allowing secondary employment can only have uneven effects among parliamentarians.

In relation to post-separation employment, it is remarkable that there is so little regulation in relation to parliamentarians. A ban like the one that used to apply to NT parliamentarians should be adopted in all jurisdictions: former parliamentarians would then be prohibited for a year after leaving office from acting as adviser or consultant (including as a lobbyist) to any company or organisation with which they had direct and significant involvement as parliamentarians in their last year in office.[57] In relation to former Ministers and parliamentary secretaries of all Australian governments, more stringent restrictions are appropriate, given the power and responsibilities they have when in office. Specifically, the federal ban is appropriate: former Ministers would then be prohibited for 18 months after leaving that office from acting for any person or entity with which they had official dealings in their last 18 months as a Minister. This prohibition should be supplemented by a general prohibition on employment that gives rise to conflicts of interest. Enacting these prohibitions should be a priority in New South Wales, Western Australia, the ACT and the Northern Territory, where there is currently no ban on post-separation lobbying for these former public officials.

Two matters are worth emphasising in relation to these measures. First, insofar as they rely upon codes of conduct, they will also rely upon effective enforcement of these codes – this was discussed in Chapter 3. Effective enforcement of the restrictions applying to secondary and post-separation employment, in particular, will depend on training and education.[58] Second, restrictions applying to secondary and post-separation employment should not be subject to waiver by current Prime Ministers or Premiers. The danger with such a power is that any indebtedness a current office-holder feels to their predecessors might result in preferential treatment. Such a risk is illustrated by the NSW ban on post-separation employment of former Ministers with companies that had (or have) contractual relationships with the NSW government. These provisions, though adopted when the Greiner government was in power, were waived in relation to Nick Greiner by his successor, John Fahey, thereby allowing Greiner to become a board director of various companies that had contracts with the NSW government.[59]

We have dealt so far with measures that deal with corruption and misconduct by public officials. It remains to discuss corruption and misconduct by lobbyists and their clients. The transparency measures recommended above would go a long way towards preventing such behaviour. In addition, it would be useful to develop codes of conduct for lobbyists that have some 'bite'. One obvious model is that in the *Integrity Act 2009* (Qld). As noted earlier, this Act empowers the Integrity Commissioner to adopt a Lobbyists' Code of Conduct (after consultation with the Commissioner's supervisory parliamentary committee).[60] Breach of this code can be a ground for refusing an application for registration[61] and for cancelling a registration.[62] Another model is that recommended by the Scottish Parliament Standards Committee: that specific principles and obligations governing the conduct of lobbyists should form a code of conduct that is policed by the Ombudsman.[63] The NSW ICAC has expressed agreement with these recommendations and called for them to be adopted in New South Wales.[64] A third model is the Canadian scheme. Under the Canadian *Lobbyist Registration Act*, lobbyists registered under the Act are bound by the Lobbyists' Code of Conduct, which lays down broad standards such as integrity, honesty, openness and professionalism, as well as specific rules relating to disclosure, confidentiality and conflict of interests. A breach of the code may result in an investigation by the Office of Ethics Commissioner.[65]

Lobbying involving unfair access and influence

The problem of lobbying involving unfair access and influence is perhaps the most intractable form of illegitimate lobbying. This is because tackling the sources of unfair access and influence is a formidable task. As explained in the previous chapter, financial power is a key source of such illegitimate lobbying, and that power results from inequalities in wealth and income. Another source is party influence: here power stems from complicated webs of relations within parties. And finally, the reasons for a lobbyist being able to maintain status as an 'insider', and therefore power, are also often a complex combination of knowledge, expertise and resources.

While regulation of lobbying cannot abolish these sources of unfair access and influence, it is not impotent. Transparency measures will deal directly with problems of unfair access and influence stemming from secret lobbying. Post-separation employment restrictions will alleviate the problem of 'insiders' having illegitimate and excessive power by limiting the ability of former Ministers, parliamentary secretaries and senior public servants to become lobbyists. Corruption-related offences will guard against the more egregious effects of unfair access and influence.

Arguably, the most effective measure against unfair access and influence through lobbying is not regulating lobbying, but giving more opportunities to lobby to those who have less resources and power. This first requires inclusive consultation procedures, procedures that are geared to ensuring that individuals and groups, especially the vulnerable and marginalised, have a real voice in the policy process. Faux consultation – consultation that has a pre-determined outcome, or that provides inadequate information or that occurs at too late a stage of policy-making – will not meet this aim.[66] Second, we need measures that ensure that these groups can effectively participate in these consultation processes. This is likely to require public funding (see Chapter 5). Appropriately designed public funding can promote the fair value of the freedom to lobby.

Conclusion

Reflecting on the lobbying conduct of Brian Burke, political scientist John Warhurst has observed: 'Would any regulation of lobbyists stop the activities of individuals like Burke? Probably not.' For Warhurst, 'Burke's case is certainly food for hard thought.'[67]

Warhurst's comments alert us to the limits of regulating lobbying. There are two types of limits: the first are the limits *to* regulating lobbying; the second are the limits *of* regulation. The first kind is a recognition of the fact that many of the vices of lobbying arise from circumstances that go beyond actual lobbying: inequalities in wealth, as already mentioned, and what Lindblom has characterised as the 'privileged position of businesses'.[68] Another development that may be contributing to the problems associated with lobbying is the declining 'health' of political parties, in particular their ability to perform their governance and agenda-setting functions. Former Victorian Premier John Cain has insightfully observed that:

> they [professional lobbyists] [are] filling a vacuum that's been
> left for the reasons that I've been talking about: the change of
> the nature of political parties. They're almost empty vessels in
> many ways, political parties, because they don't do policy work.
> So it leaves for a government, for a party that's in government,
> a very substantial vacuum to be filled by professional lobbyists,
> who know where to tap in to ... the party structure, bureaucratic
> structure and the structure of the private office to have maximum
> effect.[69]

The second kind of limits concerns the ethics of our political culture. Regulations, including those suggested above, are not self-executing and will not be effectively enforced in the absence of an ethical culture. As the WA Corruption and Crime Commission correctly observed, 'Regulations unsupported by cultural and attitudinal change are unlikely to be effective.'[70] Such cultural infrastructure is necessary within government departments and agencies and beyond

– we need a culture of vigilance built upon scrupulous monitoring and scrutiny by political parties, other NGOs, the media and the public.[71]

That kind of culture is probably the first line of defence against corruption, misconduct and unfair conduct by public officials. Regulatory measures such as those recommended above should facilitate the development and maintenance of such a culture, but they are not substitutes for it. Put differently, we will always rely, to some degree, on self-regulation by public decision-makers and lobbyists. The challenge is to establish a framework governing lobbying that is anchored in virtuous self-regulation.

10
TOWARDS A DEMOCRATIC POLITICAL FUNDING REGIME

We end as we began. The truth of Eric Roozendaal's observation that Australia's political funding regime is 'dangerously unsustainable'[1] can now be more fully appreciated. The integrity of representative government is under challenge by the current flows of private and public money. Foremost, there is a lack of transparency associated with private money. When devoted to lobbying, it can sometimes result in covert influences over the political process. When given directly to political parties and candidates, it can be shrouded in secrecy – there are no disclosure schemes at all in some states, and the federal, state and territory and local government disclosure schemes have significant weaknesses.

There is also corruption through undue influence due to the sale of access and influence, a practice fuelled by the increasing demand for campaign funds, which itself stems from the intensifying 'arms races'. Lobbying too can lead to corruption and misconduct. Neither is the provision of public money free from such afflictions – corruption through the misuse of public resources occurs when parliamentary entitlements and government advertising are used for electioneering. Corruption relating to political funding often takes the form of institutional rather than individual corruption; this especially applies to corruption through undue influence, and through the misuse of public resources involving electoral unfairness.

The flow of money into Australian politics also results in various forms of unfairness. The sale of access and influence provides another avenue for the rich to secure a greater influence over the political process because of their wealth. So does paid lobbying. Tax subsidies, which benefit the wealthier sections of society, are another source of unfairness. Private funding in general produces a funding inequality between the major parties and their competitors, a disadvantage that is severely compounded by election funding formulas that discriminate against minor parties and new candidates, and by the access of parliamentarians and parties in government to public resources such as parliamentary entitlements and government advertising which can be used for electioneering. There is also an unfair playing field in elections, with a serious imbalance between the election spending of major parties and that of minor parties, as well as a lack of 'equality of arms' between the major parties (it currently favours the ALP).

The poor health of political parties is both a cause and effect of the corrosive role of political money. With shrinking membership, the major parties turn to both plutocratic financing and more capital-intensive campaigning, developments that contribute to corruption and unfairness. As the agenda-setting ability of parties is hollowed out, the role of lobbyists is likely to become much more central. All this undermines the health of the political parties. Both the reality and the risk of corruption threaten the performance of parties' governance function. Unfairness in politics warps parties' ability to be responsive to the public, and an excessive preoccupation with fundraising diverts them from their functions more generally.

A distinguishing feature of Australia's political finance regime is the premium it places on 'freedom from' state regulation – the law generally allows all sorts of political contributions: from any sources, in any amounts; it also places few limits on political spending. It is the focus on 'freedom from' that characterises this regime as laissez-faire. These formal freedoms have, however, been ill used. The exercise of these freedoms has increased corruption (and the risk of corruption) and unfairness in politics and enervated the political parties, and has come at the cost of 'freedom to', or the fair value of political freedoms. The large amounts that are channelled to political parties are out of the reach of most citizens. As a result, meaningful election campaigns are the preserve of a handful of political parties.

There was nothing inevitable about this. A laissez-faire approach is not an invitation to vice; indeed, it can be an opportunity for virtuous self-regulation. The major parties have, however, failed to live up to this goal. Laissez-faire regulation has been accompanied by laissez-faire attitudes. The crucial issues concerning political funds are skated over, and the raising and use of such money are seen as merely questions of political strategy. Laissez-faire regulation is partly to blame, but so is a political culture that says 'anything goes' when it comes to questions of political money.

In order to protect the integrity of representative government and promote fairness in politics as well as support parties in discharging their functions while respecting political freedoms, there need to be fundamental changes to how money in Australian politics is regulated. The laissez-faire approach should be repudiated – self-regulation of political finance has failed abysmally. More democratic regulation of political funding is urgently required. This book has proposed a series of measures to advance this aim. The reform blueprint set out below collects the various recommendations made in this book.

The present political moment may very well provide the opportunity to make changes such as those recommended by this blueprint. The federal, Queensland and NSW governments have embarked upon a process of reforming their political finance regimes. There is also a growing list of politicians[2] who have publicly expressed grave concern at the role of money in Australian politics, and that list cuts across the political spectrum. Former Opposition Leader Malcolm Turnbull has called for 'root and branch' reform of the political funding regime.[3] Andrew Stoner, the leader of the NSW National Party, has called for 'fundamental reform of political fundraising'.[4] Greens Senator Bob Brown has long been an advocate for change.[5] Another former general secretary of the NSW ALP and current federal Minister for Employment Participation, Mark Arbib, has echoed Roozendaal's sentiments by calling for broad-ranging reform so as to 'ensure the integrity of Australia's political system'.[6]

There is, however, no guarantee that this opportunity for democratic reform will be seized. Standing in the way of any change are two groups. There are defenders of the status quo who would do nothing, including those in the political elite who believe that the current system benefits them and those, such as Victorian Premier John Brumby, who openly defend it based on a self-serving view of 'democracy'. There are also doubters of any change who would do very little or nothing, including some who would seize upon constitutional complications to present a supposedly conclusive argument against change and those who worry excessively about the 'unworkability' of any proposed regulation. There is also a grave risk of wrong turns. Those who adopt a 'scorched earth' approach, for instance, by proposing a complete ban on private funding of politics in favour of complete public funding, pay insufficient attention to the virtues and vices of both public and private funding (and may, in fact, be concealing a self-interested pursuit by the major parties of a stable funding base). There are also those who rely upon a (falsely) appealing notion of equality by calling for contribution limits that pay little regard to the special role of membership fees (including trade union affiliation fees). Finally, there are those who wrongly see contribution limits as the key to genuine reform; in fact it would do very little to address the key source of many of the dangers that money poses to Australian politics – the demand for campaign funds.

There is truth, but only partial truth, in all these positions. More often than not, they result from important principles being given simplistic applications, one principle being given inordinate weight at the expense of others, genuine issues in implementation being given exaggerated importance, and real challenges to the integrity of Australian politics being dealt with in a 'knee-jerk' way. But sorting out the wheat from the chaff leaves us with real hope for a more democratic political funding regime.

A reform blueprint

DISCLOSURE OF PRIVATE FUNDING (CHAPTER 2)

The Commonwealth Electoral Amendment (Political Donations and Other Measures) Bill 2009 (Cth), which introduces a biannual system of disclosure for registered parties, associated entities, donors and third parties based on a $1000 disclosure threshold, should be enacted, subject to the following changes:

- 'due diligence' defences should be available in relation to offences; and
- the definition of 'political expenditure' (which applies to third parties) should be tightened up.

Registered political parties and associated entities should be required to provide:

- expenditure disclosure returns; and
- donation reports (modelled on the British system).

Weekly donation reports should be required during the election period (beginning on the day the election is called and ending at the close of ballot).

Equivalent measures should be adopted in all states and territories.

OTHER REGULATION OF PRIVATE FUNDING (CHAPTER 4)

Bans should be imposed on political contributions from persons or companies with contracts with the federal, state or territory governments.

Parliamentary and ministerial codes of conduct should be adopted in all jurisdictions and strengthened in the following ways:

- conflict of interest provisions should be extended to both personal gifts and party funding;
- records of meetings between parliamentarians and Ministers with party contributors should be kept;
- Ministers, Shadow Ministers and parliamentarians should be banned from attending party fundraisers; and
- consideration should be given to independent enforcement of these codes (as in New South Wales).

Limits on contributions from individuals and organisations should be adopted in all jurisdictions subject to the following:

- such limits should be adopted as part of a broader package of reform which includes increased public funding and election spending limits; and
- these limits should provide for an exemption for membership fees (including affiliation fees from organisational members).

Companies and trade unions should be required to seek specific authorisation from their shareholders and members respectively every 3 years before making political contributions.

ELECTION FUNDING, TAX SUBSIDIES AND PARLIAMENTARY ENTITLEMENTS (CHAPTER 5)

Party and Candidate Support Funds should be established in all jurisdictions with the following three components:

- election funding payments with a low threshold and calculated according to a tapered scheme;
- annual allowances calculated according to the number of votes and party members; and

- policy development grants.

The Tax Laws Amendment (2008 Measures No. 1) Bill 2008 (Cth) should be enacted in order to abolish tax subsidies to political parties and candidates.

The rules governing parliamentary entitlements should:
- be made accessible and transparent; and
- clearly limit the use of such entitlements to the discharge of parliamentary duties and thus prevent their use for electioneering.

The amount of parliamentary entitlements should not be such as to confer an unfair electoral advantage on parliamentarians.

GOVERNMENT ADVERTISING (CHAPTER 6)

The outcomes budgeting framework should be tightened up in all jurisdictions.

The recommendations of the Senate Finance and Public Administration Committee in relation to the disclosure of information concerning government advertising should be adopted in all jurisdictions.

Guidelines governing government advertising should effectively provide for the following principles:
- material should be relevant to government responsibilities;
- material should be presented in an objective, fair and accessible manner; and
- material should not be directed at promoting party-political interests.

REGULATION OF ELECTION SPENDING (CHAPTER 7)

Election spending limits should be adopted in all jurisdictions, and should:
- apply for 6 months before polling day;
- apply in relation to 'electoral expenditure' (as defined by electoral statutes);
- apply separately at federal, state and constituency levels; and

- apply to political parties, their 'associated entities', candidates and third parties.

REGULATION OF LOBBYING (CHAPTERS 8 AND 9)

The current lobbyists' codes of conduct should be strengthened so that they:

- extend to all lobbyists and are not restricted to commercial lobbyists; and
- require further information to be disclosed relating to lobbying activities.

Records should be kept of meetings held between lobbyists and Ministers, parliamentary secretaries and senior public servants.

Specific information on the meetings between lobbyists and government representatives, including the name of the lobbyist/s, dates of contact, meeting attendees and a summary of issues discussed should be published at regular intervals.

Ministers should publish the list of meetings held with lobbyists:

- relating to a specific Bill when tabling the Bill; and
- when announcing government policy and decisions when lobbying relates to such actions.

Consideration should be given to banning secondary employment by parliamentarians.

A post-separation employment ban applying to former parliamentarians should be adopted prohibiting them, for 1 year after leaving public office, from being engaged to lobby on matters they had a significant dealing with in their last year in office.

In all jurisdictions, a post-separation employment ban that prohibits former Ministers and parliamentary secretaries, for 18 months after leaving those positions, from being engaged to lobby on matters they had a significant dealing with in their last 18 months in those positions, should be adopted.

NOTES

Preface

1   New South Wales, Legislative Council (2004) *Parliamentary Debates*, Eric
    Roozendaal, 21 September, 11117, viewed 28 January 2008: <http://www.
    parliament.nsw.gov.au/prod/parlment/members.nsf/0/d9ccd231bed39458ca256
    ebe0004b5ab/$FILE/Roozendaal.pdf>.

Chapter 1

1   See David Adamany & George Agree (1975) *Political Money: A Strategy for
    Campaign Financing in America*, Johns Hopkins University Press, Baltimore, 2–4.
2   Despite its self-image, Australia fares badly in terms of income inequality:
    see Rodney Tiffen & Ross Gittins (2009, 2nd edn) *How Australia Compares*,
    Cambridge University Press, Cambridge, 136–37.
3   Senator Andrew Murray & Marilyn Rock (2000) The Dangerous Art of Giving,
    Australian Quarterly, 72(3): 29.
4   See David Held (2006) *Models of Democracy*, Polity, Cambridge.
5   See, generally, K.D. Ewing (2007) *The Cost of Democracy: Party Funding in
    Modern British Politics,* Hart Publishing, Oxford, Ch. 2.
6   Royal Commission (Chair: G.A. Kennedy) (1992) *Report on WA Inc.: Part II*,
    1–10.
7   Hanna Fenichel Pitkin (1967) *The Concept of Representation*, University of
    California Press, Berkeley, 233.
8   Ibid., 234.
9   *Australian Capital Television Pty Ltd v Commonwealth* (1992) 177 CLR 106, 138
    (*ACTV*).

10 Dennis Thompson (1995) *Ethics in Congress: From Individual to Institutional Corruption*, Brookings Institution, Washington DC, 70–71.

11 Some of these disagreements stem from the complex character of political representation. See Pitkin, *The Concept of Representation*, Ch. 10. Speaking of the American context, for instance, Thompson has spoken of '[the] classic tension in representative government … [t]he dual nature of Congress – as an assembly of local representatives and as a lawmaking institution': Thompson, *Ethics in Congress*, 69.

12 Thompson, *Ethics in Congress*, 20.

13 As the following discussion indicates, there are various shades and meanings of corruption: see, for example, Editors (1989) Introduction, in Arnold J. Heidenheimer, Michael Johnston & Victor T. LeVine (eds) *Political Corruption: A Handbook*, Transaction Publishers, New Brunswick, 3, 7–13; Syed Hussein Alatas (1990) *Corruption: Its Nature, Causes and Functions*, Aldershot, Hants, 1–5; Oskar Kurer (2005) Corruption: An Alternative Approach to its Definition and Assessment, *Political Studies*, 53: 222.

14 Joint Standing Committee on Electoral Matters (1994) *Interim Report on the Inquiry into the Conduct of the 1993 Election and Matters Related Thereto: Financial Reporting by Political Parties*, para 7.

15 Commonwealth, House of Representatives (1983) *Parliamentary Debates,* Kim Beazley, Minister for Aviation, Special Minister of State and Minister Assisting the Minister for Defence, 2nd Reading Speech to Commonwealth Electoral Legislation Amendment Bill 1983, 2 November, 2215. For similar sentiments, see Electoral and Administrative Review Commission (1992) *Report on Public Registration of Political Donations, Public Funding of Election Campaigns and Related Issues*, para 2.5.

16 Thompson, *Ethics in Congress*, 7.

17 Michael McKenna & Sarah Elks (2009) 'Corrupt ex-minister Gordon Nuttall in jail facing extra charges', *The Australian*, 16 July, viewed 1 December 2009: <http://www.theaustralian.com.au/news/corrupt-ex-minister-gordon-nuttal-in-jail-facing-extra-charges/story-0-1225750676560>.

18 See Charles Beitz (1984) Political Finance in the United States: A Survey of Research, *Ethics*, 95(1): 129, 137; Burke (1997) The Concept of Corruption in Campaign Finance Law, *Constitutional Commentary*, 14: 127; Thompson, *Ethics in Congress*, 55.

19 Daniel Lowenstein (1989) On Campaign Finance Reform: The Root of All Evil is Deeply Rooted, *Hofstra Law Review*, 18: 301, 323–29.

20 Beitz, Political Finance in the United States, 129, 137; Burke, The Concept of Corruption in Campaign Finance Law, 127; Thompson, *Ethics in Congress*, 55.

21 Committee of Inquiry Concerning Public Duty and Private Interest (Chair: N.H. Bowen) (1978) *Public Duty and Private Interest*, 14.

22 See Yasmin Dawood (2006) Democracy, Power, and the Supreme Court: Campaign Finance Reform in Comparative Context, *International Journal of Constitutional Law*, 4(2): 269, 280–81.

23 Commonwealth, House of Representatives (1991) *Parliamentary Debates*, Kim Beazley, Minister for Transport and Communications, 2nd Reading Speech to Political Broadcasts and Political Disclosures Bill 1991, 9 May, 3477.

24 Ibid., 3482. For similar sentiments, see Commonwealth, House of Representatives (1983) *Parliamentary Debates*, Kim Beazley, 2nd Reading Speech to Commonwealth Electoral Legislation Amendment Bill 1983, 2213–15.
25 See Thompson, *Ethics in Congress*, 28.
26 Ibid., 103–8.
27 Ibid., 7.
28 Ibid., 25.
29 Ibid., 7.
30 Committee of Inquiry Concerning Public Duty and Private Interest, *Public Duty and Private Interest*, 11. See also Thompson, *Ethics in Congress*, 32.
31 Thompson, *Ethics in Congress,* 124.
32 Queensland Integrity Commissioner (2008) *Annual Report 2007–08*, 8.
33 Thompson, *Ethics in Congress*, 124.
34 Ibid., 124.
35 John Rawls [1972](1999) *A Theory of Justice*, Oxford University Press, Oxford, 225; John Rawls (ed. Erin Kelly) (2001) *Justice as Fairness: A Restatement*, Harvard University Press, Cambridge MA, 149. Carmen Lawrence has noted that '[d]espite the otherwise general equality in voting power, many are suspicious that not all citizens are equally able to influence their representatives': Carmen Lawrence (2000) Renewing Democracy: Can Women Make a Difference?, *The Sydney Papers*, 12(4): 54, 58.
36 Rawls, *Justice as Fairness: A Restatement*, 46.
37 Ronald Dworkin (1990) Equality, Democracy, and Constitution: We the People in Court, *Alberta Law Review*, 28(2): 324, 338.
38 Norman Daniels (1975) Equal Liberty and Unequal Worth of Liberty, in Norman Daniels (ed.) *Reading Rawls: Critical Studies on Rawls' A Theory of Justice*, Basil Blackwell, Oxford, 253–81.
39 Rawls, *Justice as Fairness: A Restatement*, 137.
40 See ibid., 149.
41 See Charles Beitz (1989) *Political Equality: An Essay in Democratic Theory*, Princeton University Press, Princeton NJ.
42 Rawls, *Justice as Fairness: A Restatement*, 150.
43 See Amy Gutmann & Dennis Thompson (2004) *Why Deliberative Democracy?*, Princeton University Press, Princeton NJ, 4–5. For a fuller discussion of the purposes of democratic deliberation, see Gutmann & Thompson, *Why Deliberative Democracy?*, 10–13 and Amy Gutmann & Dennis Thompson (1996) *Democracy and Disagreement*, Belknap Press, Cambridge MA, 41–44.
44 Beitz, *Political Equality*, 98.
45 Commonwealth, Senate (1902) *Parliamentary Debates*, Senator O'Connor, 2nd Reading Speech introducing Commonwealth Electoral Bill 1902, 30 January, 9529.
46 Harrison Moore (1902, 1st edn) *The Constitution of the Commonwealth of Australia*, John Murray, London, 329. This statement was cited with approval in *ACTV* (1992) 177 CLR 106, 139–40 (Mason CJ).
47 See discussion in Beitz, *Political Equality*, 12–14, 15–16.
48 Royal Commission, *Report on WA Inc.: Part II*, paras 1–10. See also Corruption and Crime Commission of Western Australia (2007) *Report on the Investigation of*

Alleged Public Sector Misconduct Linked to the Smiths Beach Development at Yallingup, 90.

49 The notion being emphasised here is of fair competition, not competition per se. A competitive system, even a highly competitive one, is not necessarily fair: Beitz, *Political Equality*, 200–1.

50 T.H. Marshall (1964) Citizenship and Social Class, in T.H. Marshall, *Class, Citizenship and Social Development*, Doubleday, Garden City NY, 65, 90.

51 Commonwealth, Senate (1902) *Parliamentary Debates*, Senator O'Connor, 2nd Reading Speech to Commonwealth Electoral Bill 1902, 9542.

52 Rawls, *A Theory of Justice*, 198.

53 Commonwealth, House of Representatives (1983) *Parliamentary Debates*, Kim Beazley, 2nd Reading Speech to Commonwealth Electoral Legislation Amendment Bill 1983, 2215. This specific aim is long-standing.

54 Keith Ewing (1987) *The Funding of Political Parties in Britain*, Cambridge University Press, Cambridge, 182.

55 Commonwealth, House of Representatives (1983) *Parliamentary Debates*, Kim Beazley, 2nd Reading Speech to Commonwealth Electoral Legislation Amendment Bill 1983, 2213.

56 Keith Ewing (1992) *Money, Politics and Law: A Study of Electoral Finance Reform in Canada*, Clarendon Press, Oxford, 18.

57 For this distinction, see Ian Marsh (1995) *Beyond the Two Party System: Political Representation, Economic Competitiveness and Australian Politics*, Cambridge University Press, Cambridge, 35–43.

58 Dean Jaensch (1994) *Power Politics: Australia's Party System*, Allen & Unwin, Sydney, 1–2.

59 Elmer E. Schattschneider (1942) *Party Government*, Holt, Rinehart & Winston, New York, 1. On the connection between different types of parties and democracy, see Gerald Pomper (1992) Concept of Political Parties, *Journal of Theoretical Politics*, 4(2): 143.

60 Giovanni Sartori (1976) *Parties and Party Systems: A Framework for Analysis: Volume 1*, Cambridge University Press, Cambridge, 28.

61 Ibid., ix.

62 In terms of freedom of *political* expression, the rationale based on democratic participation is the most pertinent and compelling. See Eric Barendt (2005) *Freedom of Speech*, Oxford University Press, New York, vi, 18–19. See also Tom Campbell (1994) Rationales for Freedom of Communication, in Tom Campbell & Wojciech Sadurski (eds) *Freedom of Communication*, Dartmouth, England, 17, 37–41.

63 See Beitz, *Political Equality*, 209–13.

64 See Stanley Ingber (1984) The Marketplace of Ideas: A Legitimizing Myth, *Duke Law Journal*, 1: 1.

65 This metaphor is famously used by Alexander Meiklejohn: Alexander Meiklejohn (1948) *Free Speech and its Relation to Self-Government*, Harper & Brothers, New York.

66 The connection between political finance and democratic deliberation is powerfully made by Gutmann and Thompson: Gutmann & Thompson, *Democracy and Disagreement*, 134; Gutmann & Thompson, *Why Deliberative*

Democracy, 48–49. See also Ian Shapiro (1999) Enough of Deliberation: Politics is about Interests and Power, in Stephen Macedo (ed.) *Deliberative Politics: Essays on Democracy and Disagreement*, Oxford University Press, New York, 28, 34–36.

67   Owen Fiss (1996) *The Irony of Free Speech*, Harvard University Press, Cambridge MA, 2.

68   Ibid., 4.

69   Ibid., 15. See also Beitz, Political Finance in the United States, 209–13.

70   Amy Gutmann (1998) Freedom of Association: An Introductory Essay, in Amy Gutmann (ed.) *Freedom of Association*, Princeton University Press, Princeton NJ, 3.

71   For a general argument that freedom of association is based on the idea of popular sovereignty, see Jason Mazzone (2002) Freedom's Associations, *Washington Law Review*, 77: 639.

72   See, generally, Howard Davis (2000) *Political Freedom: Associations, Political Purpose and the Law*, Continuum, London, 47.

73   For a rejection of a rights-based approach to freedom of party association and a preference for a functional analysis, see Samuel Issacharoff (2001) Private Parties with Public Purposes: Political Parties, Associational Freedoms, and Partisan Competition, *Columbia Law Review*, 101(2): 274.

74   Davis, *Political Freedom*, 45.

75   Beitz, *Political Equality*, 191.

76   The last point threads through Nathaniel Persily's argument for non-interference in the primary elections of American political parties. See Nathaniel Persily (2001) Toward a Functional Defense of Political Party Autonomy, *New York University Law Review*, 76: 751.

77   Hindess, Deficit by Design, *Australian Journal of Public Administration*, 61(1): 33.

78   Senator John Faulkner (2008) Transparency and Accountability, address, 30 October, viewed 16 December 2008: <http://www.smos.gov.au/speeches/2008/sp_20081030.html>.

79   *ACTV* (1992) 177 CLR 106.

80   Graeme Orr (2006) Political Finance Law in Australia, in K.D. Ewing & Samuel Issacharoff (eds) *Party Funding and Campaign Financing in International Perspective*, Hart Publishing, Portland OR, 99, 100.

81   K.D. Ewing & Samuel Issacharoff (2006) Introduction, in ibid., 1, 6–7.

82   See Graeme Orr (2000) The Law Comes to the Party: The Continuing Juridification of Australian Political Parties, *Constitutional Law and Policy Review*, 3: 41.

Chapter 2

1   *Electoral Act 1992* (Qld) Sch 'Election Funding and Financial Disclosure Based on Part XX of the Commonwealth Electoral Act', Div 4A, Subdiv A.

2   *Election Funding and Disclosures Act 1981* (NSW) ss 96GA–96GE.

3   *Electoral Act 2002* (Vic) ss 216–17.

4   *Electoral Act 1992* (Qld) Sch 'Election Funding and Financial Disclosure Based on Part XX of the Commonwealth Electoral Act', s 287; *Electoral Act 1907* (WA) s 175; *Electoral Act 1992* (ACT) s 198; *Electoral Act 2004* (NT) s 176.

5   *Commonwealth Electoral Act 1918* (Cth) s 287.

6   *Commonwealth Electoral Act 1918* (Cth) s 308; *Electoral Act 1992* (Qld) Sch 'Election Funding and Financial Disclosure Based on Part XX of the Commonwealth Electoral Act', s 308; *Electoral Act 2002* (Vic) s 206; *Electoral Act 1907* (WA) s 175; *Electoral Act 1992* (ACT) s 223; *Electoral Act 2004* (NT) s 199. The NSW definition of 'electoral expenditure' and the Tasmanian definition of 'election expenditure' are different from the definition commonly adopted under other schemes; see, respectively, *Election and Funding Disclosures Act 1981* (NSW) s 87 and *Electoral Act 2004* (Tas) s 5.

7   *Commonwealth Electoral Act 1918* (Cth) s 287; *Election Funding and Disclosure Act 1981* (NSW) s 84; *Electoral Act 1992* (Qld) Sch 'Election Funding and Financial Disclosure Based on Part XX of the Commonwealth Electoral Act', s 287; *Electoral Act 1907* (WA) s 175; *Electoral Act 1992* (ACT) s 198; *Electoral Act 2004* (NT) s 176.

8   There is a rather compelling view that the selling of political access, even when involving substantial fees, may not involve 'gifts', because access to and influence on political power is consideration for the fees: see Australian Electoral Commission (AEC) (2000) *Submission to the Joint Standing Committee on Electoral Matters Inquiry into Electoral Funding and Disclosure*, paras 8.2–8.4, viewed 21 January 2010: <http://www.aph.gov.au/house/committee/em/f_d/subseven. pdf>.

9   *Commonwealth Electoral Act 1918* (Cth) ss 314AB–AC.

10 *Commonwealth Electoral Act 1918* (Cth) s 314AEA.

11 *Commonwealth Electoral Act 1918* (Cth) ss 314AC, 314AE, 314AEA(5), 321A.

12 *Commonwealth Electoral Act 1918* (Cth) s 305B.

13 *Commonwealth Electoral Act 1918* (Cth) s 314AEB.

14 *Commonwealth Electoral Act 1918* (Cth) s 314AEC.

15 *Commonwealth Electoral Act 1918* (Cth) s 304.

16 *Commonwealth Electoral Act 1918* (Cth) s 309.

17 *Commonwealth Electoral Act 1918* (Cth) s 305A.

18 *Electoral Act 2002* (Vic) s 222.

19 *Electoral Act 2004* (NT) ss 195, 207, 209.

20 *Electoral Act 1907* (WA) ss 175N(5), 175NA(3)(c).

21 *Electoral Amendment Act 2008* (Qld).

22 *Election Funding Amendment (Political Donations and Expenditure) Act 2008* (NSW).

23 *Electoral Amendment Act 2008* (Qld).

24 *Election Funding Amendment (Political Donations and Expenditure) Act 2008* (NSW).

25 This section draws from Joo-Cheong Tham & Graeme Orr (2005) *Submission to the Joint Standing Committee on Electoral Matters' Inquiry into the 2004 Federal Election*, viewed 21 January 2010: <http://www.aph.gov.au/House/committee/ em/elect04/subs/sub160.pdf>.

26 AEC, *Submission to the Joint Standing Committee on Electoral Matters Inquiry into Electoral Funding and Disclosure*, para 2.10, viewed 21 January 2010: <http:// www.aph.gov.au/house/committee/em/f_d/subseven.pdf>.

27 Donor return lodged by Lord Michael Ashcroft, viewed 30 May 2007: <http://fadar.aec.gov.au/>.

28 Similar criticisms have been made by Ian Ramsay, Geof Stapledon & Joel Vernon (2001) *Political Donations by Australian Companies*, Melbourne University Research Report; Ramsay et al. (2001) Political Donations by Australian Companies, *Federal Law Review*, 29(1): 177.

29 See, generally, Colin Hughes & Brian Costar (2006) *Limiting Democracy: The Erosion of Electoral Rights in Australia*, UNSW Press, Sydney, Ch. 3.

30 Sarah Miskin & Greg Barber (2006) *Political Finance Disclosure under Current and Proposed Thresholds: Parliamentary Library Research Note No. 27/ 2006*.

31 Joint Standing Committee on Electoral Matters (2008) *Advisory Report on the Commonwealth Electoral Amendment (Political Donations and Other Measures) Bill 2008*, 33.

32 Richard Baker (2006) 'Are our politicians for sale?', *The Age*, 24 May, 15.

33 Graeme Orr (2007) Political Disclosure Regulation in Australia: Lackadaisical Law, *Election Law Journal*, 6(1): 5.

34 AEC, *Submission to the Joint Standing Committee on Electoral Matters Inquiry into Electoral Funding and Disclosure*, para 2.9.

35 AEC (2000) *Funding and Disclosure Report Following the Federal Election Held on 3 October 1998*, para 2.

36 See ibid., 15.

37 Letter from Tim Gartrell, national secretary, ALP, dated 8 November 2005.

38 Josh Gordon (2010) 'MPs pay as donations dry up', *The Age*, 7 February, viewed 8 February 2010. <http://www.theage.com.au/national/mps-pay-as-donations-dry-up-20100206-njxg.html>.

39 The Australian Greens, *Donations to the Australian Greens*, viewed 15 December 2009: <http://greens.org.au/donations_policy>.

40 *Democracy4sale*, viewed 2 February 2010: <http://www.democracy4sale.org>.

41 See comments by Graeme Orr (2003) The Currency of Democracy: Campaign Finance Law in Australia, *University of New South Wales Law Journal*, 26(1): 25–26.

42 *Local Government (Elections) Act 1999* (SA) s 80(1); *Local Government Act 1989* (Vic) s 62(1); *Local Government (Elections) Regulations 1997* (WA) reg 30B.

43 *Local Government (Elections) Act 1999* (SA) s 80(1); *Local Government Act 1989* (Vic) s 62(1).

44 *Local Government (Elections) Regulations 1997* (WA) regs 30C, 30D(2).

45 *Local Government (Elections) Act 1999* (SA) s 87; *Local Government Act 1989* (Vic) s 62A(3); *Local Government (Elections) Regulations 1997* (WA) reg 30H.

46 *Local Government Act 1993* (Qld) Ch 5, Pt 8, Div 3.

47 *Local Government Act 1993* (Tas) s 279.

48 *Election Funding and Disclosures Act 1981* (NSW) Pt 6.

49 Queensland Crime and Misconduct Commission (Queensland CMC) (2006) *Independence, Influence and Integrity in Local Government: A CMC Inquiry into the 2004 Gold Coast City Council Election*, iv.

50 Ibid., iii.

51 Ibid., v.

52 Ibid., ii.

53 Ibid., ii.

54 Details of the amount of funds set out in Merv Whelan, Inspector of Municipal Administration (2006) *Report on Investigation into Greater Geelong City Council*, 13–14.

55 Ibid., 10.

56 Ibid., 11.

57 Ibid., 15–16.

58 Royce Millar (2007) 'Geelong Mayor may face charges over planning', *The Age*, 16 February, viewed 3 June 2008: <http://www.theage.com.au/news/national/geelong-mayor-may-face-charges/2007/02/15/1171405370980.html?page=fullpage>.

59 Peter Begg (2008) 'Saunderson plans to stand for re-election', *The Geelong Advertiser*, 26 May, viewed 6 June 2008: <http://www.geelongadvertiser.com.au/article/2008/05/26/14332_news_pf.html>.

60 See *Geelong City Council*, viewed 20 November 2009: <http://www.geelongcity.vic.gov.au/council/councillor/item/DavidSaunderson.aspx>.

61 The six elected candidates were Tony Ansett, Lou Brazier, Bruce Harwood, Peter McMullin, Tom O'Connor and David Saunderson. There were 12 members of the council in total: see *Geelong City Council*, viewed 3 June 2008: <http://www.geelongcity.vic.gov.au/Accessing_Council/Councillors_and_Wards/>.

62 Quoted in Liz Minchin & Royce Millar (2006) 'King Cat: The millionaire who helps shape Geelong', *The Age*, 28 January, viewed 6 June 2008: <http://www.theage.com.au/news/national/king-cat-the-millionaire-who-helps-shape-geelong/2006/01/27/1138319450839.html?page=2#>.

63 Quoted in Minchin & Millar, 'King Cat: The millionaire who helps shape Geelong'.

64 Quoted in Queensland CMC, *Independence, Influence and Integrity in Local Government*, v.

65 Commonwealth Government (2008) *Electoral Reform Green Paper: Donations, Funding and Expenditure*, 50–56.

66 *Electoral Act 1992* (Qld), Sch 'Election Funding and financial disclosure based on part XX of the Commonwealth Electoral Act', Div 4A, Subdiv A.

67 The original Bill was the Commonwealth Electoral Amendment (Political Donations and Other Measures) Bill 2008 (Cth). This Bill was amended to take into account two of the recommendations made by the Joint Standing Committee on Electoral Matters, *Advisory Report on the Commonwealth Electoral Amendment (Political Donations and Other Measures) Bill 2008*.

68 It is unlikely that the Bill will be passed in this parliamentary term given the opposition by the Coalition parties. See Joint Standing Committee on Electoral Matters, *Advisory Report on the Commonwealth Electoral Amendment (Political Donations and Other Measures) Bill 2008*, 79–81 (Dissenting Report).

69 Commonwealth Electoral Amendment (Political Donations and Other Measures) Bill 2009 (Cth) proposed amendments to the *Commonwealth Electoral Act 1918* (Cth) ss 303A–305B, 314AA–314AEC.

70 Commonwealth Electoral Amendment (Political Donations and Other Measures) Bill 2009 (Cth) proposed amendments to the *Commonwealth Electoral Act 1918* (Cth) s 4(1).

71 Commonwealth Electoral Amendment (Political Donations and Other Measures) Bill 2009 (Cth) proposed amendments to the *Commonwealth Electoral Act 1918* (Cth) ss 304(2)–(3), 305A(3), 305B(1), 309(2)–(3), 314AB(1), 314AEA(1), 314AEB(3)(a), 314AEC(3)(a), 315(1)–(4). For details, see Joint Standing Committee on Electoral Matters, *Advisory Report on the Commonwealth Electoral Amendment (Political Donations and Other Measures) Bill 2008*, 66–70.

72 Commonwealth Electoral Amendment (Political Donations and Other Measures) Bill 2009 (Cth) proposed amendments to the *Commonwealth Electoral Act 1918* (Cth) s 306AC.

73 Commonwealth Electoral Amendment (Political Donations and Other Measures) Bill 2009 (Cth) proposed amendments to the *Commonwealth Electoral Act 1918* (Cth) s 306AC.

74 Commonwealth Electoral Amendment (Political Donations and Other Measures) Bill 2009 (Cth) proposed amendments to the *Commonwealth Electoral Act 1918* (Cth) ss 306AD(1)–(2).

75 See definition of 'permitted anonymous gift': Commonwealth Electoral Amendment (Political Donations and Other Measures) Bill 2009 (Cth) proposed amendments to the *Commonwealth Electoral Act 1918* (Cth) s 306AF. This exception is an adoption of a recommendation made in the Joint Standing Committee on Electoral Matters, *Advisory Report on the Commonwealth Electoral Amendment (Political Donations and Other Measures) Bill 2008*, 64.

76 Commonwealth Electoral Amendment (Political Donations and Other Measures) Bill 2009 (Cth) proposed amendments to the *Commonwealth Electoral Act 1918* (Cth) s 306AH.

77 Commonwealth Electoral Amendment (Political Donations and Other Measures) Bill 2009 (Cth) proposed amendments to the *Commonwealth Electoral Act 1918* (Cth) s 306AH.

78 Commonwealth Electoral Amendment (Political Donations and Other Measures) Bill 2009 (Cth) proposed amendments to the *Commonwealth Electoral Act 1918* (Cth) s 306AD(3).

79 Commonwealth Electoral Amendment (Political Donations and Other Measures) Bill 2009 (Cth) proposed amendments to the *Commonwealth Electoral Act 1918* (Cth) s 306AJ.

80 Commonwealth Electoral Amendment (Political Donations and Other Measures) Bill 2009 (Cth) proposed amendments to the *Commonwealth Electoral Act 1918* (Cth) s 315.

81 *Political Parties, Elections and Referendums Act 2000* (UK) Sch 6.

82 *Political Parties, Elections and Referendums Act 2000* (UK) ss 62–63.

83 Democratic Audit of Australia (2008) *Submission to the Joint Standing Committee on Electoral Matters' Inquiry into the Commonwealth Electoral Amendment (Political Donations and Other Measures) Bill 2008 (Cth)*, viewed 23 November 2009: <http://www.aph.gov.au/house/committee/em/taxlawbill%202/subs/sub01.pdf>; *New York Campaign Finance Board*, viewed 23 November 2009: <http://www.nyccfb.info/>.

84 See Commonwealth Electoral Amendment (Political Donations and Other Measures) Bill 2009 (Cth) proposed amendments to the *Commonwealth Electoral Act 1918* (Cth) s 315.

85 *Commonwealth Electoral Act 1918* (Cth) s 314AEB(1)(a)(ii).

86 Andrew Norton (2009) Diminishing Democracy: The Threat Posed by Political Expenditure Laws, *The Centre for Independent Studies: Issues Analysis*, no. 114, 7, viewed 23 November 2009: <http://www.cis.org.au/issue_analysis/IA114/IA114.pdf>.

87 Ibid., 9.

88 See Jeffrey Carlson & Marcin Walecki (2006) *Money and Politics Program: Guide to Applying Lessons Learned*, 11, viewed 15 December 2009: <http://www.moneyandpolitics.net/researchpubs/pdf/MAP_Guide_to_Applying_Lessons_Learned.pdf>.

89 '[T]he ethical significance of the media as the fourth estate in democratic societies' in assessing the ethics of political conduct has been noted: Editors (1998) Introduction, in Noel Preston & Charles Sampford with C-A. Bois (eds) *Ethics and Political Practice: Perspectives on Legislative Ethics*, Federation Press, Sydney, 2.

90 Sally Young (2011, forthcoming) Disclosure, Accountability and the Role of the Media, in Joo-Cheong Tham, Brian Costar & Graeme Orr (eds) *Electoral Regulation and Prospects for Australian Democracy*, Melbourne University Press, Melbourne.

91 Tiffen has observed that 'The cumulative, unintended effect of the political and media emphasis on scandals is almost certainly a long-term decline in respect for politicians, for the political system and the media': Rodney Tiffen (1999) *Scandals: Media, Politics & Corruption in Contemporary Australia*, UNSW Press, Sydney, 252.

Chapter 3

1 Joo-Cheong Tham & David Grove (2004) Public Funding and Expenditure Regulation of Australian Political Parties, *Federal Law Review*, 32(3): 397, 401.

2 Australian Government (2008) *Electoral Reform Green Paper: Donations, Funding and Expenditure*, 12.

3 AEC (2010) *Election Funding and Disclosure Report: Federal Election 2007*, 15.

4 Australian Bureau of Statistics (ABS) (August 2009) *Average Weekly Earnings, Australia: Catalogue 6302.0*, viewed 25 November 2009: <http://www.abs.gov.au/ausstats/abs@.nsf/mf/6302.0>.

5 Dean Jaensch, Peter Brent & Brett Bowden (2004) *Australian Political Parties in the Spotlight: Democratic Audit of Australia Report No. 4*, 29.

6 Tham & Grove, Public Funding and Expenditure Regulation, 402.

7 See Senate Standing Committee on Economics (2008) *Disclosure Regimes for Charities and Not-for-Profit Organisations*, viewed 26 January 2008: <http://www.aph.gov.au/senate/committee/economics_ctte/charities_08/report/>, para 7.5.

8 Richard Baker (2009) 'Rich mates fill Turnbull poll coffers', *The Age*, 15 July, 1.

9 In fact, empirical study of Australian political contributions is *generally* at an incipient stage.

10 Iain McMenamin (2008) Business, Politics and Money in Australia: Testing Economic, Political and Ideological Explanations, *Australian Journal of Political Science*, 43(3): 377, 381.

11   Ibid., 382.
12   Ian Ramsay, Geof Stapledon & Joel Vernon (2001) Political Donations by
     Australian Companies, *Federal Law Review*, 29(2): 201.
13   Ibid., 204.
14   McMenamin, Business, Politics and Money in Australia, 391.
15   Ramsay, Stapledon & Vernon, Political Donations by Australian Companies,
     201–2.
16   AEC Annual Returns for 2005–06, available from AEC website, viewed
     5 February 2010: <http://periodicdisclosures.aec.gov.au/>.
17   Nicholas Harrigan (2007) Political Partisanship and Corporate Political
     Donations in Australia, viewed 11 April 2008: <http://www.mysmu.edu/
     faculty/nharrigan/2007,%20Partisanship.doc>.
18   The disparity between the total of itemised amounts and total receipts is quite
     significant. The amounts itemised for the 2006–07 and 2007–08 financial
     years were respectively 57.49 per cent and 75.78 per cent of the total funding
     (calculated from Annual Returns to the AEC 2006–07 to 2007–08). This
     disparity might not mean significant understatement of trade union political
     contributions to the ALP, as these contributions are likely to have exceeded the
     threshold for itemisation.
19   The information contained in this paragraph was collected from two types
     of sources: information published on the websites of the various ALP state
     branches and correspondence with these branches and some unions (copies of
     correspondence on file with author).
20   Annual Returns to the AEC, 2006–07 to 2007–08.
21   Ibid.
22   Royce Millar (2009) 'Businesses pay to meet Brumby', *The Age*, 6 August,
     viewed 20 January 2010: <http://www.theage.com.au/national/brumby-
     defiant-on-alp-fundraiser-20090806-ebi0.html>.
23   See also Barry Hindess (2004) Corruption and Democracy in Australia, in
     Democratic Audit of Australia Report No. 3, 16. As late as 2009, Theophanous
     described the charges of which he was convicted as 'minor': quoted in Victoria
     Ombudsman (2009) *Whistleblowers Protection Act 2001: Investigation into the
     Alleged Improper Conduct of Councillors at Brimbank City Council*, 43.
24   Royal Commission (Chair: Judge Kennedy) (1992) *Report of the Royal
     Commission into Commercial Activities of Government and Other Matters*, WA
     Government Printer, Perth.
25   Commission of Inquiry into Possible Illegal Activities and Associated Police
     Misconduct (Chair: G.E. Fitzgerald) (1989) *Report of A Commission of Inquiry
     Pursuant to Orders in Council*, viewed 2 February 2010: <http://www.cmc.qld.
     gov.au/data/portal/00000005/content/81350001131406907822.pdf>. See also
     Queensland CMC, *The Fitzgerald Inquiry*, viewed 2 February 2010: <http://
     www.cmc.qld.gov.au/asp/index.asp?pgid=10877>.
26   Michael McKenna & Sarah Elks (2009) 'Corrupt ex-minister Gordon Nuttall
     in jail facing extra charges', *The Australian*, 16 July, viewed 2 February 2010:
     <http://www.theaustralian.com.au/news/corrupt-ex-minister-gordon-nuttal-
     in-jail-facing-extra-charges/story-0-1225750676560>.
27   NSW ICAC (2005) *Report on Investigation on the Relationship Between Certain
     Strathfield Councillors & Developers*, 43.

28 NSW ICAC (2008) *Report on Investigation of Corruption Allegations Affecting Wollongong City Council: Part 1*, viewed 3 June 2008: <http://www.icac.nsw.gov.au/files/pdf/Part_1.pdf>.

29 As the Nolan report noted, 'Deliberate corruption is, however, notoriously difficult to measure': Committee on Standards in Public Life (Chairman: Lord Nolan) (1995) *First Report: Volume 1*, 15.

30 See Shaun Carney (2005) 'Reserve Bank row threatened to put Treasurer in overdraft', *The Age*, 3 December, 9.

31 Elissa McKeand (2006) AWB's Political Donations, *Reportage: Magazine of the Australian Centre for Independent Studies*, 1 April, viewed 6 June 2007: <http://www.reportage.uts.edu.au/local/detail.cfm?ItemId=10574>. See also Richard Baker (2006) 'Embattled exporter handed out nearly $80,000 to major political parties', *The Age*, 21 January, 15.

32 See Thompson *Ethics in Congress*, 108–13.

33 See discussion in Royal Commission (Chair: Judge Kennedy), *Report of the Royal Commission into Commercial Activities of Government and Other Matters*, para 26.2.4.

34 Senate Select Committee on Ministerial Discretion in Migration Matters (2004) *Report*, Parliament of Australia, Canberra, para 6.51.

35 Cameron Houston (2008) 'Honesty issues brought up after $50,000 political gift', *The Age*, 28 May, 5.

36 As quoted in Victorian Parliament Select Committee on Public Land Development (2008) *Final Report*, 13, viewed 8 November 2008: <http://www.parliament.vic.gov.au/council/publicland/Reports/Final%20Report.pdf>.

37 As quoted in ibid., 112.

38 See Beitz, Political Finance in the United States, 95(1): 129, 137; Burke, The Concept of Corruption in Campaign Finance Law, 127; Thompson, *Ethics in Congress*, 55.

39 'Conflict of interest' situations extend beyond situations involving political contributions to instances where other kinds of interests, such as personal associations, conflict with public duty.

40 Thompson, *Ethics in Congress*, 117.

41 NSW ICAC (1990) *Investigation into North Coast Land Development: Part Five: Formal Findings and Final Observations*, 31.

42 See Karl Bitar, NSW ALP secretary (March 2008) *Submission to NSW Inquiry into Electoral and Political Party Funding*.

43 Janet Albrechtsen (2008) Common Ground: Political Donations, speech given at Centre for Policy Development, Sydney, 13 August, 2 (copy on file with author).

44 Thompson, *Ethics in Congress*, 113. Lowenstein alludes to a similar distinction in the context of American bribery offences. See Daniel H Lowenstein (1985) Political Bribery and the Intermediate Theory of Politics, *UCLA Law Review*, 32: 784, 845–47.

45 For an overview of the various theories of deliberative democracy, see, for example, J. Dryzek (2000) *Deliberative Democracy and Beyond: Liberals, Critics and Contestations*, Oxford University Press, Oxford, Ch. 1, and D. Held (2006) *Models of Democracy*, Polity, Cambridge, Ch. 9.

46 Amy Gutmann & Dennis Thompson (1996) *Democracy and Disagreement*, Belknap Press, Cambridge, 45.
47 Ibid., 3.
48 Ibid., 52.
49 Gutmann & Thompson, *Why Deliberative Democracy?*, 123.
50 Thompson, *Ethics in Congress*, 114.
51 Ibid., 114.
52 Ibid., 117.
53 For example, Amy McKay (2007) The Effect of Interest Groups' Ideology on their PAC and Lobbying Expenditure, Conference Papers – Midwestern Political Science Association 2007 Annual Meeting, 1.
54 See, for example, National Constitution of the ALP, cl 5.
55 In some cases, party rules set up a specific forum for dialogue between trade unions and the ALP. The NSW ALP's Constitution, for example, sets up a Labor Advisory Council whose role 'is to provide a formal consultative mechanism between the Party and the union movement in NSW': Rules of the Australian Labor Party (NSW) 2005–2006, cl Q.2.
56 NSW Select Committee on Electoral and Political Party Funding, *Electoral and Political Party Funding in New South Wales*, 113 (Recommendation 9).
57 *Corporations Act 2001* (Cth) s 184.
58 See discussion in Ramsay, Stapledon & Vernon, Political Donations by Australian Companies, 188–89, 196–97.
59 Harrigan, Political Partisanship and Corporate Political Donations in Australia.
60 Quoted in B. Birnbauer & D. Elias (2001) 'Coming to the party', *The Age*, 14 February, 13.
61 Millennium Forum website, viewed 7 June 2007: <http://www. millenniumforum.com.au/first.htm>. Note that this page is no longer available online. However, the more recent link to the Millennium Forum website contains a similar quotation: viewed 25 January 2010: <http://www.millenniumforum.com.au/index.php?option=com_ content&view=article&id=37:the-hon-john-howard-ac&catid=9:testimonials &Itemid=11>.
62 Millennium Forum website, viewed 7 June 2007: <http://www. millenniumforum.com.au/first.htm>. As above, this page is no longer available online.
63 E. Mychasuk & P. Clark (2001) 'Howard and his team rented by the hour', *Sydney Morning Herald*, 13 June, 1.
64 A list of the Millennium Forum's sponsors is available online, viewed 22 January 2010: <http://www.millenniumforum.com.au/index.php?option=com_conten t&view=article&id=9&Itemid=10>.
65 Andrew Clennell (2007) 'Coalition wins vote for donations inquiry', *Sydney Morning Herald*, 28 June, 4.
66 Anne Davies & Jonathan Pearlman (2006) 'Top Libs split on corporate donations', *Sydney Morning Herald*, 3 November, 1.
67 Michael Bachelard (2007) 'Taking their toll', *The Age*, 14 May, 9.
68 Information about Progressive Business is available from its website, viewed 22 January 2010: <http://www.pb.org.au/>. Details about membership fees

are also available online, viewed 22 January 2010: <http://www.pb.org.au/membership/membership.html#joinfrom>.

69 Royce Millar & Paul Austin (2009) '$10,000 to sit next to Brumby', *The Age*, 3 November, 1.

70 Details about the Millennium Forum's events are available through its website, viewed 22 January 2010: <http://www.millenniumforum.org.au/index. php?option=com_content&view=category&layout=blog&id=6&Itemid=7>.

71 Jason Koutsoukis & Misha Schubert (2004) 'Political donors put money where a mouth is', *The Sunday Age*, 1 August, 8.

72 Michelle Grattan & Katharine Murphy (2007) 'Hope in the hearts of Labor faithful', *The Age*, 27 April, 1.

73 For details, see Michelle Grattan (2007) 'Labor legal advice: PM function was a gift', *The Age*, 16 June, 2.

74 Brendan Nicholson (2007) 'Rudd open to Melbourne PM pad', *The Age*, 11 June, 5.

75 Clare Masters (2007) 'How $55,000 will buy you a slice of Malcolm', *Daily Telegraph*, 1 August, 23.

76 Alan Ramsey (2008) 'Junee farmer tables dinner time complaint', *Sydney Morning Herald*, 5 April, viewed 27 May 2008: <http://www. smh.com.au/news/opinion/junee-farmer-tables-dinner-time-complai nt/2008/04/04/1207249457708.html>.

77 Richard Baker (2006) 'Are our politicians for sale?', *The Age*, 24 May, 15.

78 Bachelard, 'Taking their toll', 9.

79 As quoted in Victorian Parliament Select Committee on Public Land Development, *Final Report*, para 383.

80 As quoted in Anthony Klan (2010) 'Political donors play to win, as the pokies saga during Bob Carr's tenure illustrates', *The Weekend Australian*, 13–14 February, 5.

81 Royal Commission (Chair: G.A. Kennedy) (1992) *Report on WA Inc.: Part II*, 1–3.

82 As David Truman correctly observed, 'power of any kind cannot be reached by a political interest group, or its leaders, without access to one or more key points of decision in the government. Access, therefore, becomes the facilitating intermediate objective of political interest groups': David Truman (1971, 2nd edn) *The Governmental Process: Political Interests and Public Opinion*, Knopf, New York, 264.

83 Details available from the Millennium Forum website, viewed 22 January 2010. <http://www.millenniumforum.com.au/>.

84 ALP website, Progressive Business, viewed 13 November 2005: <http:/// www.alp.org.au/action/progressive>. Note that this page is no longer active. The current website to view information about Progressive Business, viewed 5 February 2010, is: <http://www.pb.org.au/>.

85 Bachelard, 'Taking their toll', 9.

86 Ibid., 9.

87 The website of the organisation promises sponsors '"Off the Record" briefings that will keep you up to date with important political and economic developments that impact on your business': Bachelard, 'Taking their toll', 9.

88   Michael Walzer (1983) *Spheres of Justice: A Defense of Pluralism and Equality*, Basic Books, New York, 100.
89   Daniel Lowenstein (1989) On Campaign Finance Reform: The Root of All Evil is Deeply Rooted, *Hofstra Law Review*, 18: 301, 323–29.
90   Beitz, Political Finance in the United States: A Survey of Research, 129, 137.
91   See ibid., 137.
92   Misha Schubert (2007) 'Party hopes party won't end so soon', *The Age*, 4 June, 6.
93   Baker, 'Are our politicians for sale?', 15.
94   Ibid., 15.
95   Millar & Austin, '$10,000 to sit next to Brumby'.
96   At least for state and federal elections. The position is different with some local government elections.
97   Royce Millar (2009) 'Brumby in rethink on fund-raising', *The Age*, 8 December, 1.
98   Queensland Integrity Commissioner (2008) *Annual Report 2007–08*, 7.
99   Ibid., 7–8.
100   Quoted in Editors (2007) 'Political hubris laid bare in a tale of two lodges', *The Age: Insight*, 16 June, 8.
101   Quoted in ibid.
102   Tham & Grove, Public Funding and Expenditure Regulation of Australian Political Parties, 403–4.
103   Bachelard, Taking their toll, 9.
104   Michelle Grattan (2007) 'Liberals' treasure attacks two-bob each-way donors', *The Age*, 2 June, 2.
105   *ACTV* (1992) 177 CLR 106, 159.
106   For a similar argument in the US context, see Vincent Blasi (1994) Free Speech and the Widening Gyre of Fund-Raising: Why Campaign Spending Limits May Not Violate the First Amendment After All, *Columbia Law Review*, 94: 1281, 1283.
107   Michelle Grattan (2005) 'Our political guns for hire', *The Age*, 25 May, 21.
108   ALP (NSW Branch) (Karl Bitar) (May 2008) *Supplementary Submission: Proposals on Electoral and Political Party Funding Reform*, 2.
109   Peter Costello, 'Beware cashed-up influence peddlers', *Sydney Morning Herald*, 12 August 2009.
110   See, for example, Tony Wright (2007) 'Bold offer might help Lib reset', *The Age*, 26 November, viewed 25 February 2008: <http://www.theage.com.au/articl es/2007/11/25/1195975872419.html>.
111   See, for example, Michelle Grattan (2008) 'Lib Senate leader urges conservatives to unite', *The Age*, 26 January, viewed 25 January 2008: <http://www.theage.com.au/cgi-bin/common/popupPrintArticle.pl?path=/articl es/2008/01/25/1201157673214.html#>.
112   Maurice Duverger (trans. Barbara & Robert North) [1954] (1959, 2nd edn) *Political Parties: Their Organization and Activity in the Modern State* [translation of: *Les Partis Politiques*], John Wiley, London, 63.
113   Australian Government, *Electoral Reform Green Paper: Donations, Funding and Expenditure*, 41.

114 Angelo Panebianco (trans. Marc Silver) (1988) *Political Parties: Organization and Power*, Cambridge University Press, Cambridge, 264.

115 See Ian Ward (1991) The Changing Organisational Nature of Australia's Political Parties, *The Journal of Commonwealth and Comparative Politics*, 29(2): 153.

116 Panebianco, *Political Parties: Organization and Power*, 264.

117 Ibid., 264.

118 Ibid., 35–36.

119 Senator John Faulkner, 'Apathy and Anger: Our Modern Australian Democracy', 3rd Henry Parkes Oration, 22 October 2005, viewed 13 January 2010: <http://www.parkesfoundation.org.au/Faulkner%20oration%202005.pdf>.

Chapter 4

1 *Criminal Code 1995* (Cth) s 142.2. For a detailed discussion of these offences, see Gerald Carney (2000) *Members of Parliament: Law and Ethics*, Prospect Media, NSW, Ch. 8. See also Daniel H. Lowenstein (1990) Legal Efforts to Define Political Bribery, in Arnold J. Heidenheimer, Michael Johnston & Victor T. Levine (eds) *Political Corruption: A Handbook*, Transaction Publishers, New Brunswick, Ch. 3.

2 *Australian Capital Territory (Self-Government) Act 1988* (Cth) s 14(1)(c); *Northern Territory (Self-Government) Act 1978* (Cth) s 21(2)(3). For a discussion of these and the federal prohibition, see Carney, *Members of Parliament: Law and Ethics*, 133–40.

3 ACT Government (February 2004) *Code of Conduct for Ministers*, viewed 27 November 2008: <http://www.cmd.act.gov.au/__data/assets/pdf_file/0018/1827/codeconduct.pdf>; Australian Commonwealth Parliament (2007) *Standards of Ministerial Ethics,* viewed 22 January 2010: <http://www.dpmc.gov.au/guidelines/docs/ministerial_ethics.rtf>; NSW Department of Premier and Cabinet, *NSW Ministerial Handbook*; Queensland Department of Premier and Cabinet (September 2008) *Governing Queensland: Queensland Ministerial Handbook*, Appendix 19: Ministers' Code of Ethics (see also some parts of the main body of the document, including para 3.3, the policy on the receipt of gifts), viewed 22 January 2010: <http://www.premiers.qld.gov.au/publications/categories/policies-and-codes/handbooks/ministerial-handbook.aspx>; SA Department of Premier and Cabinet (July 2002) *Ministerial Code of Conduct*, viewed 22 January 2010: <http://www.premcab.sa.gov.au/pdf/Conduct_2002.pdf>; Tasmanian Department of Premier and Cabinet (2006) *Code of Conduct: Government Members of Parliament*, viewed 22 January 2010: <http://www.dpac.tas.gov.au/__data/assets/pdf_file/0016/53503/Government_MPs_code_of_conduct.pdf> (this Code applies to all government members of Parliament, not only Ministers. However, see, in particular, Pt 2.1.3 'Cabinet Government'); also in force in Tasmania is Department of Premier and Cabinet (February 2007) *Government Members' Handbook*, which applies to the Premier, Ministers, the Leader of the Government in the Legislative Council, the Speaker of the House of Assembly and Government Backbenchers (this is a confidential document available only on special request to the Department and

available for restricted use only); Government of Western Australia (September 2008) *Ministerial Code of Conduct*, viewed 22 January 2010: <http://www. opssc.wa.gov.au/ICG/Documents/ministerialCodeOfConduct_200809. pdf>. The author has been advised by the Department of Chief Minister and Cabinet that a Ministerial Code of Conduct for the Northern Territory is currently being drafted. In Victoria, no formal ministerial code exists, but in 2007 Victorian Premier John Brumby was reported to be considering the possibility of introducing a code similar to the 2007 Commonwealth Code: Deirdre McKeown (2009) A Survey of Codes of Conduct in Australian and Selected Overseas Parliaments, *Commonwealth Parliamentary Library Background Note*, 17, viewed 22 January 2009: <http://www.aph.gov.au/library/pubs/BN/ pol/CodesOfConduct.pdf> (document first published as an E-brief in June 2006 and Background Note in July 2007). Provisions dealing with ministerial conduct can be found in *Members of Parliament (Register of Interests) Act 1978* (Vic) ss 3(1)(e)–(f).

4   Legislative Assembly for the ACT (August 2005) Code of Conduct for All Members of the Legislative Assembly for the Australian Capital Territory (Continuing Resolution 5) in Legislative Assembly for the ACT (August 2009) Standing and Temporary Orders and Continuing Resolutions of the Assembly, viewed 22 January 2010: <http://www.parliament.act.gov.au/downloads/ standing-orders/Standing_Orders.pdf>; Parliament of NSW (May 1998, last updated June 2007) *Code of Conduct for Members and ICAC*, viewed 22 January 2010: <http://www.parliament.nsw.gov.au/prod/parlment/publications. nsf/key/LABP11>; *Legislative Assembly (Members' Code of Conduct and Ethical Standards) Act 2008* (NT) (The Code appears as a Schedule to the Act. The Act was brought into force following the adoption by the NT Legislative Assembly in 2004 of the *Members' Code of Conduct and Ethical Standards*. The Act now supersedes the 2004 Code); Legislative Assembly of Queensland (September 2004, last amended May 2009) *Code of Ethical Standards*, viewed 22 January 2010: <http://www.parliament.qld.gov.au/view/committees/ documents/MEPPC/other/ethicalStandards/Code04.pdf>; Tasmanian House of Assembly, Code of Ethical Conduct for Members of the House of Assembly and A Code of Race Ethics for Members of the House of Assembly, in *Standing and Sessional Orders and Rules* (Standing Orders 2A and 2B), viewed 22 January 2010: <http://www.parliament.tas.gov.au/ha/So&Sessionals. pdf>; *Members of Parliament (Register of Interests) Act 1978* (Vic) Pt I: Code of Conduct; WA Legislative Assembly (August 2003) *Code of Conduct for Members of the Legislative Assembly*, viewed 22 January 2010: <http://www.parliament. wa.gov.au/web/newwebparl.nsf/iframewebpages/Legislative+Assembly+- +Code+of+Conduct>. Notably, in Tasmania and Western Australia there are no codes that apply to their Legislative Councils. In South Australia and in the Commonwealth jurisdiction, there are no formal parliamentary codes of conduct.

5   On Australian codes of conduct, see generally Carney, *Members of Parliament: Law and Ethics*, 256–62; McKeown, *A Survey of Codes of Conduct in Australian and Selected Overseas Parliaments*. For discussion of past proposals to institute a parliamentary code of conduct at the federal level, see Michael Beahan (1998)

Parliamentary Ethics, Political Realities, in Preston & Sampford with Bois (eds) *Ethics and Political Practice: Perspectives on Legislative Ethics*, 127, 129–33.

6   Tasmanian House of Assembly, Code of Ethical Conduct for Members of the House of Assembly.

7   SA Department of Premier and Cabinet, *Ministerial Code of Conduct*, cll 4.9, 11; ACT Government, *ACT Code of Conduct for Ministers*, cll 4, 8.

8   Australian Commonwealth Parliament, *Standards of Ministerial Ethics*, para 1.4. For a similar injunction, see *Members of Parliament (Register of Interests) Act 1978* (Vic) ss 3(1)(a)(i), (1)(f).

9   Queensland Department of Premier and Cabinet, *Governing Queensland: Queensland Ministerial Handbook*, para 3.3 (This is excerpted from the main body of *Governing Queensland* rather than from Appendix 19, the Ministers' Code. Part 3 of *Governing Queensland*, covering the policy on received gifts, specifically states that the schedule applies to 'Ministers and their staff'). See also South Australia, *Ministerial Code of Conduct*, cll 4.9, 11.

10 Parliament of NSW, *Code of Conduct for Members and ICAC,* cl 3b. See also WA Legislative Assembly, *Code of Conduct for Members of the Legislative Assembly*, cl 5(b). For a similar provision, see Queensland Parliament, *Code of Ethical Standards: Legislative Assembly of Queensland*, 7(1)(j).

11 *Local Government Act 1989* (Vic) ss 1, 78C, 79(6). These amendments were inserted by the *Local Government Amendment (Councillor and Other Matters) Act 2008* (Cth), which adopted many of the recommendations made in Victorian Department of Planning and Community Development (2007) *Better Local Governance: Consultation Paper.*

12 *Local Government Act 1993* (NSW) s 451.

13 *Local Government Act 1993* (Qld) s 244.

14 *Local Government Act 1999* (SA) ss 73–74.

15 *Local Government Act 1993* (Tas) s 48.

16 *Local Government Act* (NT) ss 73–74.

17 *Local Government Act 1993* (NSW) s 442; *Local Government Act* (NT) s 73; *Local Government Act 1993* (Qld) s 6; *Local Government 1999* (SA) s 73; *Local Government Act 1993* (Tas) s 49.

18 *Federal Election Campaign Act (FECA)* (1971) s 441c.

19 Victorian Parliament Select Committee on Public Land Development (2008) *Final Report*, 13, viewed 5 February 2010: <http://www.parliament.vic.gov.au/council/publicland/Reports/Final%20Report.pdf>.

20 *Election Funding and Disclosures Act 1981* (NSW) ss 96GA–GE.

21 Meredith Burgmann (1999) Constructing Legislative Codes of Conduct, lecture given in the Department of the Senate Occasional Lecture Series, Canberra, 23 July, 8–9.

22 Andrew Brien (1998) A Code of Conduct for Parliamentarians?, *Commonwealth Parliamentary Library Research Paper No. 2*, 1998–1999, viewed 12 January 2009: <http://www.aph.gov.au/library/pubs/rp/1998-99/99rp02.htm>.

23 Committee of Inquiry Concerning Public Duty and Private Interest (Chair: N.H. Bowen) (1978) *Public Duty and Private Interest*, 20, 32.

24 Noel Preston (1998) Legislative Ethics: Challenges and Prospects, in Preston & Sampford with Bois, *Ethics and Political Practice: Perspectives on Legislative Ethics*, 143–49.

25   Brien, *A Code of Conduct for Parliamentarians?*
26   Burgmann, Constructing Legislative Codes of Conduct, 3.
27   Committee of Inquiry Concerning Public Duty and Private Interest (Chair: N.H. Bowen), *Public Duty and Private Interest*, 21.
28   See Thompson, *Ethics in Congress*, 131.
29   Ministerial codes of conduct can be promulgated through executive conduct while parliamentary codes can be enacted pursuant to the powers of the various Australian parliaments to regulate and discipline their members and to enact standing rules and orders. On the latter, see generally Carney, *Members of Parliament: Law and Ethics*, 178–81; Enid Campbell (2003) *Parliamentary Privilege*, Federation Press, Sydney, Ch. 11.
30   Ministerial staff should be covered by these obligations as they can in some circumstances wield considerable executive power: see generally Anne Tiernan (2007) *Power Without Responsibility: Ministerial Staffers in Australian Governments from Whitlam to Howard*, UNSW Press, Sydney.
31   The British Nolan report, for instance, recommended that records be kept of meetings between public officials (including ministers) and lobbyists: see Committee on Standards in Public Life (Chairman: Lord Nolan) (1995) *Standards in Public Life: First Report of the Committee on Standards in Public Life: Volume 1*.
32   AAP (2009) 'Bligh slaps bans on fundraising functions', *Brisbane Times*, 2 August, viewed 14 January 2010: <http://www.brisbanetimes.com.au/queensland/bligh-slaps-ban-on-fundraising-functions-20090802-e5kb.html>.
33   Tasmanian House of Assembly, *Code of Ethical Conduct for Members of the House of Assembly*, Preamble.
34   Australian Commonwealth Parliament, *Standards of Ministerial Ethics*, para 1.3.
35   Queensland Department of Premier and Cabinet, *Governing Queensland: Queensland Ministerial Handbook*, Appendix 19: Ministers' Code of Ethics.
36   SA Department of Premier and Cabinet, *Ministerial Code of Conduct*, cl 1.1.
37   See generally Brien, *A Code of Conduct for Parliamentarians?*.
38   Australian Commonwealth Parliament, *Standards of Ministerial Ethics*, para 7.
39   SA Department of Premier and Cabinet, *Ministerial Code of Conduct*, cl 1.4; Queensland Department of Premier and Cabinet, *Governing Queensland: Queensland Ministerial Handbook*, Appendix 19: Ministers' Code of Ethics. Note that Queensland Ministers may also seek the advice of the Integrity Commissioner. The ACT code does not specifically discuss enforcement, but does note that '[i]t is not intended that issues relating to compliance or non-compliance with this Code be determined or reviewed by any court, tribunal or other body': ACT Government (February 2004) *Code of Conduct for Ministers*. The NSW code does not explicitly discuss enforcement but notes that Ministers are 'subject to the civil and criminal law as holders of public office': NSW Department of Premier and Cabinet, *NSW Ministerial Handbook*. In the Tasmanian code, enforcement is not specified: Tasmanian Department of Premier and Cabinet (2006) *Code of Conduct: Government Members of Parliament*, Introduction. The WA code notes that the administration of the code is the responsibility of the Cabinet Secretary, who is responsible to the Premier; however, it does not specifically discuss enforcement: Government of Western Australia (September 2008) *Ministerial Code of Conduct*.

40 With the Victorian and WA parliamentary codes of conduct, there are express
    provisions stating so: see *Members of Parliament (Register of Interests) Act 1978* (Vic)
    s 9; WA Legislative Assembly (2003) *Code of Conduct for Members of the Legislative
    Assembly*. In relation to the Tasmanian Code of Ethical Conduct for Members
    of the House of Assembly and the ACT Code of Conduct for All Members of
    the Legislative Assembly for the ACT, this situation results from the code being
    in the form of standing rules and orders. For a general discussion of the powers
    of Australian parliaments to discipline their members, see Carney, *Members of
    Parliament: Law and Ethics*; Campbell, *Parliamentary Privilege*.
41 *Parliament of Queensland Act 2001* (Qld) ss 90–93.
42 *Independent Commission Against Corruption Act 1988* (NSW) s 72E.
43 See *Integrity Act 2009* (Qld), Ch. 2. See generally, Integrity Commissioner of
    Queensland website, viewed 25 January 2010: <http://www.integrity.qld.gov.
    au/page/integrity-regime/index.shtml>.
44 NSW Legislative Assembly (2009) *Effective House Membership: A Short Guide
    to the Procedures of the New South Wales Legislative Assembly*, Ch. 14, viewed
    2 March 2009: <http://www.parliament.nsw.gov.au/prod/la/precdent.nsf/
    V3ListShortGuideToProcedure>. The document also details the role of the
    Advisor and the power to disclose records of advice.
45 Legislative Assembly for the ACT, *Standing Orders and Continuing Resolutions of
    the Assembly*, 76–77, viewed 27 November 2008: <http://www.parliament.act.
    gov.au/downloads/standing-orders/standing_orders.pdf>.
46 The following ministerial codes of conduct are available publicly online:
    ACT Government, *Code of Conduct for Ministers*; Australian Commonwealth
    Parliament, *Standards of Ministerial Ethics*; Queensland Department of Premier
    and Cabinet, *Governing Queensland: Queensland Ministerial Handbook*, Appendix
    19: Ministers' Code of Ethics; SA Department of Premier and Cabinet,
    Ministerial Code of Conduct; Department of Premier and Cabinet Tasmania
    (2006) *Code of Conduct: Government Members of Parliament* (note, however,
    that the *Government Members' Handbook* is not available publicly, see below);
    Government of Western Australia (2008) *Ministerial Code of Conduct* (note that
    the WA *Ministerial Code of Conduct* was brought into force by the then Carpenter
    Labor Government. It has been difficult to obtain a clear statement from the
    WA Department of Premier and Cabinet indicating that this code has been
    adopted by the current Barnett Government, however, but as at 11 November
    2008 it appears that the Barnett Government was continuing to follow the
    Carpenter Code: Legislative Assembly of Western Australia (2008) *Parliamentary
    Debates*, Mr E.S. Ripper and Premier Barnett, 11 November 2008, 83). The
    following codes were made available on request: NSW Department of Premier
    and Cabinet, *NSW Ministerial Handbook*; Tasmanian Department of Premier and
    Cabinet, *Government Members' Handbook* (applies to the Premier, Ministers, the
    Leader of the Government in the Legislative Council, the Speaker of the House
    of Assembly and Government Backbenchers; this confidential document was
    made available for restricted use only with any publication of any of its contents
    requiring formal permission). As noted above, there is no Ministerial code
    operating in the Northern Territory or in Victoria at present.
47 ACT Government, *Code of Conduct for Ministers*, 'Conformity with the Principles
    of Accountability and Financial and Collective Responsibility' and 'Disclosure

and Management: Cabinet Deliberations', 2, 6; Australian Commonwealth Parliament, *Standards of Ministerial Ethics*; NSW Department of Premier and Cabinet, *NSW Ministerial Handbook*, 4.1: Queensland Department of Premier and Cabinet, *Governing Queensland: Queensland Ministerial Handbook*, Appendix 19: Ministers' Code of Ethics, 'Accountability': SA Department of Premier and Cabinet, *Ministerial Code of Conduct*, Pt 2.9; Department of Premier and Cabinet Tasmania, *Code of Conduct: Government Members of Parliament*, para 2.1.3; Government of Western Australia, *Ministerial Code of Conduct*, Pt 9.

48   ACT Government, *Code of Conduct for Ministers*, 5, 7; Australian Commonwealth Parliament, *Standards of Ministerial Ethics*, paras 2.1, 2.19; NSW Department of Premier and Cabinet, *NSW Ministerial Handbook*, 4.2; Queensland Department of Premier and Cabinet, *Governing Queensland: Queensland Ministerial Handbook*, Appendix 19: Ministers' Code of Ethics, 'Integrity', Responsibility'; SA Department of Premier and Cabinet, *Ministerial Code of Conduct*, Pt 5; Department of Premier and Cabinet Tasmania, *Code of Conduct: Government Members of Parliament*, para 2.2.2; Government of Western Australia, *Ministerial Code of Conduct*, Pt 9.

49   Committee of Inquiry Concerning Public Duty and Private Interest (Chair: N.H. Bowen), *Public Duty and Private Interest*, 110–12.

50   Parliament of the United Kingdom, Parliamentary Commissioner for Standards, viewed 22 January 2010: <http://www.parliament.uk/about_commons/pcfs. cfm>. The establishment of the position of Commissioner was the result of the recommendation made by the Nolan Committee, see Committee on Standards in Public Life (Chairman: Lord Nolan), *Standards in Public Life*, 43–45. Another variant is the Ethics Commission suggested by Dennis Thompson, which is to be made up of seven distinguished citizens well versed in legislative ethics, with the key function of investigating individual complaints and tabling its findings for a parliamentary committee which then decides upon punishment: see Thompson, *Ethics in Congress*, 159–65. See also Meredith Burgmann (1998) Constructing Codes: Pitfalls and Challenges, in Preston & Sampford with Bois (eds), *Ethics and Political Practice: Perspectives on legislative ethics*, 118, 122–24.

51   See, for example, *Fair Work (Registered Organisations) Act 2009* (Cth), s 5(3)(d).

52   *Fair Work (Registered Organisations) Act 2009* (Cth), s 141(1)(b)(ix)–(xi).

53   *Fair Work (Registered Organisations) Act 2009* (Cth) s 149.

54   Rules of the Automotive, Food, Metals, Engineering, Printing and Kindred Industries Union (as at 7 October 2008), cl 21.

55   Rules of the Communication, Electrical, Electronic, Energy, Information, Postal, Plumbing and Allied Services Union of Australia (as at 3 March 2009), cl 19.

56   Rules of the Liquor, Hospitality and Miscellaneous Workers' Union (as at 7 July 2008), cl 31.

57   Rules of the Construction, Forestry, Mining and Energy Union (as at 29 August 2008), c 49.

58   See, for example, *Fair Work (Registered Organisations) Act 2009* (Cth), ss 143–44.

59   Robert Michels (1962) *Political Parties: A Sociological Study of the Oligarchical Tendencies of Modern Democracy*, Collier Books, New York.

60   See, for example, the study by Seymour Martin Lipset, Martin Trow and James Coleman of the International Typographical Union, where the authors

concluded: 'We have shown that there is much more variation in the internal organization of associations than the notion of an iron law of oligarchy would imply, but nevertheless, the implications of our analysis for democratic organizational politics are almost as pessimistic as those postulated by Robert Michels': Lipset, Trow & Coleman (1956) *Union Democracy: The Internal Politics of the International Typographical Union*, Free Press, Glencoe, 405. For discussion of the Australian situation, see Stephen J. Deery & David H. Plowman (1991) *Australian Industrial Relations*, McGraw-Hill, Sydney, 247–53; Peter Fairbrother (1991) Union Democracy in Australia: Accommodation and Resistance, in Lawson Savery & Norman Dufty (eds) *Readings in Australian Industrial Relations*, Harcourt Brace Jovanovich, Sydney, 297; Carol Fox, William Howard & Marilyn Pittard (1995) *Industrial Relations in Australia: Development, Law and Operation*, Longman Australia, Melbourne, 209–15.

61 Mathew Dunckley (2009) 'ALP peace deal falls foul of unions', *Australian Financial Review*, 19 January; Paul Austin with Marc Moncrief (2009) '"Peace" deal has ALP in turmoil', *The Age*, 20 January.

62 Andrew Leigh (2006) How Do Unionists Vote? Estimating the Causal Impact of Union Membership on Voting Behaviour from 1966 to 2004, *Australian Journal of Political Science*, 41(4): 537.

63 Lipset, Trow & Coleman, *Union Democracy*, 5.

64 See Ramsay, Stapledon & Vernon, Political Donations by Australian Companies, 186–87, 189–90.

65 Phillip Coorey (2007) 'Exposed: the secret business plot to wreck Labor', *Sydney Morning Herald*, 20 June, 1.

66 See Australian Shareholders' Association (2004) *Political Donations: Policy Statement*, viewed 19 February 2008: <http://www.asa.asn.au/PolicyStatements/PoliticalDonations.pdf>.

67 See Democrats Senator Andrew Murray (2006) 'Dissenting Report' in Joint Standing Committee on Electoral Matters, *Funding and Disclosure: Inquiry into Disclosure of Donations to Parties and Candidates*, para 2.2 (trade unions) and para 5.5 (corporations) viewed 3 June 2008: <http://www.aph.gov.au/house/committee/em/donations/report/dissent_murray.pdf>.

68 Former section 97P of the *Industrial Relations Act 1979* (WA). This requirement was in force from 1997 to 2002.

69 For the requirements applying to trade union political expenditure, see discussion in Ewing, *The Cost of Democracy*, Ch. 3; and Keith Ewing (1982) *Trade Unions, the Labour Party and the Law: A Study of the Trade Union Act 1913*, Edinburgh University Press, Edinbourgh.

70 See Bitar, *Submission to NSW Inquiry into Electoral and Political Party Funding*.

71 Malcolm Turnbull (2005) *Submission to the Joint Standing Committee on Electoral Matters Inquiry into the 2004 Federal Election*.

72 See Report of Proceedings Before the Select Committee on Electoral and Political Party Funding: Inquiry into Electoral and Political Party Funding (3 March 2008), viewed 22 January 2010: <http://www.parliament.nsw.gov.au/prod/parlment/committee.nsf/0/dfc9200362cf2c4aca257402000e38aa/$FILE/080303%20corrected%20hearing%20transcript.pdf>.

73 Queensland Premier Anna Bligh (2009) 'Sweeping reforms deliver Queensland strong integrity and accountability', media release, 10 November,

viewed 27 November 2009: <http://statements.cabinet.qld.gov.au/MMS/StatementDisplaySingle.aspx?id=67319>.

74 NSW Select Committee on Electoral and Political Party Funding (NSW Select Committee) (2008) *Electoral and Political Party Funding in New South Wales*, 105 (Recommendation 7).

75 *Election Funding and Disclosures Act 1981* (NSW) ss 96GA–GE.

76 *Electoral Act 2002* (Vic) ss 216–217.

77 John Rawls has referred to restrictions on contributions as a possible means for ensuring fair value of political liberties: see John Rawls (1996) *Political Liberalism*, Columbia University Press, New York, 357–58; Rawls, *Justice as Fairness: A Restatement*, 149.

78 See Ewing, *The Cost of Democracy: Party Funding in Modern British Politics*, 227–30.

79 NSW Select Committee, *Electoral and Political Party Funding in New South Wales*, 113 (Recommendation 9).

80 Ibid.

81 See Editors (2010) 'Voters betrayed by failure to clean up party funding', *The Age*, 14 February, viewed 3 February 2010: <http://www.theage.com.au/opinion/editorial/voters-betrayed-by-failure-to-clean-up-party-funding-20100113-m6uj.html>.

82 Janet Albrechtsen (2008) 'End the stench of political donations', *The Australian*, 24 February, viewed 25 February 2008: <http://blogs.theaustralian.news.com.au/janetalbrechtsen/index.php/theaustralian/comments/end_the_stench_of_political_donations/>.

83 See Samuel Issacharoff & Pamela Karlan (1999) The Hydraulics of Campaign Finance Reform, *Texas Law Review*, 77: 1705, 1714–15.

84 See also Ewing, *Trade Unions, the Labour Party and Political Funding*, paras 4.6–4.7. This is not to deny that the ALP is already influenced by pressure group politics. For a case study, see Philip Mendes (2004) Labourists and the Welfare Lobby: The Relationship Between the Federal Labor Party and the Australian Council of Social Service (ACOSS), *Australian Journal of Political Science*, 39(1): 145.

85 Editors (2008) 'Limit political donations: Carr', *The Australian*, 4 May, viewed 21 May 2008: <http://www.theaustralian.news.com.au/story/0,25197,23643124-2702,00.html>.

86 Mark Aarons (2008) The Unions and Labor, in Robert Manne (ed.) *Dear Mr Rudd: Ideas for A Better Australia*, Black Inc. Agenda, Melbourne, 86, 91.

87 Ibid., 88.

88 Ibid.

89 In 2007, union density stood at 19 per cent of the Australian workforce: ABS (2007) *Employee Earnings, Benefits and Trade Union Membership, Australia, August 2007* (cat. no. 6310.0).

90 This point is made well by Bolton: John Bolton, Constitutional Limitations on Restricting Corporate and Union Political Speech, *Arizona Law Review*, 22:417.

91 This would include political advisers, some of whom have been criticised as exercising 'power without responsibility': Anne Tiernan (2007) *Power Without Responsibility: Ministerial Staffers in Australian Governments from Whitlam to Howard*, UNSW Press, Sydney. Tiernan's study was focused on ministerial advisers.

92 For figures, see Gary Johns (2006) Party Organisation and Resources: Membership, Funding and Staffing, in Ian Marsh (ed.) (2006) *Political Parties in*

Transition?, Federation Press, Sydney, 46, 47; Ian Ward (2006) Cartel Parties and Election Campaigns, in Marsh, *Political Parties in Transition?*, 70, 73–75.

93   Ward, Cartel Parties and Election Campaigns, 70, 72, 85–88. On the power of trade unions within the ALP, see Kathryn Cole (1982) Unions and the Labor Party, in Kathryn Cole (ed.) (1982) *Power, Conflict and Control in Australian Trade Unions*, Penguin, Melbourne, where it was concluded that 'the power of unions within the ALP is far more circumscribed than is commonly believed and the process [through] which each of the party's two sections (i.e. industrial and political wings) accommodates to the demands and needs of the other is complex and tortuous': Cole, *Power, Conflict and Control in Australian Trade Unions*, 100.

94   Robert Michels (1962) *Political Parties: A Sociological Study of the Oligarchical Tendencies of Modern Democracy*, Collier Books, New York, 365. Michels' iron law is better understood as pointing to the 'oligarchical tendencies' of organisations. The title of the last part of Michels' book is, in fact, 'Synthesis: The Oligarchical Tendencies of Organizations'.

95   Michels, *Political Parties*, 61. Schattscheider has similarly observed that 'People do not usually become formidable to governments until they are organised': E.E. Schattscheider (1942) *Party Government*, Holt, Rinehart & Winston, New York, 28.

96   Lindblom, *Politics and Markets*, 141.

97   Aarons, The Unions and Labor, 86, 89.

98   Andrew Parkin (1983) Party Organisation and Machine Politics: The ALP in Perspective, in Andrew Parkin & John Warhurst (eds) (1983) *Machine Politics in the Australian Labor Party*, George Allen & Unwin, Sydney, 15, 22.

99   Aarons has argued that problems with 'trade union bosses' require review of the funding provided by trade unions to the ALP: Mark Aarons (2008) 'Rein in union strongmen's ALP power', *The Australian*, 18 March, viewed 19 May 2008: <http://www.theaustralian.news.com.au/story/0,25197,23391595-7583,00.html>.

100 Affidavit of Keith Ewing to IDSA litigation. See also Howard Davis (2000) *Political Freedom: Associations, Political Purpose and the Law*, Continuum, London, 46.

101 See, for example, Constitution and Regulations of the Liberal Party of Australia (NSW), cl 2.1.

102 See, for example, Constitution and Rules of the National Party of Australia (NSW), cl 2.

103 See, for example, Rules of the Australian Labor Party (NSW) 2005–2006, cll A.2–A.3.

104 Constitution of the Greens (NSW), cl 2.1.

105 Constitution of the National Party of Australia (Cth), cl 71. Before 1945, various farmers' organisations had formal relationships with the Country Party, the predecessor of the National Party: Keith O. Campbell (1968), Australian Farm Organizations and Agricultural Policy, in Colin Hughes (ed.) *Readings in Australian Government*, University of Queensland Press (UQP), Brisbane, 438.

106 Constitution of The Shooters Party (NSW), By-law (2).

107 In the case of The Shooters Party, this is made clear by its Constitution, which states that one of its aims is '*To exert a discipline through shooting organizations and clubs and within the non-affiliated shooting community*, to curb the lawless and

dangerous element; and to help shooters understand that they hold the future of their sport in their own hands by their standards of conduct' (emphasis added): Constitution of The Shooters Party (NSW), cl 2(g). In relation to the 2003 NSW state election, the Shooters Party received thousands of dollars in contributions from various hunting and pistol clubs including the Federation of Hunting Clubs Inc., Singleton Hunting Club, St Ives Pistol Club, Illawarra Pistol Club and the NSW Amateur Pistol Association: Election Funding Authority (NSW) (2003) *Details of Political Contributions of More than $1,500 Received by Parties that Endorsed a Group and by Independent Group at the Legislative Council 2003*, viewed 5 February 2008: <http://www.efa.nsw.gov.au/__data/assets/pdf_file/0008/30140/2003PartyContributions.pdf>.

108 For fuller explanations of direct and indirect party structures, see Duverger, *Political Parties: Their Organization and Activity in the Modern State*, 6–17.

109 For fuller discussion, see Ewing, *The Cost of Democracy*, 35–38.

110 This seems to be the position in relation to the Canadian New Democratic Party, which still allows trade unions to affiliate on a collective basis: see Harold Jansen & Lisa Young (2005) Solidarity Forever? The NDP, Organised Labour, and the Changing Face of Party Finance in Canada, paper presented to the Annual Meeting of the Canadian Political Science Association, London, Ontario, 2–4 June, viewed 21 May 2008: <http://www.partyfinance.ca/publications/OrganizedLabour.pdf>. See also the discussion in Ewing, *The Cost of Democracy*, 220–21.

111 Matthew Bodah, Steve Ludlam & David Coates (2003) The Development of an Anglo-American Model of Trade Union and Political Party Relations, *Labor Studies Journal*, 28(2): 45, 46; see also Steve Ludlam, Matthew Bodah & David Coates (2002) Trajectories of Solidarity: Changing Union-Party Linkages in the UK and the USA, *British Journal of Politics and International Relations*, 4(2): 222, 233–41. For an application of the typology to the Australian context, see Gerard Griffin, Chris Nyland & Anne O'Rourke (2004) Trade Unions, the Australian Labor Party and the Trade-Labour Rights Debate, *Australian Journal of Political Science*, 39(1): 89.

112 See, for example, Rules of the Australian Labor Party (NSW) cl B.25(a), B.26; Rules of the Australian Labor Party (Victorian Branch), cl 6.3.2.

113 See, for example, Rules of the Australian Labor Party (NSW), cl B.2; Rules of the Australian Labor Party (Victorian Branch), cl 6.2.

114 National Constitution of the ALP, cl 5(b).

115 National Constitution of the ALP, cl 7(a).

116 NSW Select Committee, *Electoral and Political Party Funding in New South Wales*, 107–8, 113 (Recommendation 9).

117 Ibid., 113.

118 See, for example, Dean Mighell (2010) 'Unions must leave Labor', *The Age*, 11 February, viewed 8 March 2010: <http://www.theage.com.au/opinion/politics/unions-must-leave-labor-20100210-nsat.html>.

119 Joo-Cheong Tham (2010) *Towards a More Democratic Political Funding Regime in New South Wales: A Report Prepared for the New South Wales Electoral Commission*, 95–102, viewed 22 February 2010: <http://www.efa.nsw.gov.au/__data/assets/pdf_file/0009/66465/Towards_a_More_Democratic_Political_Finance_Regime_in_NSW_Report_for_NSW_EC.pdf>.

120 *Lange v Australian Broadcasting Corporation* (1997) 189 CLR 520, 566–67.

121 *Lange v Australian Broadcasting Corporation* (1997) 189 CLR 520, 571–72. See also *ACTV v Commonwealth* (1992) 177 CLR 106, 142 (Mason CJ), 168–69 (Deane and Toohey JJ), 215–17 (Gaudron J); *Coleman v Power* (2004) 220 CLR 1, 45 (McHugh J).

122 The test was stated in *Lange v Australian Broadcasting Corporation* (1997) 189 CLR 520, 571–72 as modified by a majority in *Coleman v Power* (2004) 220 CLR 1, 50 (McHugh J), 78 (Gummow and Hayne JJ), 82 (Kirby J).

123 See, for example, *ACTV* (1992) 177 CLR 106, 144–45 (Mason CJ).

124 Harrison Moore (1902) *The Constitution of the Commonwealth of Australia*, John Murray, London, 329. This statement was cited with approval in *ACTV* (1992) 177 CLR 106, 139–40 (Mason CJ).

125 *ACTV* (1992) 177 CLR 106, 15 (Brennan J).

126 *Coleman v Power* (2004) 220 CLR 1, 52–53 (McHugh J).

127 *ACTV* (1992) 177 CLR 106, 143 (Mason CJ), 234–235 (McHugh J).

128 *Levy v Victoria* (1997) 189 CLR 579, 598.

129 *Coleman v Power* (2004) 220 CLR 1, 31 (Gleeson CJ).

130 *Attorney-General (Cth); Ex rel McKinlay v Commonwealth* (1975) 135 CLR 1, 57 (Stephen J).

131 *ACTV* (1992) 177 CLR 106, 144–45 (Brennan J).

Chapter 5

1 The book does not examine all types of public funding of political parties. See generally Gary Johns (2006) Party Organisation and Resources: Membership, Funding and Staffing, in Marsh, *Political Parties in Transition?*, 46; Sally Young & Joo-Cheong Tham (2006) *Political Finance in Australia: A Skewed and Secret System*, Democratic Audit of Australia, Canberra, Chs 3–4.

2 For a classification, see Andrew Murray (2009) Submission in response to the Australian Government's December 2008 *Electoral Reform Green Paper: Donations, Funding and Expenditure*, Section 5.

3 *Election Funding and Disclosures Act 1981* (NSW) (*EFA*) s 97C.

4 *EFA* (NSW) s 97D.

5 *EFA* (NSW) s 97C(2).

6 *EFA* (NSW) s 97E.

7 Commonwealth, House of Representatives (1983) *Parliamentary Debates*, Kim Beazley, 2nd Reading Speech for the Commonwealth Electoral Legislation Amendment Bill 1983, 2215.

8 Ibid.

9 Ibid., 2213.

10 Ewing has also noted that equality of electoral opportunity requires that 'no candidate or party should be permitted to spend more than its rivals by a disproportionate amount': Ewing, *Money, Politics and Law*, 18.

11 See discussion in Australian Government, *Electoral Reform Green Paper: Donations, Funding and Expenditure*, Ch. 4.

12 See also discussion in Graeme Orr (2003) The Currency of Democracy: Campaign Finance Law in Australia, *University of New South Wales Law Journal*, 26: 1, 27.

13 For similar sentiments, see ibid., 21.

14 David Tucker & Sally Young (2001) Public Financing of Election Campaigns – A Solution or a Problem?, in Glenn Patmore (ed.) *Labor Essays 2002: The Big Makeover: A New Australian Constitution*, Pluto Press in association with the Australian Fabian Society, Sydney, 60, 69.

15 Ibid., 67.

16 Even with robust regulation of campaign expenditure, public funding is still likely to fuel the parties' expenditure in other areas: for example, through the employment of increased numbers of party staff members and more expensive party events such as conferences.

17 Stephen Mills (1986) *The New Machine Men: Polls and Persuasion in Australian Politics*, Penguin, Melbourne, 189–90.

18 UK Electoral Commission (2003) *The Funding of Political Parties: Background Paper*, 22. See also Committee on Standards in Public Life (1998) *Fifth Report: The Funding of Political Parties in the United Kingdom*, Cm 4057–I, 91–92 (often referred to as the Neill Committee Report after its Chair, Lord Neill). For similar sentiments, see Sally Young (2003) Killing Competition: Restricting Access to Political Communication Channels in Australia, *AQ: Journal of Contemporary Analysis*, 75: 9–11.

19 Arguments based on 'purification' have been made by UK proponents of increased state funding: see Committee on Standards in Public Life, *Fifth Report*, 90–91.

20 See Dean Jaensch, Party Structures and Processes, in Marsh, *Political Parties in Transition?*, 24, 30. Blondel has also raised the prospect that public funding of parties might diminish their 'fighting spirit': Jean Blondel (1978) *Political Parties: A Genuine Case for Discontent?*, Wildwood House, London, 91.

21 Joint Standing Committee on Electoral Matters (2008) *Advisory Report on the Commonwealth Electoral Amendment (Political Donations and Other Measures) Bill 2008*, 14.

22 Rawls, *Political Liberalism*, 357–58; Rawls, *Justice as Fairness*, 149.

23 For instance, whereas a 2 per cent threshold used to apply in relation to the ACT funding and disclosure regime, the threshold is now 4 per cent: *Electoral Act 1992* (ACT) s 208.

24 *Political Parties, Elections and Referendum Act 2000* (UK) s 12.

25 This section of the chapter draws upon Joo-Cheong Tham & Stephen Sempill (April 2008) *Submission to Joint Standing Committee on Electoral Matters' Inquiry into Schedule 1 of the Tax Laws Amendment (2008 Measures No. 1) Bill 2008 – Political Contributions and Gifts*.

26 *ITAA 1997* s 30–243, as amended by the *Electoral and Referendum Amendment (Electoral Integrity and other Measures) Act 2006* (Cth).

27 Explanatory Memorandum to the Tax Laws Amendment (2008 Measures No. 1) Bill 2008, 3.

28 For similar sentiments, see Lowenstein, On Campaign Finance Reform: The Root of All Evil is Deeply Rooted, 18: 301, 364–65.

29 See Ewing, *The Funding of Political Parties in Britain*, 139.

30 See Ewing, *The Cost of Democracy*, 194.

31 Lisa Young (2004) Regulating Campaign Finance in Canada: Strengths and Weaknesses, *Election Law Journal*, 3(3): 444, 452.

32 Young, Regulating Campaign Finance in Canada, 447, 459.

33 See Louis Massicotte (2006) Financing Parties at the Grass-Roots Level: The Quebec Experience, in Ewing & Issacharoff, *Party Funding and Campaign Financing in International Perspective*, 151, 159–60.

34 Massicotte, Financing Parties at the Grass-Roots Level, 173.

35 Ibid., 172.

36 Similar points are made by Ewing: K.D. Ewing (2002) *Trade Unions, the Labour Party and Political Funding: The Next Step: Reform with Restraint*, Catalyst, London, 39–40.

37 See, generally, Joint Standing Committee on Electoral Matters (2008) *Advisory Report on Schedule 1 of the Tax Laws Amendment (2008 Measures No. 1) Bill 2008 (Cth)*.

38 See NSW Parliament – Department of the Legislative Council (April 2007) *Legislative Council Members' Guide*; NSW Parliament – Department of the Legislative Council (November 2008) *Members' Handbook: A Guide to the Support Available to Members of the New South Wales Legislative Assembly*, viewed 27 January 2010: <http://www.parliament.nsw.gov.au/prod/la/lahandbook2008. nsf/PDFs/Full+Handbook/$File/Handbook.pdf>; Parliamentary Service of Queensland Parliament (as at October 2009) *Members' Entitlements Handbook: Benefits Afforded Members and Former Members of the Queensland Legislative Assembly*, viewed 27 January 2010: <http://www.parliament.qld.gov.au/ publications/view/legislativeAssembly/documents/entitlements/Members%20 Entitlements%20Handbook.pdf>; SA Legislative Council (as at 20 April 2009) *Handbook for Members of the Legislative Council of South Australia* (copy on file with author); *Parliamentary Allowances Regulations 2003* (Vic); Legislative Assembly for the ACT (as at 24 October 2008) *Members' Guide: Guide to Services, Facilities and Entitlements for Non-Executive Members and Their Staff* (copy on file with author); Northern Territory of Australia Remuneration Tribunal (2000) *Report on the Entitlements of Assembly Members and Determination No. 1 of 2009*.

39 Queensland parliamentarians are not entitled to an electorate allowance but are provided similar allowances, namely, the General and Miscellaneous Allowances: Parliamentary Service of Queensland Parliament, *Members' Entitlements Handbook*, 5, 7. Similarly, there is no specific electorate allowance for members of the ACT Legislative Assembly. These members are, however, entitled to a similar allowance, an annual Discretionary Office allocation. For members other than the Speaker or the Leader of the Opposition, the amount of the allocation is $4600 per annum: Legislative Assembly for the ACT, *Members' Guide*, 120.

40 *Parliamentary Remuneration Act 1990* (SA) s 4(1); *Parliamentary Salaries, Superannuation and Allowances Act 1973* (Tas) s 4, Sch 1, Sch 2; *Salaries and Allowances Act 1975* (WA) s 6; *Australian Capital Territory (Self-Government) Act 1988* (Cth) s 73(2).

41 *Parliamentary Remuneration Act 1989* (NSW) s 4.

42 *Assembly Members and Statutory Officers (Remuneration and Other Entitlements) Act 2006* (NT) s 3.

43 *Parliamentary Remuneration Act 1989* (NSW) ss 6B, 9; *Assembly Members and Statutory Officers (Remuneration and Other Entitlements) Act 2006* (NT) s 4.

44 *Parliamentary Remuneration Act 1989* (NSW) s 10(1).

45 *Parliamentary Remuneration Act 1990* (SA) s 4(4).

46 *Parliament of Queensland Act 2001* (Qld) s 109.

47 Parliamentary Service of Queensland Parliament, *Members' Entitlements Handbook: Benefits Afforded Members and Former Members of the Queensland Legislative Assembly*.

48 *Parliamentary Salaries and Superannuation Act 1968* (Vic) ss 3, 6(1)(a)–(b).

49 *Parliamentary Salaries and Superannuation Act 1968* (Vic) s 6(1)(c).

50 *Parliamentary Salaries and Superannuation Act 1968* (Vic) s 8(1)(c).

51 *Remuneration and Allowances Act 1990* (Cth) ss 6–7, Schs 3–4.

52 *Parliamentary Entitlements Act 1990* (Cth) s 4, Sch 1.

53 *Parliamentary Entitlements Act 1990* (Cth) s 5(1)(b).

54 *Parliamentary Entitlements Regulations 1997* (Cth) reg 3AA.

55 *Parliamentary Allowances Act 1952* (Cth) s 4; *Remuneration Tribunal Act 1973* (Cth) ss 7(1), 7(4).

56 For similar sentiments, see Thompson, *Ethics in Congress*, 74.

57 Ibid., 73.

58 NSW ICAC (2003) *Report on an Investigation into the Conduct of the Hon. Malcolm Jones MLC*, 28.

59 See Victoria Ombudsman (2009) *Whistleblowers Protection Act 2001: Investigation into the Alleged Improper Conduct of Councillors at Brimbank City Council*, 148–49.

60 Australian National Audit Office (ANAO) (2009) *Administration of Parliamentarians' Entitlements by the Department of Finance and Deregulation: Auditor-General Report No. 3 / 2009–2010*, 141.

61 For another statement of principles, see Department of Finance and Deregulation (2009) *Submission to the Committee for the Review of Parliamentary Entitlements*, 3.

62 The Commonwealth Auditor-General has recommended that this handbook be made publicly available: ANAO, *Administration of Parliamentarians' Entitlements*, 24.

63 Ibid., 54–67.

64 Ibid., 19–20.

65 Ibid., 21.

66 See, for example, Legislative Assembly for the ACT, *Members' Guide*, 119, 123.

67 Ibid., 129–30.

68 NSW ICAC (2005) *Report on Investigation into the Conduct of the Hon Peter Breen MLC*, 50.

69 Ibid., 50.

70 *Parliamentary Remuneration Act 1989* (NSW) s 3. These duties include any duties prescribed by regulation to be included and excludes those that are deemed by regulations to fall outside the definition.

71 See NSW Parliamentary Remuneration Tribunal (NSW PRT) (May 2009) *Annual Report and Determination of Additional Entitlements for the Members of the Parliament of New South Wales*, 14, viewed 20 October 2009: <http://

www.remtribunals.nsw.gov.au/__data/assets/pdf_file/0020/50609/2009_
Parliamentary_Annual_Report_and_Determination.pdf>.

72 Ibid., 14–19.

73 Ibid., 16.

74 NSW Parliament – Department of the Legislative Council, *Legislative Council
Members' Guide*, para 5.17.

75 *Parliamentary Entitlements Act 1990* (Cth) Sch 1, Pt 1, Item 3.

76 ANAO (2001) *Parliamentarian Entitlements: 1999–2000*, paras 2.61–2.68; ANAO
(2009) *Administration of Parliamentarians' Entitlements*, 15.

77 ANAO (2003) *Administration of Staff Employed Under the Members of Parliament
(Staff) Act 1984: Auditor-General Audit Report No. 15 / 2003–2004*, 16.

78 The printing entitlement has now been merged with the communications
allowance: see *Parliamentary Entitlements Regulations 1997* (Cth) reg 3AA.

79 *Parliamentary Entitlements Regulations 1997* (Cth) regs 3(1)(c), 3A(1)(c) (repealed).

80 ANAO, *Administration of Parliamentarians' Entitlements*, 146.

81 Ibid., 148.

82 Ibid., 147.

83 Ibid., 163.

84 Ibid., 165–66.

85 Ibid., 36–37. See also 199–214.

86 Ibid., 18.

87 *Parliamentary Entitlements Regulations 1997* (Cth) reg 3AC(2).

88 *Parliamentary Entitlements Regulations 1997* (Cth) reg 3AB(6).

89 *Parliamentary Entitlements Regulations 1997* (Cth) regs 3AA(3)–(4).

90 *Parliamentary Entitlements Regulations 1997* (Cth) reg 3AA(11).

91 *Parliamentary Entitlements Regulations 1997* (Cth) reg 3AA(3).

92 *Parliamentary Entitlements Regulations 1997* (Cth) reg 3AA(10).

93 Senator Joe Ludwig, Cabinet Secretary and Special Minister of State (2009)
'Reform of Parliamentary Entitlements', media release, 8 September, viewed
22 October 2009: <http://www.smos.gov.au/media/2009/mr_352009.html>.

94 *Parliamentary Entitlements Amendment Regulations 2009 (No. 2)* (Cth), Sch 1, reg 1.

95 Senator Joe Ludwig, Cabinet Secretary and Special Minister of State (2009)
'Government Welcomes Submissions to Parliamentary Entitlements Review
Committee', media release, 9 October, viewed 22 October 2009:
<http://www.smos.gov.au/media/2009/mr_402009.html>.

96 ANAO, *Administration of Parliamentarians' Entitlements*, 11, 45–46.

97 ANAO (2001) *Parliamentarian Entitlements: 1999–2000*, paras 2–3.

98 Tham & Grove, Public Funding and Expenditure Regulation of Australian
Political Parties, 401 (calculated from Table 1).

99 Young & Tham, *Political Finance in Australia*, 58 (Table 3.7).

100 NSW Department of Legislative Council, *Legislative Council Members' Guide*, 51;
NSW Department of Legislative Assembly, *Members' Handbook*, para 8B.1.5.

101 Parliamentary Service of Queensland Parliament, *Members' Entitlements
Handbook*, 62.

102 SA Legislative Council, *Handbook for Members of the Legislative Council of South
Australia*, Pt 3 'Salaries and Allowances'.

103 *Commonwealth Electoral Act 1918* (Cth) ss 273 (Senate) and 274 (House of Representatives).

104 Figures derived from the AEC website, viewed 28 January 2004: <http://www.aec.gov.au/_content/when/past/2001/results/>. Historical election result data also available from Parliament of Australia, Parliamentary Library website, viewed 27 January 2010: <http://www.aph.gov.au/library/Pubs/RB/2004-05/05RB11-1f.HTM>.

105 *Commonwealth of Australia Constitution Act 1900* (Cth) s 24.

106 Leesha McKenny and Lisa Carty (2009) 'Rees sets own agenda', *Sydney Morning Herald*, 15 November.

107 Brian Robins (2009) 'Election campaign funding hits hurdle', *Sydney Morning Herald*, 2 January; ABC Television, Interview with Kristina Keneally, *Stateline* (transcript), 4 December 2009, viewed 27 January 2010: <http://www.abc.net.au/news/video/2009/12/04/2762677.htm>.

108 See Richard Katz & Peter Mair (1995) Changing Models of Party Organizations and Party Democracy: The Emergence of the Cartel Party, *Party Politics*, 1(1): 5–28; Mark Blyth & Richard Katz (2005) From Catch-all Politics to Cartelisation: The Political Economy of the Cartel Party, *West European Politics*, 28(1): 33–60.

109 The plausibility of this thesis in its application to Australian political parties is contested. See the various contributions in Marsh, *Political Parties in Transition?*. On the funding of parties specifically, Gary Johns has argued that the cartel thesis has 'its use ... but does not fully explain the Australian case': Gary Johns (2006) Party Organisations and Resources: Membership, Funding and Staffing, in Marsh, *Political Parties in Transition?*, 66. See also Ian Ward, Cartel Parties and Election Campaigning in Australia, in the same collection.

110 Katz, Party Organizations and Finance, 123.

111 Josh Gordon (2010) 'MPs pay as donations dry up', *The Age*, 7 February, viewed 8 February 2010: <http://www.theage.com.au/national/mps-pay-as-donations-dry-up-20100206-njxg.html>.

Chapter 6

1 This was originally the title of an opinion piece that I co-wrote: G. Orr and J. Tham (2007) 'Turning taxes into spin', *The Age*, 17 May, 14.

2 See Sally Young (2006) Government and the Advantages of Office, in Young & Tham, *Political Finance in Australia: A Skewed and Secret System*, 62–65.

3 Young, Government and the Advantages of Office, 74.

4 Senate Finance and Public Administration References Committee (2005) *Government Advertising and Accountability*, 16–17, viewed 29 January 2010: <http://www.aph.gov.au/senate/committee/fapa_ctte/completed_inquiries/2004-07/govtadvertising/report/report.pdf>.

5 Senate Finance and Public Administration References Committee, *Government Advertising and Accountability*, 17.

6 NSW Auditor-General (2007) *Performance Audit: Government Advertising – Department of Premier and Cabinet, Department of Commerce*, 2, viewed 29 January

2010: <http://www.audit.nsw.gov.au/publications/reports/performance/2007/advertising/government_advertising.pdf>.

7   The figures for the specific years are $123 million for 2002–03; $147.1 million for 2003–04; $161.3 million for 2004–05: Victorian Auditor-General (2006) *Government Advertising*, 4, viewed 29 January 2010: <http://www.audit.vic.gov.au/reports__publications/reports_by_year/2006/20060914_advertising.aspx>.

8   Senate Finance and Public Administration References Committee, *Government Advertising and Accountability*, 6–7.

9   See Sally Young (2007) A History of Government Advertising in Australia, in Sally Young (ed.) *Government Communication in Australia*, Cambridge University Press, Cambridge, 181, 185–190.

10   See, generally, Senate Finance and Public Administration References Committee, *Government Advertising and Accountability*, 31–32.

11   Sally Young (2004) *The Persuaders: Inside the Hidden Machine of Political Advertising*, Pluto Press, Melbourne, 124–25.

12   For fuller details, see ANAO (1998) *Performance Audit: Taxation Reform: Community Education and Information Program*, 8, 20–21. For comment, see Geoffrey Lindell (1999) Parliamentary Appropriations and the Funding of the Federal Government's Pre-Election Advertising in 1998, *Constitutional Law and Policy Review*, 2(2): 21.

13   Senate Finance and Public Administration References Committee, *Government Advertising and Accountability*, xv. For fuller details of the expenditure, see 47.

14   For fuller detail, see ibid., 50–51.

15   Elements of this objection can be found in Liberal MP Petro Georgiou's objection to federal government advertising being subject to a guideline that '[m]aterial should not be liable to misrepresentation as party political', on the basis that 'in a highly combative political system, materials which are totally non-partisan are open to misrepresentation as party political': see Joint Committee of Public Accounts and Audit (2000) *Report 377: Guidelines for Government Advertising*, 3.

16   SA Auditor-General (1998) *Report of the Auditor-General for the Year Ending 30 June 1997*, Part A.4.

17   Ibid.

18   See, for example, Petro Georgiou's dissent at Joint Committee of Public Accounts and Audit, *Report 377*, 3.

19   Victorian Auditor-General (2002) *Report on Public Sector Agencies*, 306–307, viewed 29 January 2010: <http://download.audit.vic.gov.au/files/PSA_report_2002.pdf>.

20   Senate Finance and Public Administration References Committee, *Government Advertising and Accountability*, 51.

21   See, generally, NSW Auditor-General, *Performance Audit*, 28.

22   For equivalent provisions in other jurisdictions, see *Constitution Act 1902* (NSW) s 45; *Constitution of Queensland Act 2001* (Qld) s 66; *Public Finance and Audit Act 1987* (SA) s 6; *Public Accounts Act 1986* (Tas) s 8; *Constitution Act 1975* (Vic) s 92; *Constitution Act 1889* (WA) s 72; *Financial Management Act 1996* (ACT) ss 6, 8; *Financial Management Act 1995* (NT) s 5(2).

23 For a recent article examining these provisions, see Charles Lawson (2008) Reinvigorating the Accountability and Transparency of the Australian Government's Expenditure, *Melbourne University Law Review*, 32: 879.

24 *Brown v West* (1990) 169 CLR 195, 205.

25 For excellent analyses of this decision, see Lotta Ziegert (2006) Does the Public Purse Have Strings Attached? *Combet & Anor v Commonwealth of Australia & Ors*, *Sydney Law Review*, 28: 387; Geoffrey Lindell (2007) The *Combet Case* and the Appropriation of Taxpayers' Funds for Political Advertising – An Erosion of Fundamental Principles?, *Australian Journal of Public Administration*, 66(3): 307; Graeme Orr (2007) Government Communication and the Law, in Young, *Government Communication in Australia*, 22–24.

26 *Combet v Commonwealth* (2005) 224 CLR 494, 530.

27 *Combet v Commonwealth* (2005) 224 CLR 494, 565 (Gummow, Hayne, Callinan and Heydon JJ).

28 *Combet v Commonwealth* (2005) 224 CLR 494, 564–65 (Gummow, Hayne, Callinan and Heydon JJ).

29 *Combet v Commonwealth* (2005) 224 CLR 494, 532 (McHugh J), 605–08 (Kirby J).

30 *Combet v Commonwealth* (2005) 224 CLR 494, 532.

31 *Combet v Commonwealth* (2005) 224 CLR 494, 535.

32 *Combet v Commonwealth* (2005) 224 CLR 494, 610.

33 See Lindell, The *Combet Case*, 307.

34 See, for example, discussion at Senate Standing Committee on Finance and Public Administration (2007) *Transparency and Accountability of Commonwealth Public Funding and Expenditure*, 46–49.

35 Senator Andrew Murray (June 2008) *Review of Operation Sunlight: Overhauling Budgetary Transparency*, 86.

36 Ibid.

37 Australian Government (December 2008) *Operation Sunlight: Enhancing Budget Transparency*.

38 Ibid., 4.

39 Ibid.

40 Ibid., 5–6.

41 Murray, *Review of Operation Sunlight*, 87.

42 They are the Commonwealth Joint Committee of Public Accounts and Audit; NSW Public Accounts Committee; Queensland Public Accounts Committee; SA Economic and Finance Committee; Tasmanian Parliamentary Public Accounts Committee; Victorian Public Accounts and Estimates Committee; WA Legislative Assembly Public Accounts Committee; WA Legislative Council Estimates and Financial Operations Committee; ACT Standing Committee on Public Accounts; NT Public Accounts Committee.

43 The Victorian Auditor-General has commented on the lack of readily available information on government advertising in Victoria: see Victorian Auditor-General, *Government Advertising*, 4.

44 Department of Premier and Cabinet, State Government of Tasmania (July 2008) *Whole of Government Communications Policy*, Version 8.0, 11–12, viewed 1 December 2009: <http://www.communications.tas.gov.au/__data/assets/

pdf_file/0009/43866/CURRENT_WoGCommsPolicy_V8_July2008_web. pdf>.

45   Ibid.

46   NSW Government (2009) *NSW Government Advertising Guidelines*, 10, viewed 5 May 2009: <http://www.services.nsw.gov.au/advertising/pdf/NSWGovernme ntAdvertisingGuidelines.pdf>.

47   NSW Auditor-General's Report, *Performance Audit*, 4.

48   *Commonwealth Electoral Act 1918* (Cth) s 311A.

49   *Commonwealth Electoral Act 1918* (Cth) s 321A.

50   Commonwealth Department of Finance and Deregulation, Asset Management Group (March 2009) *Campaign Advertising by Australian Government Departments and Agencies Half Year Report 1 July to 31 December 2008*; Commonwealth Department of Finance and Deregulation, Asset Management Group (September 2009) *Campaign Advertising by Australian Government Departments and Agencies: Full Report 2008–2009*, viewed 19 October 2009: <http://www. finance.gov.au/advertising/campaign_advertising_2008–09.html>.

51   *Government Agencies (Campaign Advertising) Act 2009* (ACT) s 17.

52   ANAO, *Performance Audit*, 57–60; Joint Committee of Public Accounts and Audit, *Report 377*, 4–7; Victorian Auditor-General, *Report on Public Sector Agencies*, 314–15; Senate Finance and Public Administration References Committee, *Government advertising and Accountability*, 123–26; NSW Auditor-General's Report, *Performance Audit*, 36–37.

53   Victorian Auditor-General, *Government Advertising*, 8–9.

54   NSW Auditor-General, 2–3, 30–1.

55   Australian Government (June 2008) *Guidelines on Campaign Advertising by Australian Government Departments and Agencies*, para 12.

56   See *Government Agencies (Campaign Advertising) Act 2009* (ACT) ss 12, 14–15.

57   Australian Government, *Guidelines on Campaign Advertising by Australian Government Departments and Agencies*, para 6. It should be noted that the Cabinet Secretary can exempt a campaign from compliance with the guidelines on the grounds of 'a national emergency, extreme urgency or other extraordinary reasons the Cabinet Secretary considers appropriate'. Such exemption must, however, be notified to the Auditor-General and recorded in Parliament: Australian Government, *Guidelines on Campaign Advertising by Australian Government Departments and Agencies*, para 7.

58   Statement by Senator Joe Ludwig, Special Minister of State and Cabinet Secretary (2010) *Changes to the Framework for Government Advertising* , viewed 20 April 2010: <http://www.smos.gov.au/publications/2010/docs/100331-Ministerial-Statement-Government-Advertising.pdf>.

59   Auditor-General's letter to Senator Joe Ludwig, Special Minister of State (29 March 2010), viewed 20 April 2010: <http://www.finance.gov.au/ advertising/docs/Attachment-A-Auditor-General-to-SMOS.pdf>.

60   Graeme Orr (2010) *Submission to the New South Wales Joint Standing Committee on Electoral Matters' Inquiry into Public Funding of Election Campaigns*, viewed 9 March 2010: <http://www.parliament.nsw.gov.au/Prod/parlment/committee.nsf/0 /9885328db7edcd28ca2576bc00835c75/$FILE/%2323%20Ass%20Prof%20 Graeme%20Orr.pdf>.

Chapter 7

1   See AEC 2007, *Funding and Disclosure Handbook for Candidates*, viewed
     2 December 2009: <http://www.aec.gov.au/pdf/political_disclosures/
     handbooks/2007/candidates/candidates_handbook_2007.pdf>.
2   Australian Government, *Electoral Reform Green Paper: Donations, Funding and
     Expenditure*, 11.
3   Ibid.
4   AEC (2005) *Funding and Disclosure Report: Election 2004*, 28.
5   Senator John Faulkner (2008) Message from the Special Minister of State in
     Australian Government, *Electoral Reform Green Paper*, 1.
6   I owe this insight to Keith Ewing.
7   See discussion in Ian Ward (2006) Cartel Parties and Election Campaigning in
     Australia, in Marsh, *Political Parties in Transition?*, 70, 75–79.
8   Committee on Standards in Public Life (1998) *Fifth Report: The Funding of
     Political Parties in the United Kingdom*, 117.
9   Sally Young (2002) Spot On: The Role of Political Advertising in Australia,
     Australian Journal of Political Science, 37: 81, 91.
10   James Forrest (1991) Campaign Spending in the New South Wales Legislative
     Assembly Elections of 1984, *Australian Journal of Political Science*, 26: 526, 526.
11   Beitz, *Political Equality*, 199.
12   Young, Spot On, 81, 89.
13   Justin Fisher (2002) Next Step: State Funding for the Parties?, *Political Quarterly*,
     73: 392, 396.
14   R.J. Johnston & P.J. Perry (1983) Campaign Spending and Voting in the New
     Zealand General Election 1981: A Note, *New Zealand Geographer*, 39: 81.
15   Ron Johnston & Charles Pattie (2008) Money and Votes: A New Zealand
     Example, *Political Geography*, 27: 113.
16   Marie Rekkas (2007) The Impact of Campaign Spending on Votes in
     Multiparty Elections, *Review of Economics and Statistics*, 89(3): 573.
17   R.J. Johnston, C.J. Pattie & L.C. Johnston (1989) The Impact of Constituency
     Spending on the Result of 1987 British General Election, *Electoral Studies*, 8:
     143; R.J. Johnston & C.J. Pattie (2006) *Putting Voters in their Place: Geography and
     Elections in Great Britain*, Oxford University Press, Oxford.
18   R.J. Johnston (1979) Campaign Expenditure and the Efficacy of Advertising
     at the 1974 General Election, *Political Studies*, 27: 114; R.J. Johnston (1983)
     Campaign Spending and Voting in England: Analysis of the Efficacy of Political
     Advertising, *Environment and Planning C: Government and Policy*, 1: 117; R.J.
     Johnston (1986) Information Flows and Votes: An Analysis of Local Campaign
     Spending in England, *Geoforum*, 17: 69; Justin Fisher (1999) Party Expenditure
     and Electoral Prospects: A National Level Analysis of Britain, *Electoral Studies*,
     18: 519.
19   G.C. Jacobson (1985) Money and Votes Reconsidered: Congressional Elections,
     1972–1982, *Public Choice*, 47: 7; Charles Pattie, Ronald Johnston & Edward
     Fieldhouse (1995) Winning the Local Vote: The Effectiveness of Constituency
     Campaign Spending in Great Britain, 1983–1992, *American Political Science
     Review*, 89(4): 969; R.J. Johnston & C.J. Pattie (1998) Campaigning and

Advertising: An Evaluation of the Components of Constituency Activism at Recent British General Elections, *British Journal of Political Science*, 28: 677.

20 Johnston & Pattie, Money and Votes, 130–32.

21 Rekkas, The Impact of Campaign Spending on Votes in Multiparty Elections, 573.

22 See D.P. Green & J.S. Krasno (1988) Salvation for the Spendthrift Incumbent: Reestimating the Effects of Campaign Spending in House Elections, *American Journal of Political Science*, 32: 884; R.B. Grier (1989) Campaign Spending and Senate Elections 1978–84, *Public Choice*, 63: 201; D.P. Green & J.S. Krasno (1990) Rebuttal to Jacobson's 'New Evidence for Old Arguments', *American Journal of Political Science*, 34: 363.

23 As Forrest has noted, 'one area ... largely if not totally ignored in the Australian context surrounds the impact on voter behaviour of party spending during the course of an election campaign': Forrest, Campaign Spending in the New South Wales Legislative Assembly Elections of 1984, 526.

24 J. Forrest, R.J. Johnston & C.J. Pattie (1999) The Effectiveness of Constituency Campaign Spending in Australian State Elections During Times of Electoral Volatility: the New South Wales Case, 1988–95, *Environment and Planning A*, 31: 1119, 1127.

25 The summary of Forrest's research has been distilled from the following: Forrest, Campaign Spending in the New South Wales Legislative Assembly Elections of 1984, 531–32; James Forrest (1992) The Geography of Campaign Funding, Campaign Spending and Voting at the New South Wales Legislative Assembly Elections of 1984, *Australian Geographer*, 23: 66, 75; James Forrest (1997) The Effect of Local Campaign Spending on the Geography of the Flow-of-the-Vote at the 1991 New South Wales State Election, *Australian Geographer*, 28(2): 229, 229, 234; James Forrest & Gary Marks (1999) The Mass Media, Election Campaigning and Voter Response: The Australian Experience, *Party Politics*, 5: 99, 110.

26 Forrest & Marks, The Mass Media, Election Campaigning and Voter Response, 110.

27 This is part of the difficulty in developing criteria for fairness. See Stanley Ingber (1984) The Marketplace of Ideas: A Legitimizing Myth, *Duke Law Journal*, 1: 1, 51–55.

28 R. Hasen (2003) *The Supreme Court and Election Law: Judging Equality from Baker v. Carr to Bush v. Gore*, NYU Press, New York, 111.

29 See, generally, K. Muir (2008) *Worth Fighting For: Inside the Your Rights At Work Campaign*, UNSW Press, Sydney, Chs 3–5.

30 Muir, *Worth Fighting For*, 179–82. In insisting that the Your Rights at Work campaign be controlled or directed by the ALP, the approach taken by this article bears some affinity to the concept of 'coordinated expenditure' under US campaign finance laws: see Samuel Issacharoff, Pamela Karlan & Richard Pildes (2007) *The Law of Democracy: Legal Structure of the Political Process*, Foundation Press, New York, 353–54.

31 *Electoral Act 2004* (Tas) s 159.

32 *Electoral Act 2004* (Tas) s 160.

33   See Deborah Cass & Sonia Burrows (2000) Commonwealth Regulation of
     Campaign Finance – Public Funding, Disclosure and Expenditure Limits,
     Sydney Law Review, 22: 477, 484–85, 491.
34   New South Wales, Legislative Council (2004), *Parliamentary Debates*, Eric
     Roozendaal, 21 September, 11118, viewed 28 January 2008: <http://www.
     parliament.nsw.gov.au/prod/parlment/members.nsf/0/d9ccd231bed39458ca256
     ebe0004b5ab/$FILE/Roozendaal.pdf>.
35   Commonwealth, Senate (1902) *Parliamentary Debates*, Senator O'Connor, 2nd
     Reading Speech to Commonwealth Electoral Bill 1902, 30 January, 9542.
36   Johnston & Pattie, Money and Votes, 132.
37   Kevin Milligan & Marie Rekkas (2008) Campaign Spending Limits, Incumbent
     Spending, and Election Outcomes, *Canadian Journal of Economics*, 41(4): 1351–74.
38   There are, of course, other factors that influence fundraising, including
     incumbency (in assisting in raising funds) and the marginality of a seat (that
     is, the more marginal, the more emphasis on fundraising). See Forrest, The
     Geography of Campaign Funding, Campaign Spending and Voting at the New
     South Wales Legislative Assembly Elections of 1984, 67.
39   Select Committee on Electoral and Political Party Funding (2008) *Electoral and
     Political Party Funding in New South Wales*, para 8.8.
40   Keith Ewing (2003) Promoting Political Equality: Spending Limits in British
     Electoral Law, *Election Law Journal*, 2: 499, 507.
41   Committee on Standards in Public Life, *Fifth Report*, 116–17.
42   Rawls, *Justice as Fairness: A Restatement*, 150.
43   Committee on Standards in Public Life, *Fifth Report*, 172.
44   Commonwealth of Australia (Chair: C.W. Harders) (1981) *Inquiry into Disclosure
     of Electoral Expenditure*, 8–9, 13.
45   Committee on Standards in Public Life, *Fifth Report*, 172.
46   Before they were repealed, the Australian expenditure limits were, in fact,
     subject to widespread non-compliance. For example, 433 out of 656 candidates
     for the 1977 federal elections did not file returns disclosing their expenditure:
     Commonwealth of Australia (Chair: C.W. Harders), *Inquiry into Disclosure of
     Electoral Expenditure*, 18. However, this is largely because the laws were left to
     decay. Indeed, as early as 1911 the Electoral Office and the Attorney-General's
     Department signalled lax compliance in a policy of not prosecuting unsuccessful
     candidates for failure to make a return: Patrick Brazil (ed.) (1981) *Opinions of
     the Attorneys-General of the Commonwealth of Australia: Vol. 1 1901–14*, Australian
     Government Publishing Service, Canberra, 499–500.
47   The principle of subjecting 'front organisations' to the same obligations that
     apply to political parties dates back to the Joint Select Committee on Electoral
     Reform, Parliament of Australia (1983) *First Report*, 166.
48   See Committee on Standards in Public Life, *Fifth Report*, 118.
49   *Lange v Australian Broadcasting Corporation (Lange v ABC)* (1997) 189 CLR 520,
     566–67.
50   The test stated in *Lange v ABC* (1997) 189 CLR 520, 571–72 as modified by a
     majority in *Coleman v Power* (2004) 220 CLR 1, 50 (McHugh J), 78 (Gummow
     and Hayne JJ), 82 (Kirby J).
51   (1992) 177 CLR 106.

52   (1992) 177 CLR 106.

53   (1992) 177 CLR 106.

54   David Tucker (1994) Representation-Reinforcing Review: Arguments about Political Advertising in Australia and the United States, *Sydney Law Review*, 16: 274, 284.

55   Sarah Joseph (2001) Political Advertising and the Constitution, in Patmore, *The Big Makeover: A New Australian Constitution*, 53.

56   Joseph, Political Advertising and the Constitution, 53.

57   Tucker, Representation-Reinforcing Review, 283–86.

58   Deborah Cass (1994) Through the Looking Glass: The High Court of Australia and the Right to Political Speech, in Tom Campbell & Wojciech Sadurski (eds) *Freedom of Communication*, Aldershot, Dartmouth, 170, 193.

59   See, generally, Tom Campbell (1994) Democracy, Human Rights, and Positive Law, *Sydney Law Review*, 16: 195.

60   Tucker, Representation-Reinforcing Review, 283–84.

61   Campbell, Democracy, Human Rights, and Positive Law, 202–3.

62   The latter would often characterise judicial decisions on the protection of rights: see Jeremy Waldron (1999) *Law and Disagreement*, Clarendon Press, Oxford, Chs 10–13.

63   *ACTV* (1992) 177 CLR 106, 161.

64   *R (On The Application of Animal Defenders International) v Secretary of State For Culture, Media and Sport* [2008] UKHL 15.

65   George Williams (2004), *Submission to the Joint Standing Committee on Electoral Matters' Inquiry into Disclosure of Donations to Political Parties and Candidates*, viewed 2 December 2009: <http://www.aph.gov.au/house/committee/em/donations/subs/sub4.pdf>.

66   *ACTV* (1992) 177 CLR 106, 145.

67   *Coleman v Power* (2004) 220 CLR 1, 52 (McHugh J).

68   *ACTV* (1992) 177 CLR 106, 129.

69   *ACTV* (1992) 177 CLR 106,146 (Mason CJ), 239 (McHugh J).

70   *Commonwealth Constitution* ss 7, 24.

71   *Lange v ABC* (1997) 189 CLR 520, 560 (adopting Dawson J's dicta in *ACTV* (1992) 177 CLR 106, 187).

72   *Lange v ABC* (1997) 189 CLR 520, 560 (adopting Dawson J's dicta in *ACTV* (1992) 177 CLR 106, 187).

73   *ACTV* (1992) 177 CLR 106, 158.

74   For fuller discussion of the constitutional issues concerning specifically designed election spending limits, see Tham, *Towards a More Democratic Political Funding Regime in New South Wales*, 101–9.

75   See Elections Canada, The Electoral System of Canada, viewed 8 February 2009: <http://www.elections.ca/content.asp?section=gen&document=part1&dir=ces&lang=e&anchor=3&textonly=false#3>; Elections New Zealand, General Election Date and Timetable, viewed 8 February 2009: <http://www.elections.org.nz/rules/timetable-overview.html>. It should be noted that after the 2009 Canadian general election, there will be fixed four-year term elections: *Canada Elections Act 2000* (c. 9) s 56.

76 Expenses are 'campaign expenditure' if they fall within one of the eight separate categories of expenses listed in Schedule 8 of the PPERA: party political broadcasts, advertising, unsolicited material, manifestos and other documents, market research, press conferences and dealings with the media, transport, and rallies and other events.

77 *Canada Elections Act* 2000 (c. 9) s 441(3), (10).

78 Issacharoff & Karlan, The Hydraulics of Campaign Finance Reform, 1705, 1714–15.

79 Twomey Report, 2.

80 Twomey Report, 32–37.

81 See *Levy v Victoria* (1997) 189 CLR 579, 598 (Brennan CJ); *Coleman v Power* (2004) 220 CLR 1, 48 (McHugh J).

82 For example, see discussion of *Bowman v United Kingdom* (1998) 26 EHRR 1 in Twomey Report, 35–36.

83 See, for example, discussion of *Harper v Canada* [2004] 1 SCR 827 in Twomey Report, 33–35.

Chapter 8

1 For one of the few Australian publications acknowledging such a link, see Liquor, Hospitality and Miscellaneous Union (2009) *Democracy Pty Ltd: The Case for Election Campaign and Political Party Finance Reform*, Sydney.

2 Quoted in Clay Lucas (2007) 'State "caved in" to Richardson's pleas', *The Age*, 9 October, 5.

3 Cameron Houston (2008) 'Honesty issues brought up after $50,000 political gift', *The Age*, 28 May, 5.

4 See Royal Commission (Chair: G.A. Kennedy) (1992) *Report on WA Inc.: Part I*.

5 Corruption and Crime Commission of Western Australia (CCC WA) (2007) *Report on the Investigation of Alleged Public Sector Misconduct Linked to the Smiths Beach Development at Yallingup*, 3.

6 For the list of charges, see Warwick Stanley & Robert Taylor (2008) 'Former WA premier Brian Burke, ex-ministers on corruption charges', *The Age*, 7 November, 3. See also CCC WA (2008) 'Charges Laid Over Lobbying Hearings', media release, 6 November, viewed 18 February 2009: <http://www.ccc.wa.gov.au/media_statements.php?id=155 >; CCC WA, 'Two Charged as a Result of Smiths Beach', media release, 9 November, viewed 18 February 2009: <http://www.ccc.wa.gov.au/media_statements.php?id=126>.

7 See, for example, ABC Television (2003) 'WA Govt bans ministers from meeting former premier', *ABC News*, 10 April, viewed 29 January 2010: <http://www.abc.net.au/news/stories/2003/04/10/829055.htm>; Steven Pennels (2003) 'Burke ban divides WA Labor', *The West Australian*, 21 April.

8 Amanda O'Brien (2008) 'Burke blamed for shock poll loss', *The Australian*, 16 December; ABC Radio, David Webber (reporter) (2008) 'Bitter election lessons for Labor', *PM* (transcript), 15 December, viewed 2 March 2009: <http://www.abc.net.au/pm/content/2008/s2447002.htm>; AAP (2008) 'WA Labor had election shocker: Ray', 15 December.

9   Patrick Hanks (ed.) (1979) *Collins Dictionary of the English Language*, 862.

10   NSW ICAC (1990) *Investigation into North Coast Land Development: Part Five: Formal Findings and Final Observations*, 29.

11   For the range of activities that come under the rubric of 'lobbying', see John Warhurst (August 1987) Lobbyists and Policy Making in Canberra, *Current Affairs Bulletin*, 13; Julian Fitzgerald (2006) *Lobbying in Australia: You Can't Expect Anything to Change If You Don't Speak Up*, Rosenberg Publishing, Dural NSW, Ch. 2; John Warhurst (2007) *Behind Closed Doors: Politics, Scandals and the Lobbying Industry*, UNSW Press, Sydney, 14–20, Ch. 2; Peter Sekuless (1991) *Lobbying Canberra in the Nineties: The Government Relations Game*, Allen & Unwin, Sydney; Peter Cullen (1991) *No is Not an Answer: Lobbying for Success*, Allen & Unwin, Sydney.

12   Committee on Standards in Public Life (2000) *Reinforcing Standards: Sixth Report of the Committee on Standards in Public Life: Review of the First Report of the Committee on Standards in Public Life*, 86.

13   CCC WA (2008) *Corruption and Crime Commission Report on Behalf of the Procedure and Privileges Committee of the Legislative Assembly: Inquiry Conducted into Alleged Misconduct by Mr John Edwin McGrath MLA, Mr John Robert Quigley MLA and Mr Benjamin Sana Wyatt MLA*, Report No. 5 of 2008, 44.

14   For example, Bryan McQuide (2007) 'Interest Group Informational Lobbying: Policy vs Political', Conference Papers – Midwestern Political Science Association 2007 Annual Meeting, 8.

15   Ian Marsh (1999) 'Opening Up the Policy Process', in Marian Sawer & Sarah Miskin (eds), *Representation and Institutional Change: 50 Years of Proportional Representation in the Senate*, Papers on Parliament No. 34, Parliament of Australia, Department of the Senate, Canberra, 187, 189–91.

16   The main types of interest groups are producer groups (e.g. business and trade unions), welfare state client groups (e.g. NGOs representing interests of pensioners, veterans and the homeless), welfare state provider groups (e.g. organisations providing social services), and other professional groups. The main groupings of issue movements are the women's, peace, environment, consumer, gay rights, animal liberation, ethnic and 'New Right' movements: see Ian Marsh (1997) 'Interest Group Analysis', in Dennis Woodward, Andrew Parkin & John Summers (eds) *Government Politics, Power & Policy in Australia*, Addison Wesley Longman, Melbourne, 314–33.

17   Marsh has argued that 'The proliferation of interest groups and social movements is arguably the single most significant change in the character of post-war domestic politics': Marsh, 'Opening Up the Policy Process', 187, 193.

18   See, generally, Ian Ward (2006) Lobbying and Political Communication: A Review Article', *Australian Journal of Communication*, 33(2–3): 163.

19   CCC WA, *The Smiths Beach Development at Yallingup*, 101.

20   NSW ICAC (2005) *Report on Investigation into Planning Decisions Relating to the Orange Grove Centre*, 8.

21   CCC WA, *The Smiths Beach Development at Yallingup*, 98–99.

22   This is also one of the main complaints of former ALP President, Carmen Lawrence, who has argued that '[i]n Australia … we're in the dark about these

influences': Carmen Lawrence (2007) *Railroading Democracy*, Democratic Audit of Australia Discussion Paper 6/07, 8.

23 Warhurst, *Behind Closed Doors: Politics, Scandals and the Lobbying Industry*.

24 See Clive Hamilton (with research assistance from Christian Downie) (2007) *Scorcher: The Dirty Politics of Climate Change*, Black Inc. Agenda, Melbourne, 3.

25 See Hamilton, *Scorcher: The Dirty Politics of Climate Change*, Ch. 1.

26 See Senate Finance and Public Administration (2008) *Knock, Knock ... Who's There? The Lobbying Code of Conduct*, para 2.8, viewed 29 January 2010: <http://www.aph.gov.au/Senate/committee/fapa_ctte/lobbying_code/report/index.htm> (contra see Senate Finance and Public Administration, *Knock, Knock ... Who's There? The Lobbying Code of Conduct*, Coalition Senators' Minority Report, para 1.27). See also Scottish Parliament Standards Committee (2002) *Report on Lobbying*, 4–5.

27 Jennifer Victor (2007) Strategic Lobbying, *American Politics Research*, 35(6): 826, 827.

28 See, for example, Rachael Brown (2008) 'Graphic anti-abortion pamphlets spark emotional debate', *ABC News*, 13 March, viewed 2 March 2009: <http://www.abc.net.au/news/stories/2008/03/13/2188181.htm>; ABC (2008) 'Restraint urged after anti-abortion letter drop', *ABC News*, 12 March, viewed 2 March 2009: <http://www.abc.net.au/news/stories/2008/03/12/2187137.htm>; see also David Rood (2008) 'Churches unite to fight abortion law', *The Age*, 4 September.

29 CCC WA (2008) *Report on Issues Relating to Record Keeping in the Ministerial Office of the Hon John James Mansell Bowler MLA* (Report on Behalf of the Procedure and Privileges Committee of the Legislative Assembly), para 122, viewed 8 November 2008: <http://www.ccc.wa.gov.au/pdfs/Recordkeeping%20Report.pdf>.

30 Ibid., para 127.

31 Ibid., para 130.

32 Ibid., para 154.

33 John Warhurst (1990) Political Lobbying in Australia, *Corruption and Reform*, 5:173, 182.

34 CCC WA (2008) *Report on the Investigation of Alleged Misconduct concerning Dr Neale Fong, Director General of the Department of Health*, 5.

35 Warhurst, Political Lobbying in Australia, 173, 182.

36 CCC WA, *The Smiths Beach Development at Yallingup*, 6–7.

37 Royal Commission (Chair: G.A. Kennedy) (1992) *Report on WA Inc.: Part II*, 1–2.

38 Committee on Standards in Public Life, *Standards in Public Life: First Report of the Committee on Standards in Public Life: Volume 1*, 14.

39 There are three such statutes: *Independent Commission Against Corruption Act 1988* (NSW); *Crime and Misconduct Commission Act 2001* (Qld); and *Corruption and Crime Commission Act 2003* (WA).

40 See *Independent Commission Against Corruption Act 1988* (NSW) ss 7–9; *Crime and Misconduct Commission Act 2001* (Qld) ss 14–15; and *Corruption and Crime Commission Act 2003* (WA) s 4.

41 CCC WA, *The Smiths Beach Development at Yallingup*, 100.

42 NSW ICAC, *North Coast Land Development*, 33.

43 NSW ICAC, *The Orange Grove Centre*, 101.
44 Ibid.
45 Ibid.
46 Ibid.
47 See generally NSW ICAC (2003) *Regulation of Secondary Employment for Members of the NSW Legislative Assembly*.
48 See ABC (2008) 'Mark Vaile freelancing in Middle East', *AM* (transcript), 5 March, viewed 12 November 2008: <http://www.abc.net.au/am/content/2008/s2180137.htm>.
49 NSW ICAC, *Strategies of Managing Post Separation Employment Issues*, 3.
50 NSW ICAC, *Managing Post Separation Employment*, 7.
51 Ibid., 9–11.
52 NSW ICAC, *Strategies of Managing Post Separation Employment Issues*, 4. See also Committee of Inquiry Concerning Public Duty and Private Interest (Chair: N.H. Bowen) (1978) *Public Duty and Private Interest*, 115.
53 CCC WA, *The Smiths Beach Development at Yallingup*, 6.
54 Ibid., 80.
55 NSW ICAC, *The Orange Grove Centre*, 101.
56 See *Independent Commission Against Corruption Act 1988* (NSW) ss 7–9; *Crime and Misconduct Commission Act 2001* (Qld) ss 14–15; and *Corruption and Crime Commission Act 2003* (WA) s 4.
57 See CCC WA, *Dr Neale Fong, Director General of the Department of Health*.
58 CCC WA (2008) *Report on the Investigation of Alleged Misconduct concerning Rezoning of Land at Whitby*, paras 4–5, viewed 8 November 2008: <http://www.ccc.wa.gov.au/pdfs/Report%20on%20the%20Investigation%20of%20Alleged%20Misconduct%20Concerning%20Rezoning%20of%20Land%20at%20Whitby.pdf>.
59 Ibid., para 13.
60 Ibid., para 18.
61 Ibid., para 19.
62 Ibid., para 25.
63 Ibid., xii (Recommendation 2).
64 CCC WA (2008) 'Former Senior Public Servant Charged', media release, 12 November, viewed 17 November 2008: <http://www.ccc.wa.gov.au/media_statements.php?id=156>.; AAP (2009) 'WA: Burke goes to trial with public servant on disclosure charge', *AAP General News*, 8 September.
65 There was more than a hint of such behaviour in some of the conduct associated with WA Inc. For example, the conclusions of the Royal Commission on WA Inc. included the following:

> Some ministers *elevated personal or party advantage over their constitutional obligation to act in the public interest*. The decision to lend government support to the rescue of Rothwells in October 1987 was principally that of Mr Burke as Premier. Mr Burke's motives in supporting the rescue were not related solely to proper governmental concerns. They derived in part from his well-established relationship with Mr Connell, the chairman and major shareholder of Rothwells, and from *his desire to preserve the standing of the Australian Labor Party in the eyes*

of those sections of the business community from which it had secured much financial support (emphasis added): Royal Commission (Chair: G.A. Kennedy), *Report on WA Inc.: Part II*, 1–2.

66 CCC WA, *Mr John Edwin McGrath MLA, Mr John Robert Quigley MLA and Mr Benjamin Sana Wyatt MLA*, 46.

67 CCC WA (2008) 'Charges Laid Over Lobbying Hearings', media release, 6 November, viewed 8 November 2008: <http://www.ccc.wa.gov.au/media_statements.php?id=155>. AAP (2009) 'WA: Burke goes to trial with public servant on disclosure charge', 8 September. Burke and Grill both pleaded not guilty when they appeared before the WA Supreme Court on 3 September 2009; they will face a judge-only trial, an application not opposed by the WA DPP: Debbie Guest (2009) 'Pressure on accused lobbyist', *The Australian*, 4 September.

68 Hindess, Corruption and Democracy in Australia, 25.

69 Ibid., 27.

70 See *Independent Commission Against Corruption Act 1988* (NSW) ss 7–9; *Crime and Misconduct Commission Act 2001* (Qld) ss 14–15. The *Corruption and Crime Commission Act 2003* (WA) appears to be directed only at public officials, see s 4.

71 NSW Government, *New South Wales Government Lobbyist Code of Conduct*, cl 1, viewed 11 November 2008: <http://www.dpc.nsw.gov.au/publications/news/stories/?a=32066>; WA Department of Premier and Cabinet, *Contact with Lobbyists Code*, cl 1, viewed 11 November 2008: <https://secure.dpc.wa.gov.au/lobbyistsregister/index.cfm?event=contactWithLobbyistsCode>.

72 Australian Government (2008) *Lobbying Code of Conduct*, cl 8.1, viewed 4 November 2008: <http://lobbyists.pmc.gov.au/lobbyistsregister/index.cfm?event=contactWithLobbyistsCode>; British Association of Professional Political Consultants, *Code of Conduct*, cl 2, viewed 6 November 2008: <http://www.appc.org.uk/index.cfm/pcms/site.membership_code_etc.Code_of_Conduct/>; Office of the Commissioner of Lobbying of Canada, *Lobbyists' Code of Conduct*, section entitled 'Principles', viewed 6 November 2008: <http://www.ocl-cal.gc.ca/epic/site/lobbyist-lobbyiste1.nsf/en/nx00019e.html>.

73 Australian Government, *Lobbying Code of Conduct*, cl 8.1; British Association of Professional Political Consultants, *Code of Conduct*, cl 4, viewed 6 November 2008: <http://www.appc.org.uk/index.cfm/pcms/site.membership_code_etc.Code_of_Conduct/>; Office of the Commissioner of Lobbying of Canada, *Lobbyists' Code of Conduct*, Section entitled 'Principles', Rule 1.

74 Australian Government, *Lobbying Code of Conduct*, cl 8; British Association of Professional Political Consultants, *Code of Conduct*, cll 3, 6; Office of the Commissioner of Lobbying of Canada, *Lobbyists' Code of Conduct*, Rule 2.

75 Australian Government, *Lobbying Code of Conduct*, cl 8; British Association of Professional Political Consultants, *Code of Conduct*, cll 8, 11, 12; Office of the Commissioner of Lobbying of Canada, *Lobbyists' Code of Conduct*, Rules 6, 7.

76 Office of the Commissioner of Lobbying of Canada, *Lobbyists' Code of Conduct*, Section entitled 'Principles', Rules 4, 5.

77 British Association of Professional Political Consultants, *Code of Conduct*, cl 7; Office of the Commissioner of Lobbying of Canada, *Lobbyists' Code of Conduct*, Rule 8.

78 NSW ICAC, *North Coast Land Development*, 29.

79 Ibid., 32.

80 CCC WA, *Mr John Edwin McGrath MLA, Mr John Robert Quigley MLA and Mr Benjamin Sana Wyatt MLA*, 44.

81 As Greg Palast, journalist with *The Observer*, correctly observed: 'When Government gives special access to business interests, the rest of the public is left outside the door: in this power industry story, I can list the advocates for poor people ... who were turned down flat on requests for meetings on utility charges. They had no lobbyist, no cash, and as a result, no access': quoted in Committee on Standards in Public Life (2000) *Reinforcing Standards: Sixth Report of the Committee on Standards in Public Life*, 85.

82 NSW ICAC, *The Orange Grove Centre*, 101.

83 NSW ICAC, *North Coast Land Development*, 31.

84 CCC WA, *Mr John Edwin McGrath MLA, Mr John Robert Quigley MLA and Mr Benjamin Sana Wyatt MLA*, 47, 50–51.

85 Lindblom, *Politics and Markets*, Ch. 13.

86 It can be added that trade union officials are also dependent on the decisions of business for their ability to maintain the support of their membership, with the welfare of their constituency profoundly shaped by the decisions of business on how to use and deploy its capital.

87 Lindblom, *Politics and Markets*, 175.

88 Tony Wright (2010) 'The worker's mate has a day on the piste with Kerry', *The Age*, 18 February, 6.

89 Jason Dowling & Royce Millar (2009) 'Opposition U-turn on Crown expansion', *The Age*, 5 December, 5.

90 See NSW ICAC, *The Orange Grove Centre*, 7–8.

91 Barry Fitzgerald & Ari Sharp (2009) 'Argus and Co. never far from seats of power', *The Business Age*, 16 October, 1.

92 Stephen Bell & John Warhurst (1993) Business Political Activism and Government Relations in Large Companies in Australia, *Australian Journal of Political Science,* 28: 201, 212.

93 Ibid., 212.

94 Ibid., 208–9.

95 Fitzgerald & Sharp, 'Argus and Co. never far from seats of power', 1.

96 See, generally, Matthew Darke (1997) Lobbying by Law Firms: A Study of Lobbying by National Law Firms in Canberra, *Australian Journal of Public Administration* 56(4): 32–46.

97 Bronwen Dalton & Mark Lyons (2005) Representing the Disadvantaged in Australian Politics: The Role of Advocacy Organisations, *Democratic Audit of Australia Report No. 5*. See also Sarah Maddison & Richard Denniss (2005) Democratic Constraint and Embrace: Implications for Progressive Non-Government Advocacy Organisations in Australia, *Australian Journal of Political Science*, 40(3): 373, 376–80; Marian Sawer (2002) Governing for the Mainstream: Implications for Community Representation, *Australian Journal of Public Administration*, 61(1): 39–49; and Sarah Maddison & Clive Hamilton (2007) Non-Government Organisations, in Clive Hamilton & Sarah Maddison (eds) (2007) *Silencing Dissent*, Allen & Unwin, Sydney, Ch. 5.

98   Wyn Grant (2004) Pressure Politics: The Changing World of Pressure Groups, *Parliamentary Affairs*, 57(2): 408. There are different types of insider groups – core insider groups dealing with a wide range of topics, specialist insider groups and peripheral insider groups – all of which would enjoy varying levels of influence: Grant, Pressure Politics, 409.

99   While the distinction between insider and outsider groups does not precisely map the level of influence, insider group strategies are generally seen to be more successful: Grant, Pressure Politics, 409–12.

100 There are groups that are outsiders by necessity and those who are outsiders by choice: Grant, Pressure Politics, 409.

101 NSW ICAC, *Managing Post Separation Employment*, 15–16.

102 Darke, Lobbying by Law Firms, 32, 35.

103 Hamilton, *Scorcher: The Dirty Politics of Climate Change*, 3–4.

104 Bell & Warhurst, Business Political Activism and Government Relations in Large Companies in Australia, 211.

105 Warhurst, *Behind Closed Doors*, 64.

106 Ian Holland (2002) *Post-Separation Employment of Ministers*, Department of Parliamentary Library, Research Note No. 40/2002, 1.

107 Katharine Murphy (2008) 'Beazley now lobbyist', *The Age*, 18 October, 8.

108 Adele Ferguson & Eric Johnston (2010) 'Lobbyist control plans in disarray', *The Age*, 6 February, 7.

109 NSW ICAC (1992) *Second Report on Investigation into the Metherell Resignation and Appointment*, 3.

Chapter 9

1   See Scottish Parliament Standards Committee (2002) *Report on Lobbying*, 3.

2   See Clive Thomas (1998) Interest Group Regulation Across the United States: Rationale, Development and Consequences, *Parliamentary Affairs*, 51(4): 500.

3   For an excellent account of regulatory models in Australia and elsewhere, see Gareth Griffin (2008) *The Regulation of Lobbying*, NSW Parliamentary Library Research Service, Briefing Paper No. 5/08.

4   Australian Government (2007) *Standards of Ministerial Ethics*, cll 8.3–8.4, viewed 20 April 2009: <http://www.dpmc.gov.au/guidelines/docs/ministerial_ethics.pdf>.

5   Australian Government, *Standards of Ministerial Ethics*, cl 8.5; NSW Government, Department of Premier and Cabinet (2009) *NSW Government Lobbyist Code of Conduct*, cl 4.1, viewed 20 April 2009: <http://www.dpc.nsw.gov.au/__data/assets/pdf_file/0017/32066/NSW_Government_Lobbyist_Code_of_Conduct.pdf>; Public Sector Commission of Western Australia (2008) *Contact with Lobbyists Code*, Commission Circular, cl 4, viewed 20 April 2009: <https://secure.dpc.wa.gov.au/lobbyistsregister/index.cfm?event=contactWithLobbyistsCode>.

6   Parliament of NSW, *Code of Conduct for Members and ICAC*, cl 7, viewed 20 April 2009: <http://www.parliament.nsw.gov.au/prod/parlment/publications.nsf/key/LABP11>.

7 The NT *Legislative Assembly (Members' Code of Conduct and Ethical Standards) Act 2008* (NT), Schedule 'Code of Conduct and Ethical Standards', cl 4.
8 The codes are the parliamentary codes of conduct in New South Wales, Queensland, Victoria and the ACT: Parliament of New South Wales, *Code of Conduct for Members and ICAC*; Legislative Assembly of Queensland, *Code of Ethical Standards*, viewed 20 April 2009: <http://www.parliament.qld.gov.au/view/committees/documents/MEPPC/other/ethicalStandards/Code04.pdf>; *Members of Parliament (Register of Interests) Act 1978* (Vic) Pt I – Code of Conduct; *Code of Conduct for All Members of the Legislative Assembly for the Australian Capital Territory*, in ACT Government, *Code of Conduct for Ministers*, viewed 20 April 2009: <http://www.cmd.act.gov.au/__data/assets/pdf_file/0018/1827/codeconduct.pdf>. Interestingly, while the Northern Territory Code (a legislative Code that appears as a Schedule to the *Legislative Assembly (Members' Code of Conduct and Ethical Standards) Act 2008* (NT)) does not contain any restriction on post-separation employment, the previous Code (adopted by the Legislative Assembly in March 2004) did prohibit former parliamentarians from acting as adviser or consultant (including as a lobbyist) to any company or organisation with which they had had direct and significant involvement as parliamentarians: 2004 Code, cl 16. The legislative Code now supersedes the 2004 Code.
9 Government of Tasmania, *Code of Conduct Government Members of Parliament*, cl 2.2.3, viewed 20 April 2009: <http://www.dpac.tas.gov.au/__data/assets/pdf_file/0016/53503/Government_MPs_code_of_conduct.pdf>.
10 It should be noted that, under the NSW code, Ministers who are still in office are required to obtain advice from the Parliamentary Ethics Adviser before they accept any post-separation employment or engagement, or agree to provide services to a third party/ies if the work 'relates to or related to their portfolio responsibilities' over the preceding two years. The code also requires former Ministers who no longer hold office to obtain advice from the Parliamentary Ethics Adviser before they accept any employment or engagement, or agree to provide services to a third party/ies (unless the employment/engagement is with the NSW Government) if the work relates/ed to their former portfolio responsibilities during the last two years in which they held office for the first 12 months after leaving office: NSW Government, Department of Premier and Cabinet, *Ministerial Code of Conduct*, [7.4]-[7.5], quoted in Deirdre McKeown, A Survey of Codes of Conduct in Australian and Selected Overseas Parliaments, *Commonwealth Parliamentary Library Background Note*, 15, viewed 22 January 2009: <http://www.aph.gov.au/library/pubs/BN/pol/CodesOfConduct.pdf> (first published as an E-brief in June 2006 and as a Background Note in July 2007).
11 ACT Government, *Code of Conduct for Ministers*, cl 4 – Integrity: Post-Separation Employment.
12 ACT Government, *Code of Conduct for Ministers*, cl 4.
13 *Ministers' Code of Ethics* in Queensland Government, *The Queensland Ministerial Handbook: Governing Queensland*, Appendix 19, viewed 20 April 2009: <http://www.premiers.qld.gov.au/publications/categories/policies-and-codes/handbooks/ministerial-handbook/assets/appendix-19.pdf>; Australian Government, *Standards of Ministerial Ethics*, cl 2.19.

14 ACT Government, *Code of Conduct for Ministers*, cl 4 – Integrity: Use of Information Obtained in the Course of Official Duties.

15 Institute of Public Administration (Ireland) (2004) *Regulation of Lobbyists in Developed Countries: Current Rules and Practices*, 3.

16 For accounts of this episode, see John Warhurst (1987) Lobbyists and Policy Making in Canberra, *Current Affairs Bulletin*, August: 13, 14; John Warhurst (1998) Locating the Target: Regulating Lobbying in Australia, *Parliamentary Affairs*, 51(4): 538, 543–45; Warhurst, *Behind Closed Doors*, 22–23. The guidelines governing this scheme are reproduced in Peter Sekuless (1991) *Lobbying Canberra in the Nineties: The Government Relations Game*, Allen & Unwin, Sydney, 84–88.

17 Australian Government (2008) *Lobbying Code of Conduct*, cl 5.3, viewed 1 February 2010: <http://lobbyists.pmc.gov.au/lobbyistsregister/index.cfm?event =contactWithLobbyistsCode>.

18 Australian Government, *Lobbying Code of Conduct*, cl 3. For equivalent provisions in state codes, see NSW Government, *New South Wales Government Lobbyist Code of Conduct*, cl 3; Government of South Australia (2009) *Department of Premier and Cabinet Circular: Lobbyist Code of Conduct*, cl 3, viewed 7 December 2009: <http://www.premcab.sa.gov.au/pdf/circulars/pc032_lobbyist_code_ of_conduct.pdf>; Tasmanian Government (2009) *Lobbying Code of Conduct*, cl 3, viewed 7 December 2009: <http://lobbyists.dpac.tas.gov.au/__data/assets/ pdf_file/0020/105509/Tasmanian_Government_Lobbying_Code_of_Conduct. pdf>; Victorian Government (2009) *Professional Lobbyist Code of Conduct*, cl 3, viewed 7 December 2009: <http://www.lobbyistsregister.vic.gov.au/ lobbyistsregister/documents/Vic_Gov_Professional_Lobbyist_Code_of_ Conduct_Sept_2009.PDF>; Public Sector Commission of WA, *Contact with Lobbyists Code*, cl 3.

19 Australian Government, *Lobbying Code of Conduct*, cl 3.

20 The other exclusions from 'lobbyist' are charitable, religious and other organisations endorsed as deductible gift recipients; members of trade delegations visiting Australia and persons registered under a federal scheme regulating the work of particular professions (for example, registered tax agents and auditors) in their normal dealings with government: Australian Government, *Lobbying Code of Conduct*, cl 3. For equivalent provisions, see NSW Government, *New South Wales Government Lobbyist Code of Conduct*, cl 3; Government of South Australia, *Lobbyist Code of Conduct*, cl 3; Tasmanian Government, *Lobbying Code of Conduct*, cl 3; Victorian Government, *Professional Lobbyist Code of Conduct*, cl 3; Public Sector Commission of Western Australia, *Contact with Lobbyists Code*, cl 3.

21 The other exclusions from 'lobbying activities' are communications with a committee of the Parliament or in response to a call for submissions, a request for tender or requests by government representatives for information and statements made in a public forum: Australian Government, *Lobbying Code of Conduct*, cl 3. For equivalent provisions, see NSW Government, *Lobbyist Code of Conduct*, cl 3; Government of South Australia, *Lobbyist Code of Conduct*, cl 3; Tasmanian Government, *Lobbying Code of Conduct*, cl 3; Victorian Government, *Professional Lobbyist Code of Conduct*, cl 3; Public Sector Commission of Western Australia, *Contact with Lobbyists Code*, cl 2.

22 Australian Government, *Lobbying Code of Conduct*, cl 5.1. For equivalent provisions, see NSW Government, *New South Wales Government Lobbyist Code of Conduct*, cl 5; Government of South Australia, *Lobbyist Code of Conduct*, cl 5.1; Tasmanian Government, *Lobbying Code of Conduct*, cl 5.1; Victorian Government, *Professional Lobbyist Code of Conduct*, cl 5.1; Public Sector Commission of Western Australia, *Contact with Lobbyists Code*, cl 5.1.

23 Australian Government, *Lobbying Code of Conduct*, cl 5.4.

24 Ibid., cl 5.5.

25 Ibid., cl 6.1. For equivalent provisions, see NSW Government, *New South Wales Government Lobbyist Code of Conduct*, cl 6; Government of South Australia, *Lobbyist Code of Conduct*, cl 6.1; Tasmanian Government, *Lobbying Code of Conduct*, cl 6.1; Victorian Government, *Professional Lobbyist Code of Conduct*, cl 6.1; Public Sector Commission of Western Australia, *Contact with Lobbyists Code*, cll 5.2–5.5, 6.

26 Australian Government, *Lobbying Code of Conduct*, cl 8.1. For equivalent provisions, see NSW Government, *New South Wales Government Lobbyist Code of Conduct*, cl 7; Government of South Australia, *Lobbyist Code of Conduct*, cl 8; Tasmanian Government, *Lobbying Code of Conduct*, cl 8; Victorian Government, *Professional Lobbyist Code of Conduct*, cl 8.1; Public Sector Commission of Western Australia, *Contact with Lobbyists Code*, cl 7.

27 Australian Government, *Lobbying Code of Conduct*, cl 5.

28 Ibid., above n 13, cl 8.1. For equivalent provisions, see NSW Government, *New South Wales Government Lobbyist Code of Conduct*, cl 8; Government of South Australia, *Lobbyist Code of Conduct*, cl 9; Tasmanian Government, *Lobbying Code of Conduct*, cl 10; Victorian Government, *Professional Lobbyist Code of Conduct*, cl 9.2; Public Sector Commission of Western Australia, *Contact with Lobbyists Code*, cl 8.

29 Australian Government, *Lobbying Code of Conduct*, cl 10.4.

30 Ibid., cl 4.

31 See NSW Government, *New South Wales Government Lobbyist Code of Conduct*, cl 8; Government of South Australia, *Lobbyist Code of Conduct*, cl 9; Victorian Government, *Professional Lobbyist Code of Conduct*, cl 9.2; Public Sector Commission of Western Australia, *Contact with Lobbyists Code*, cl 8.

32 Tasmanian Government, *Lobbying Code of Conduct*, cll 10.4–10.5.

33 Marissa Calligeros (2009) 'Premier bans lobbyists from State Government boards', *Brisbane Times*, 5 August.

34 Matthew Moore (2009) 'Lobbyists to lose government jobs', *Sydney Morning Herald*, 16 November.

35 *Integrity Act 2009* (Qld) Ch 4, Pt 2.

36 *Integrity Act 2009* (Qld) s 44.

37 *Integrity Act 2009* (Qld) s 49(3)(b)(ii).

38 *Integrity Act 2009* (Qld) s 68.

39 *Integrity Act 2009* (Qld) s 69.

40 Australian Government, *Lobbying Code of Conduct*, cl 1.

41 NSW Government, *New South Wales Government Lobbyist Code of Conduct*, cl 1.

42 For similar principles, see Committee on Standards in Public Life (Chairman: Lord Nolan) (1995) *Standards in Public Life: First Report of the Committee on Standards in Public Life: Volume 1*, 36; Committee on Standards in Public Life

(Chairman: Lord Neill of Bladen) (2000) *Reinforcing Standards: Sixth Report of the Committee on Standards in Public Life: Review of the First Report of the Committee on Standards in Public Life*, 9; Scottish Parliament Standards Committee (2002) *Report on Lobbying*, 9; NSW ICAC, *The Orange Grove Centre*, 101.

43   Australian Government, *Lobbying Code of Conduct*, cl 1.

44   Senator John Faulkner (2008) 'Transparency and Accountability', public address, 30 October, viewed 16 December 2008: <http://www.smos.gov.au/speeches/2008/sp_20081030.html> (emphasis added).

45   Senate Standing Committee on Finance and Public Administration, *Knock, Knock ... Who's There? The Lobbying Code of Conduct*, 21–2.

46   Senate Standing Committee on Finance and Public Administration, *Knock, Knock ... Who's There?*, 24.

47   For an account of debates leading up to enactment of the original version of the statute, see Andrew Stark (1992) 'Political-Discourse' Analysis and the Debate over Canada's Lobbying Legislation, *Canadian Journal of Political Science*, 25(3): 513–34. See also Michael Rush (1998) The Canadian Experience: The Lobbyist Registration Act, *Parliamentary Affairs* 51(4): 516 for an account of the operation of the Act from the time it came into operation (1989) to 1998.

48   The requirement to register also arises when the aggregate of communications with a public office–holder by several employees would constitute a significant part of the duties of a single employee. According to the Office of Lobbyist Registrar, 20 per cent of an employee's time is generally considered to be a significant part of his or her duties (but the requisite proportion may be less if the employee is a senior officer of the organisation): Colin Feasby, Canada, in Thomas Grant (ed.) (2005) *Lobbying, Government Relations and Campaign Finance Worldwide: Navigating the Laws, Regulations and Practices of National Regimes*, Oceana Publications, New York, 57, 75–76.

49   See US House of Representatives, Office of the Clerk, *Lobbying Disclosure Act Guidance,* viewed 1 February 2010: <http://lobbyingdisclosure.house.gov/amended_lda_guide.html>. See, generally, Trevor Potter & Paul Ryan, United States, in Grant, *Lobbying, Government Relations and Campaign Finance Worldwide*, 557, 583–84.

50   Potter & Ryan, United States, 583–84.

51   Feasby, Canada, 57, 75–76. For an argument that the Canadian scheme should be 'a useful starting point' for Australian reform, see Lawrence, *Railroading Democracy*, 8.

52   This was recommended by the NSW Legislative Council General Purpose Standing Committee, *Badgerys Creek Land Dealings and Planning Decisions*, 60.

53   NSW ICAC, *The Orange Grove Centre*, 101.

54   Committee on Standards in Public Life (Chairman: Lord Nolan), *Standards in Public Life: First Report: Volume 1*, 36; Committee on Standards in Public Life, *Reinforcing Standards: Sixth Report*, 4.

55   House of Commons Public Administration Select Committee (2009) *Lobbying: Access and Influence in Whitehall: Government Response to the Committee's First Report of Session 2008–09: Eighth Special Report of Session 2008–09*, 10, viewed 28 January 2010: <http://www.publications.parliament.uk/pa/cm200809/cmselect/cmpubadm/1058/1058.pdf>.

56 On British 'cash for questions' controversy, see, generally, Committee on Standards in Public Life (Chairman: Lord Nolan), *Standards in Public Life: First Report: Volume 1*, 39; Grant Jordan, Toward Regulation in the UK: From 'General Sense' to 'Formalised Rules', *Parliamentary Affairs*, 51(4): 524, 525–33.

57 Legislative Assembly of the Northern Territory, *Members' Code of Conduct and Ethical Standards*, cl 16 (now superseded).

58 See, generally, NSW ICAC, *Strategies for Managing Post Separation Employment Issues*, Ch 3.

59 See NSW ICAC, *Managing Post Separation Employment*, 22.

60 *Integrity Act 2009* (Qld) s 68.

61 *Integrity Act 2009* (Qld) s 55(b).

62 *Integrity Act 2009* (Qld) s 62(b).

63 Scottish Parliament Standards Committee (2002) *Report on Lobbying*, 16.

64 NSW ICAC, *The Orange Grove Centre*, 102.

65 Feasby, Canada, 57, 74.

66 See Jacob Rowbottom (2010) *Democracy Distorted: Wealth, Influence and Democratic Politics*, Cambridge University Press, Cambridge, 102–3.

67 Warhurst, *Behind Closed Doors*, 64.

68 Lindblom, *Politics and Markets*, Ch 13.

69 ABC Radio (2009) Political Parties Through the Crystal Ball, *Future Tense* (transcript), 3 December, viewed 9 December 2009: <http://www.abc.net.au/rn/futuretense/stories/2009/2755323.htm#transcript>. John Cain made similar comments in a debate broadcast by Radio National: ABC Radio (2009) Dollars and Democracy, *In the National Interest* (transcript), 21 August, viewed 9 December 2009: <http://www.abc.net.au/rn/nationalinterest/stories/2009/2663074.htm>.

70 CCC WA, *The Smiths Beach Development at Yallingup*, 102.

71 Justin Greenwood & Clive Thomas (1998) Introduction: Regulating Lobbying in the Western World, *Parliamentary Affairs*, 51(4): 487, 498–99.

Chapter 10

1 New South Wales, Legislative Council (2004) *Hansard*, Eric Roozendaal, 21 September, viewed 28 January 2008: <http://www.parliament.nsw.gov.au/prod/parlment/members.nsf/0/d9ccd231bed39458ca256ebe0004b5ab/$FILE/Roozendaal.pdf>.

2 See also Carmen Lawrence (2005) *The Democratic Project*, Progressive Essays, viewed 22 February 2008: <http://www.progressiveessays.org/files/The%20Democratic%20Project.pdf>; Senator Andrew Murray (2006) Dissenting Report in Joint Standing Committee on Electoral Matters, *Funding and Disclosure: Inquiry into Disclosure of Donations to Parties and Candidates*, viewed 3 June 2008: <http://www.aph.gov.au/house/committee/em/donations/report/dissent_murray.pdf>.

3 Tony Bartlett (2009) 'Campaign finance needs reform: Turnbull', *WA Today*, 3 August. See also Malcolm Turnbull (2005) *Submission to the Joint Standing Committee on Electoral Matters Inquiry into the 2004 Federal Election*.

4   Andrew Stoner (2007) 'Counting the cost of political advertising', *Daily Telegraph*, 27 September, 1.

5   Bob Brown (2000) 'Corporate Donations are a Cancer on Australian Politics', media release, 14 April.

6   Simon Benson (2006) 'When politicians are under the influence', *Daily Telegraph*, 2 February, 28.

INDEX

Note: Page numbers in *italics* refer
to tables and graphs.

500 Club, Liberal Party *64*, 82

Abbott, Tony 87, 90
Albrechtsen, Janet 76, 111
associated entities
    disclosure obligations 27–30,
        32–39, 42, 44–46, 52–53, 56
    revenue received 63, *63*, *64*

barometer equality 191
Bligh, Anna 102, 108, 155
bribery 4–5, 7
    criminal offences 73, 97
Brumby, John 71, 82, 87, 259
    government 233
Burke, Brian 84, 217–18, 222–24,
   226–29, 232, 241, 243, 247, 254
    Bowler, John 222–23, 227
    Busselton Shire councillors 217,
      224
    Fong, Neale 224, 227
    Smiths Beach development 217,
      224–26
    Stokes, Gary 227–28
    Urban Pacific 227
businesses
    political contributions 62, 65–67
    internal accountability 104–108
    third party spending 180, 185,
      186, *192*, 193, 201, 212–13

campaign expenditure limits
    case for 195–202
    corruption 198–99
    design 208–13
    fairness 189–95
    generally 11–12
    implied freedom of political
      communication 202–08
cartel thesis 155–56
codes of conduct
    lobbying 229–30, 241, 243–50
    ministerial 98–99, 100–01, 103
    parliamentary 98–99, 100–01,
      102–03
Commonwealth Electoral Amendment
   (Political Donations and Other
   Measures) Bill 2009 (Cth) 27, 52–53,
   54–55, 134, 260
conflicts of interest
    generally 5–7
    regulation 97–104
contribution limits
    case for 108–10
    exemption for membership fees
      110–16
    freedom of political association
      116–20
    generally 22
corruption
    election funding 130–31, 133–35
    election spending limits 198–99
    electoral processes 4
    government advertising 158,
      162–63
    graft 4–8, 21, 61, 71–76
    individual 7–8, 75–76